MAKING PEACE
with AUTISM

MAKING PEACE

with AUTISM

ONE FAMILY'S
STORY OF
STRUGGLE,
DISCOVERY,
AND
UNEXPECTED
GIFTS

SUSAN SENATOR

TRUMPETER
Boston & London
2005

Trumpeter Books
an imprint of Shambhala Publications, Inc.
Horticultural Hall
300 Massachusetts Avenue
Boston, Massachusetts 02115
www.shambhala.com

9 8 7 6 5 4 3 2 1

First Edition
Printed in the United States

Designed by Ruth Kolbert

⊗ This edition is printed on acid-free paper that meets the
American National Standards Institute Z39.48 Standard.

Distributed in the United States by Random House, Inc.,
and in Canada by Random House of Canada Ltd

Library of Congress Cataloging-in-Publication Data

Senator, Susan.
Making peace with autism: one family's story of struggle,
discovery, and unexpected gifts / Susan Senator.—1st ed.
p. cm.
Includes bibliographical references.
ISBN 1-59030-244-3 (hardcover: alk. paper)
1. Senator, Susan. 2. Parents of autistic children—United
States—Biography. 3. Autistic children—United States—
Family relationships. I. Title.
RJ506.A9S457 2005
362.196'85882'0092—dc22

2005007870

Dedicated to
Ned, Max, Ben, and Nat

CONTENTS

PREFACE

Chances are you already know somebody who is dealing with autism. Perhaps you have a child who was recently diagnosed, or a close friend or family member told you her son or daughter has been diagnosed. It's likely that your children know an autistic child at school or in the neighborhood, or that autistic adults work in your supermarket, library, or office mail room.

Autism is a complex and little-understood developmental disorder. Today it is commonly referred to as "autism spectrum disorder" (ASD) because its severity varies greatly from person to person. (I use the term *autism* as a shorthand throughout this book.) Autism Spectrum Disorders, which are also called Pervasive Development Disorders (PDD), are in fact a diverse range of disabilities characterized by impaired social interaction and communication ability, as well as by unusual behavior. They are also sometimes accompanied by cognitive deficits.

Even if you don't know someone directly affected by autism, you will soon be confronted with it on some level. According to the National Alliance for Autism Research, autism currently occurs in one out of 166 births—nearly a tenfold increase over just ten years ago. Scientists are puzzled about this dramatic increase. Compelling theories abound, but as of yet there are no clear answers. Many parents are convinced that thimersol, a mercury-based preservative previously used in some childhood vaccines, triggered their child's autism. Others believe that an intolerance to wheat and dairy products caused profound changes in their child's brain chemistry, which made their child autistic. Still others believe that autism develops in the twentieth week of gestation, as a result of trauma to the fetus. And finally, there are those who believe autism is a genetic disorder, inevitable in some of us, but inexplicably occurring in greater numbers today. The bottom line is that more children are being diagnosed with autism than ever before, and they need help, and so do their families.

Despite its increasing prevalence, autism is not well understood by most people. To many it is the Greta Garbo of disabilities. Those affected seem mysterious and appear to be living in their own worlds; they "want to be alone," and those around them don't always understand why. Although there is some truth behind it, the idea that autistic people possess extraordinary skills (such as the uncanny mathematical abilities of the main character in the movie *Rain Man*) is a stereotype that does little to alleviate the pain of families contending with a loved one's unpredictable tantrums and other bizarre behaviors, as well as social, language, and cognitive deficits. And for those with autism, these myths preserve the notion of autistic people as unknowable and perverse, odd-genius types who warrant our curiosity, perhaps, but not necessarily our help or understanding.

Making Peace with Autism is the story of a family, my family— a husband, wife, and three sons—and our struggle to incorporate our oldest son's autism into our lives. It traces our son's autism from the very beginning, from the early days of wondering and not knowing; to the pain of diagnosis; and finally to the process of understanding, acceptance, and positive action. This book looks honestly at each family member's part in the fabric of family life, a look at how we interact with each other and what we have learned from daily activities like playing together, taking vacations, going to the doctor, and going to school, as well as the bigger crises—all of them colored by autism.

Without prescribing any particular method or formula, this book offers insight, understanding, and hope for parents and family members. It also seeks to educate those who wonder what it's like to live with an autistic person, and perhaps it will offer inspiration for those who are living with other kinds of adversity but are forging ahead anyway. (While all the stories and anecdotes in this book involve real people, most names and identifying details have been changed to protect privacy.)

Tolstoy wrote, "All happy families are alike; every unhappy family is unhappy in its own way." I must respectfully disagree. Our family is happy and yet quite unique. Every family facing autism, or any major adversity, must draw on its courage, creativity, and humor to find its own particular way through. With this book I hope to convey that despite the tremendous challenges that autism brings, you can find happiness as a family— even if you don't find a miracle cure. Here's how we've done it.

PROLOGUE

IT'S 4:30 P.M. THURSDAY, and I notice it's raining. *Oh, no,*
I think. *How am I going to do this?* I set my coffee cup down, get
up, and walk into the playroom. Ben, five, my youngest child, is
sitting on the big yellow chair, absorbed in a video. His brother
Nat, fourteen, is sitting on the floor at Ben's feet, also watching
the video, which is Disney's *Pocahontas.* My gaze lingers on
them idly for a moment. I notice, as I often do, that the two
boys, one large, one small, have exactly the same profile, the
same blond bowl haircut, the same intense stare. The same
movie interests. I take in the action on the television screen to
gauge where they are in the movie. I hear the Indians singing
"Steady as the Beating Drum," and I sigh in despair. It has only
just started, and I have to interrupt them; because of the rain, I
have to get Max, their middle brother, from his play rehearsal. I
have to change the routine.

The rain is now coming down hard, absurdly so. I clear my
throat. "Guys." Nat looks up immediately, already wary. Ben
does not even seem to hear me. I consider for a second an ironic

question: *Which one is autistic here, and which one is normal?* "We have to get Max now," I tell them, hoping that my tone of voice conveys just the right mix of authority and empathy so that I can avoid a fight. This is, after all, an unpredicted change in schedule.

Ben has heard me, of course. "Aw, Mom," he says, but he is sliding off the chair, *Pocahontas* soon to be forgotten. Nat is out of sight, presumably fetching his shoes. Maybe I am out of the woods. But as I turn to gather my keys, I jump at the sound of a sharp, loud scream coming from the closet, like the yelp of a dog: *"AAARGH!"* He is coming out of the closet with his shoes.

"Stop it, Nat!" I say. No empathy this time. My response comes from pure frustration and annoyance.

Nat comes back into the room. He looks at me and says, "Get Max now" in a voice close to tears. Then he screams again. The sound cuts right through me. I clench my teeth. I have to gain control—of myself, of him. I focus on the distress in his sapphire blue eyes and hoarse voice, and from way down inside somewhere, I summon my tired but immutable love for him, my fragile firstborn.

"Nat. We have to get Max. It's raining. I'm sorry I didn't tell you. I didn't know."

"AAARGH!" Again.

My compassion evaporates. I take a step toward him, menacing. "Stop that," I say through my teeth, as angered by my inability to reach him as by the screams.

He draws back and says, "Get Max! *AAARGH!*" His pupils are so dilated that his violet eyes are now black. "Nat. Stop. We have to go." I sigh and wonder how the hell I'm going to get him into the car.

"AAARGH!" Now he runs past me, stomping loudly. My heart thumps hard. I remember the red pinch marks he left on Ben's arm, just two weeks ago. I race over to stand between Nat and Ben, who is standing at the top of the stairs to the basement.

"No, Nat!" Ben shouts fiercely. Nat is twice his size, but Ben is ready to defend himself. But Nat barrels past us, down the basement steps. We hear the slam of the back door in the basement. Ben and I follow him to the car. The rain is pouring down our necks like water from an open faucet. Nat is waiting in the driveway, sucking his thumb, drenched and oblivious. I settle the two boys into the back seat of the car.

"After Max, watch *Pocahontas*," Nat says tearfully, "After Max, watch *Pocahontas.*" His mood has shifted suddenly. For whatever reason, it's over; he will cooperate now.

"'That's right, sweetheart." I sigh in relief. I pull out onto the street, windshield wipers flapping crazily. I turn down the next block. There, walking toward me, head down against the rain, is a tall boy with thick blond hair that sticks out from under a camouflage hat. It is Max, looking as though he's showered in his clothes. I pull up to the curb and open the car door.

"Oh, honey, why did you walk in this? Why didn't you wait? Or call me?"

Max slides into the car, and the air fills with the scent of sweaty, wet boy. "I don't know," he says, shrugging, sounding almost apologetic. He takes in huddled Nat and angry Ben, understanding all, expertly adding up the inconveniences he feels he has caused. "I didn't think I could. You told me this morning I had to walk. So I walked."

As often happens when I deal with Max, I am flooded by mixed feelings: guilt and sadness that he has learned to be so self-reliant so early in life. That he understands what I had to go through to come and pick him up and that he tried to spare me by walking home in the rain. At the same time, I'm filled with pride and happiness that he is so mature and thoughtful. Even though he's only eleven, having him there in the car with me makes me feel stronger and happier. Safer. I start to relax, releasing my tight grip of the steering wheel.

"*AAARGH!*"

Max and I whip our heads around. "Nat! Cut it out!" we shout together.

"Mommy will drive," Nat insists.

I, of course, comply. *I will if you would stop screaming!* I think. But then I feel a softening, and a small inner smile. As we head home, I realize the hard part is over, we're OK, and I'm pretty sure that it looks as if it's beginning to clear off to the east.

Nat is, and has always been, an insoluble puzzle to us. Now fifteen, he is difficult to know, apparently in need of no one. Though he walks, talks, eats, sleeps, laughs, and goes to school, he will never be a "regular" kid like his brothers. No matter how much time has passed since his diagnosis, when I think about the things he will never have or be in life because of his autism, the pain of it fills me anew.

When I meet fifteen-year-olds and hear them talk, when I hear their teenage bravado and see their adolescent awkwardness, a part of me shrivels up in misery and in envy of their parents. When I look at their rooms, messy and filled with posters, outgrown toys, expensive sneakers, meticulously chosen ugly clothes, I know that such things will never be an issue between Nat and us, and I mourn that. His room is full of things that we, his parents, have chosen for him, many of them long ago. His posters are of frogs or Curious George, not Brittany Spears or the Celtics. His sneakers are expensive, but we tie them for him. His clothes have the labels cut out of them because he can't tolerate even the tiniest scrape of one against his neck. With Nat there is no swagger, no adolescent angst. Nat's room is a capsule of who he is: stuck at different ages, flashes of toddlerhood mixed with various attempts to broaden him.

There is no real knowing how Nat's autism affects our two younger boys. Max, who by personality and birth order is a peacemaking, tolerant middle child, is forced also to assume the mantle of the oldest. He is of necessity a trailblazer, because his big brother cannot show him the way, telling him which teachers in his school are nice or cluing him in on puberty. Even though we're determined not to let him put his needs aside because his brother is so needy, I suspect that somewhere along the way he has learned to keep a lot to himself, to struggle quietly on his own with growing up.

And little Ben is just beginning to realize that his oldest brother rarely answers him, may laugh at him when he cries, and breaks apart his Lego structures but has no interest in building anything. Recently he asked me if Nat's brain is "broken." He is learning the hard way that his biggest brother is someone to avoid, a dead end, even; also that sometimes life can be painful and make no sense.

We as a family are frequently hamstrung by Nat's unpredictability, our plans held hostage by autism. We can never simply go to a concert, a movie, a friend's party without first wondering, "Can Nat handle it?" Despite intensive schooling and our Herculean efforts, he still has tantrums, and even when he doesn't, he can be just plain unpleasant, unhappy, or embarrassing in public.

This certainly isn't what Ned and I expected when we began our life together. Having Nat has tested our marriage, forcing us to stick together even when we have been tempted to run. Ned has had to adjust his career; he has chosen to be a family man rather than a company man. He says he's never looked back, and I believe him.

Sometimes, though, I wonder what life would have been like if Nat had been normal. I try not to get to that question, but inevitably it comes up. I look back, I look forward, and sometimes all I see are sad and scary realities. But still I look, because that is how I learn, and how I get through a day. By looking at it all honestly, I come to understand how we function as a family, what has worked for us and what hasn't, and, maybe, I can get a sense of what might be coming next.

1

WONDERING

The Early Days

$\mathbb{T}$HE SADDEST DAY OF THE YEAR for me is November 15, Nat's birthday. My feelings about that day have never changed in all these years, although so many other things have.

Of course, Ned and I are happy to *celebrate* Nat's birthday, going to great lengths to come up with presents that catch his quicksilver attention and baking a cake slathered with frosting because the frosting is the only part he'll eat. We invite all the family members who can make it. But no friends, because Nat has none.

No, as far as we've come being Nat's parents, we cannot say we enjoy his birthday. Ned feels it's because Nat's birthday makes no difference to Nat himself. It's just another day of the year to him. Another day when people have somewhat mystifying expectations of him. In this case, he's expected to tear paper off boxes containing new and incomprehensible things, but also not to be too interested in ripping the paper.

Each year, Max, our middle child, has watched with envy as Nat opens Lego kits he'll never build with, books and

7

videos that he immediately drops on the table. Ben, the youngest, watches with disgust and confusion as his very big brother actually has to be reminded to open the remaining presents. We all probably act happier than we are feeling, each of us harboring our own particular disappointments. Yet not to mark the day at all would be far worse, as even Ben must realize at some level.

On that day more than others, I think about his early days, although I would rather not, and how I was back then. How I didn't know what was about to hit me. But also how I suffered with so much self-doubt that I did not fully recognize his problems until after he was two years old.

Those days just before delivery, I would look down at my pregnant belly, occasionally racked by early labor contractions, knowing I was on the brink of something momentous; little did I know just *how* momentous. When I think of what little idea I had of how our lives were going to be, of the autism and all, I am enormously sad. On Nat's birthday, I find myself wondering, *When did I first know? Why didn't I do something about my early intuitions?* And unfortunately, most of all, *What would he be like today if he were normal?*

When I go back to those early days, I'm trying to get some clarity. Only by looking unflinchingly at the challenging beginnings of our family life, and what followed, can I arrive at an understanding of the positive way we function today. I reopen my heart, sift through my memories, in the hope that that by looking back on Nat's milestones, the family culture, the surfacing doubts, I will come up with a story that finally satisfies me, and releases me.

Ned and I had waited five years into our youthful marriage to have a baby. Never had I wanted something more. Having a baby had been my idea, but Ned went along with it readily enough. We did all of the fervent preparation typical of high-achieving, semi-neurotic, upper-middle-class couples, even though we made fun of other couples we knew who had done the same things. Looking back on my innocence, I understand that we—like so many of our peers—were focused on, even tormented by, unimportant things. The things that people naturally obsess about when they don't realize how complex life can become! Together Ned and I interviewed ob-gyns to determine whether they performed too many C-sections and how committed they were to natural childbirth. I talked and read to the baby in utero. I read all kinds of mother-to-be books. We were so well prepared that we didn't think anything could go wrong. This illusion was deepened by our comfortable backgrounds and the fact that we lived in a society that promoted the idea of family life as a Hallmark card.

In my socioeconomic class, and in my family, everyone expected the American dream, the great career, the beautiful home, the drug-free natural childbirth that produces the perfect child. And why not? Misfortune was for other people. I did know of one distant cousin who had been "institutionalized"—the word was always spoken in a sad whisper. But this boy, who was much older than I, had been born so severely retarded that no one ever saw him.

As a child I had been both drawn to and repulsed by disability. I had read *Wren* and *Karen* by Marie Killilea, two children's books about a girl with cerebral palsy, and a biography of Helen Keller. I was moved and impressed by that heart-stopping moment when the teacher, Anne Sullivan, runs water over Helen's hand and then spells "water" into her palm, and Helen understands. I wanted to be this kind of teacher. When we were eight years old, a childhood friend and I made plans to open a school for the deaf when we grew up.

But there was also a dark side to my relationship with disabled people. In fifth grade, I met my first retarded person, Clayton, who one afternoon urinated accidentally on the classroom floor. My friends and I smirked about the accident, although a part of me also wanted to cry when I realized what the puddle was near my feet. Clayton was thin, fragile, with wide, scared eyes. Frightened by how different he was, I didn't want to look at him, especially after his accident. This was how I personally dealt with "inclusion" (the practice of educating disabled children in the most typical circumstances possible for them). As for my school system, it educated children like Clayton along with their typical peers, just as the newly enacted federal disabilities law required, in as normal an environment as possible. But the school did nothing to educate the rest of us about Clayton, or kindness, or what we could possibly learn from him.

In college I had another brush with a disabled person. A roommate, Karen, was a different kind of person from anyone I'd met. She spoke strangely, as if she always had food in her mouth, and with a slight British accent, although she wasn't British. She never made eye contact and stayed in her room, from which an odd smell emanated. When the phone rang, she'd call out, from behind her closed door, "I'll get it, I'll get it," but she never got it. "So get it!" I would yell, picking up the phone. The calls were never for Karen, anyway.

My friends and I laughed nervously about her. "What's with Karen?" we'd ask each other. None of us knew. No one had explained her particular issues to us and, self-absorbed, privileged college kids that we were, we lacked the time or desire to find out.

I never thought twice about Clayton or Karen, except to feel a cringing kind of pity deep inside, a feeling that I was lucky not to be like them, but also an arrogance that what I had was only what I and the people in my circle deserved in life. I was probably not much worse than most people who never have confronted a major personal misfortune.

As an expectant mother I read nothing about what is normal to feel about your newborn baby, and what is not. I didn't think about developmental milestones, what parents should do if they feel something is wrong, how to take action and not be paralyzed by fear. And why would I have focused on such things? I was only twenty-six; Down's syndrome is uncommon when the mother is that young. And autism? This was fifteen years ago, 1989; we knew of no one with autism. The pro-football star Doug Flutie had not yet raised national awareness of this disorder. His autistic son had not yet been born. Back then, doctors still cited an incidence of two in 10,000 births, compared with today's one in 166. (For more information, visit the website of the National Alliance for Autism Research at *www.naar.org*.)

I dreamed about my baby, yearned for his arrival, but in a straight-out-of-Hollywood way. If I had entertained the possibility that things could go wrong, if I had perhaps made a pact with Ned that we would explore any doubts we had about our boy rather than judge them as silly or pray for everything to be OK, maybe we would have gotten help sooner.

But of course, we had made no such pact, and we interpreted any jitters I had as normal pre-childbirth worries. And so Nat was born, induced after three days of early labor and then nine hours of more urgent labor, including three hours of lackluster pushing after getting an epidural. Sometime during the pushing, the doctor became concerned about the level of oxygen in Nat's blood, and took a sample from his scalp. Rushing from the labor-and delivery room with the vial of fetal blood, he nearly collided with my anxious mother, who looked at his serious face and in her nervous state of mind thought, "Susan's dead." I was not, but my dragging labor was making me wish I were. The doctor pressed the elevator button with his free hand and then didn't even wait for it but took the stairs instead. I will always wonder if Nat should have been born by C-section, if he spent too much time in the birth canal without enough oxygen. But at the time I had made it very clear to the doctor that I was hoping for a vaginal birth, based on all of my prenatal "research."

I never did find out the results of that blood test, but the doctor was more cheerful after he had completed it and jokingly urged me to finish before his shift was over. I obliged, my body finally making me realize just how hard I was supposed to push.

Nat was a beautiful baby, with tufts of white blond hair and violet eyes. A docile infant, he was so enchanting that people often stopped me to admire him. My first moments with him were ecstasy. He had warm pink skin, he smelled salty and sweet. Ned said he was like a ball with a face painted on it. He was all potential. Autism was not yet even a cloud on the horizon. But almost immediately, there was the rumble of distant thunder.

Normal Postpartum Depression, Or Was It?

We couldn't wait to get home from the hospital and start our life as a family. But when we did get home, I was hit with a big feeling of "OK, now what?" My high expectations of motherhood plummeted as I saw my days turn into a twenty-four hour blur of feedings, changings, and naps. I didn't realize that many women struggle both physically and emotionally when they bring home their first child. Few women let on what it's really like to mother a newborn, and I had no close friends at the time, being new to town.

Early on, one friend of my mother's, upon visiting us, exclaimed, "Did you ever feel such love?" And I remember thinking, "Huh?" This did not feel like love to me. What I felt instead was fear of doing things wrong, along with exhaustion, boredom, and disappointment that I was getting nothing back from this baby.

When I said this to Ned, he said, "What can you expect to get back from a baby?" I didn't know how to describe this feeling I was having about Nat, and I had no way of knowing how normal it was. Even now, I don't know how much of Nat's behavior was normal and how much was particular to Nat and the earliest signs of autism.

Nat's problems would have been hard for anyone to discern, especially in the early weeks. At the beginning, the signs were always fleeting, with a now-you-see-them, now-you-don't quality. Everything I noticed or felt was subtle, flickering, momentary. All my questions were so easily answered, my fears so quickly dismissed by doctors, family, Ned, and even me.

Looking back, I can see that in the very beginning, I was on my own in dealing with Nat's nascent autism. It was only later, as we approached Nat's first neurological evaluation, that Ned and I began to work together as a team, sharing the burden the way we do now. But during Nat's infancy, it was as if I were alone most of the time. Ned's role was simply to play with Nat and to comfort and reassure me, make me happy again, the daddy-knight on the white stallion.

Find the Autism

When did I first know something was amiss with Nat? Almost immediately. Something inside me told me that mothering a newborn was not supposed to feel so flat. Sometimes I look at the old videos of baby Nat, and I grimly play "find the autism." I look for signs of lack of affect, eye contact, affection. It is so tough to pinpoint. Yet there is indeed something missing when I watch him—what, I still cannot say. Do I see it because I now know to look?

At first the autism came in little bursts, bad moments here and there, sprinklings of disappointment in what he did or didn't do. Nat startled easily and often, though this could have been just a newborn thing; I have no way of knowing. Another possible sign: He didn't actually look at me for any length of time until his fifth day of life, when suddenly his eyes were opened almost absurdly wide. My sister Laura visited us that day. A medical student, and an aunt for the first time, she was thrilled with this chance to bond with a baby, especially mine. Nat was fully alert and experiencing this world, and it was a noisy, chaotic place for him. Laura and I noted his wide-eyed stare, thinking it was cute.

During Nat's first week, I did express a few misgivings about the way he would throw up his hands at the slightest jostling or sound. "Why does he do that?" I asked my sister. It was easier asking her, a med student, than calling the pediatrician, whom I felt I was already calling too much.

"That's his startle reflex," Laura explained. "Infants have that to protect themselves, to let them know something's around."

But why did he do it so often? The least little thing would set him off. Arms shooting up, eyes wide. His body would explode in reaction to every sudden move or loud noise. It didn't seem right to me, no matter what I was told about it.

But Ned was not worried about Nat. His confidence made me feel both reassured and lonely. He pointed out that Nat *did* smile at us, after all. In fact, Nat displayed a sense of comfort and ease around all the adults in his life. So Ned focused on this rather than on the piece that somehow did not feel right to me. Ned has always been one to quietly accept the foibles of others, baby Nat included. But although he could quiet my fears about Nat, after a while they would inevitably reemerge.

Ned recently asked me, "How could I have known? Why would I have thought there was something wrong with Nat? What did I know about babies?" But whether he knew something about babies or not, Ned had an unassailable sense that all was well, and he was simply delighted with his new baby. It was not that he was blinded by love or in denial. He has always possessed a certain solid faith in the world, not easily explained in light of his parents' bitter divorce when he was five. Perhaps it was his mother's early reliance on him as the oldest, the "man" of the house, that gave him so much faith in himself and the world. Ned thought at first that his baby was perfect, and, as Nat developed, Ned saw him as a quirky but still normal enough child. Ned's awakening about Nat was gradual, while my alarm was almost constant, flashing on and off steadily.

The first time I left Nat for a few hours with Ned, to go shopping for something to wear at Laura's wedding, I felt certain the baby would die with me gone. I called Ned within the first hour of my outing. I imagined Ned's teary voice explaining that, yes, Nat had died, because he was so fragile and young.

When Ned answered the phone, he didn't sound surprised to hear my voice. "Yeah, he's fine," he said.

"*Really?*" I replied in disbelief.

"Yeah, Sue, why wouldn't he be?" He sounded amused but also slightly annoyed about my hysterics.

Ned couldn't understand why I was frequently so unhappy and worried. I was letting minor things get to me, he thought, and I needed something outside myself to occupy my mind. Maybe a friend or a job would help. It bothered him that I couldn't just enjoy Nat, though he did not often say so.

Ned's stomach hurt a lot in those early days, and he started popping antacids. He said the problem was that he wasn't getting enough sleep. I think he connected all of his own anxiety in those days to to his lack of sleep. He would emerge like a bear out of hibernation for the 5:00 A.M. feedings, so uncharacteristically grumpy that I took those over, leaving him the midnight feedings, which worked better for him. He had had no expectations about what fatherhood should feel like, except that it should be fun. He had entered both marriage and parenthood making it all up as he went along. He hadn't bargained for things starting to feel so out of control. He hadn't realized how despondent one can become as a result of exhaustion and a constantly worried wife.

Once Nat's sleeping schedule settled down, however, Ned reemerged as his usual cheerful, unflappable self. He would grab Nat, play with him, and holding the boy out in front of him, say, "Baby!" in mock surprise. I was surprised, even awed, by the sure, easy way Ned handled Nat. Even though he's a computer geek, a mathematician, a numbers guy, he plays around like a dumb jock. When Nat and Ned played, things felt better to me, as if maybe there was nothing wrong, after all. After the long days, the evenings came as a relief to me, the two of us together with our baby, laughing and admiring his beauty and sweetness. Ned's buoyant presence balanced out my anxiety, helped it all make sense.

Growing Doubts

In the early spring, I did make a friend. It had been surprisingly difficult for me, even though this new neighborhood of ours was supposed to be full of young families. We had bought a house in a nearby suburb and left a nice condo in a more interesting city so that we could provide Nat with a yard and other kids to play with. But I hadn't connected with anyone there, and thus I spent my days burying my anxiety and loneliness by fixing up the house and planting a garden. Then, when Nat was five months old, a woman named Merle from our childbirth class brought her baby, Quinn, over to visit. Quinn was very interested in the world around him—almost ridiculously so, it seemed to me at the time. He squirmed and flailed his fat legs, apparently in frustration that he hadn't learned to crawl yet. He also made conversational noises. Seeing Quinn added to my concern about Nat and his lack of interest in the world and toys. But I hadn't observed too many peers of Nat's yet, so I thought Quinn might be the unusual one.

Merle was a godsend during this lonely and anxious time. A southerner and a very traditional kind of mother, she got all her child-rearing information from two places: her own mother and Dr. Spock. She didn't go in for any of the new childhood specialists: no Penelope Leach or Brazelton for her. She would tell me how frustrated she was with Quinn's overeager temperament, and she would comment on how quiet and shy Nat was, "like a little gentleman." She was right about Quinn; he wasn't shy. He would look at me, look at his mother, look at Nat. His face registered understanding of things. He was making connections. He would look at a ball differently than Nat did. Even at five months he seemed to understand that there was something you could do with a ball other than put it in your mouth.

Even though Nat hit the major developmental milestones on time, such as rolling over, crawling, standing, walking, and even speaking his first words, his lack of interest in people and toys would gnaw at me. It wasn't so much that he didn't make eye contact, but more that he didn't follow through. He would watch as you did something but quickly lose interest. It made me want to stuff so much into every interaction, so as to get it all in before he looked away.

As for toys, he would set up his Fisher-Price dolls in a perfect line, but then he would simply stare at them and suck his thumb. If you took one away or messed up the line, he would fight to get it back in the right place. I waited for him to do more with the dolls, like making them ride in toy cars or making them talk to one another. I would show him how to do these things time and again, but it never took. He never played with the dolls; he only wanted to line them up, and there they stayed on his rug, like little soldiers forever waiting for the call.

"He just doesn't need stupid toys to make him happy," my sister said one day in his defense. How could I argue with such an assessment? I liked thinking Nat was unique. Ned readily agreed; why did every child have to be the same as all the others? He himself had been content with little as a child. His mother was fond of saying, "Give Ned a couple of pencils, and he'd be happy for hours." Ned felt that Nat was the same kind of kid.

Yet it still pained me that Nat was this way. For one thing, it was not much fun to have a baby who didn't play. For another, it was strange, and it worried me. As his first birthday approached, I especially disliked being asked what kind of toys he liked playing with. My mother in particular never tired of the question, being such an enthusiastic grandmother. But I had no answer. What could I say? That he held onto his bunny and sucked his thumb? Sometimes I said he liked toy trucks, and he did, to the extent of putting them in his mouth or lining them up.

So when we celebrated Quinn's first birthday, Ned's and my happy feelings were mixed with concern because we couldn't believe how many different toys Quinn was interested in. There were Winnie-the-Pooh figurines, trucks, and videotapes, to name a few. Ned and I did not know that a child Nat's age could sit and watch something like a Disney Sing-Along video. I had never thought to try showing Nat videos, not until our second child started watching TV. We talked with each other about Nat's lack of interest in toys and television, but we never did anything about it. Ned's confidence and my unnamed fear kept us in this limbo.

The first time Ned felt even a flutter of concern was when he realized that Nat could not hold up his bottle—at almost one year of age. Sitting, Nat would hold the bottle tipped downward instead of up, finally throwing it away because he wasn't getting anything from it. "He hasn't figured out how to hold it up by himself," Ned remarked in surprise. Shaking his head over yet another odd-but-cute action of Nat's, Ned laid him on his back, a position that allowed him to use his bottle successfully. Problem solved. Being Ned, he didn't feel the need to connect this behavior to a bigger picture. His overall confidence that all was well remained intact for some time after.

The vague dread I felt intensified as Nat reached eighteen months, the age when children start structured play activities. A dogged 'first-time mother, I tried things like mother-and-tot swim class. That only lasted a single session. Nat spent the class floating on his back with my hands under him, staring up at the ceiling and sucking his thumb. The experience was probably too intense for him. He has always been fascinated with water. As he lay there, he probably felt overwhelmed by all the new sensations—the feeling of being immersed in the water, the other kids' laughter and splashing and screams. Perhaps he was terrified, even to the point of shutting down. If he sucked his thumb and stared straight at the ceiling, he could block out everything going on around him and feel calm again.

By then he had apparently learned the defense of blocking out stimuli that were too much for him. But to me, it was the most bizarre behavior. All the other kids were having fun; they seemed so much older, so much more capable than Nat. I looked around, trying to make eye contact with the other mothers, to find a friendly face. But they were all so involved with their own children, so interested in what their children were doing. I felt so terrible about Nat's apparent indifference, so ashamed that I couldn't even get my baby to enjoy a pool, that I never went back, never tried again.

"Why did he do that? Why doesn't he like anything?" I wondered aloud later with Ned.

Ned shrugged. "He's different. It's OK. You're not doing anything wrong." Frustrated by my constant uncertainty but still not entirely convinced by his own words, he repeated his mantra, hoping it would sink in, trying to prove to me that Nat was fine. He would even get down on his hands and knees to play with him, showing me that our child was really OK. In this game Ned would stalk an unsuspecting Nat in the living room, yell "Yah!" and, to our delight, Nat would turn around, squealing with laughter, understanding the game. Once, Nat even turned around and began crawling after Ned. Ned pretended not to notice and let Nat "get" him. After that, they played this game often. Sometimes I did it, too.

The game was enjoyable to Nat because it was one-on-one and exciting, but in a predictable way; he liked peek-a-boo for the same reason. Games like these involved a clear expectation and didn't involve a lot of distracting factors, so they were comfortable for him. The fact that Nat could play these games told us that he was intelligent and that he had some ability to relate, yet we did not discuss this observation because we hadn't yet agreed that there was any real reason for concern—other than my perpetual anxiety. For Ned, the crawling-monster game strengthened his certainty that Nat was fine, just different from what I had expected in a baby. According to this theory, the problem was with me, not Nat, though Ned and the others in my life never said this explicitly. I felt it, though, and I resented it.

The conversations would go something like this: "I just wish he would play this way with Quinn," I would say.

"Sue, he will," Ned would reply. "Just give him time. He knows how, anyway."

"But Quinn already plays so much. Nat should be able to do more."

Silence. And then: "Well, he can't. He's his own person, that's all. Don't compare them."

"I can't help it. It doesn't seem right. He can't play."

"He can play! He just did!"

This tension between us continued to grow, and Ned's explanations reassured me less and less as Nat's development continued on its atypical path. And Ned's theories didn't work once Nat was outside our small family circle. At the neighborhood playgroup, the other children were too noisy, too active for him. They liked *Sesame Street,* and Nat had no interest in the show. It moved too quickly for him. He couldn't focus on it long enough to understand what was happening on-screen.

For the longest time I thought of other children—like the playgroup kids or Quinn—as "out of control" because they were so bouncy and chatty, not realizing that they were behaving typically. I blamed the mothers around me for being lax parents. Unlike their children, Nat was easily deterred from explorations that were unsafe, destructive, or annoying. While my friends complained of power struggles with their babies over cabinet doors and electrical outlets, Nat responded well to "No." This was a point of pride for us: Nat's excellent behavior. Nobody thought he was *too* compliant. My sister Laura made up a slogan, "He's Mini-Man, he does what he can." We called him Mini-Man because he was so serene, even when you would have expected him to fuss.

On the day he got his first vaccine, he smiled his wide toothless smile at the doctor. His brow furrowed as the needle went into his soft arm, but when the needle came out, he smiled again, though there were tears in his eyes. "Oh, you're still smiling at me, you good little guy!" the doctor said, impressed. Mini-Man, smiling through his shot. Sometimes I was able to take real pleasure in his uniqueness, and it was like the sun breaking through.

Into Nat's second year, though, I was increasingly at odds with Ned because he didn't see what I saw and he sometimes acted impatient about it. He rationalized away my observations, dismissed my complaints, and generally acted defensive about Nat. By this time there was an atmosphere of growing sadness in our home, as if a mold were seeping into the walls around us, sickening our relationship. I talked a lot about moving. I yearned to get away from our new neighborhood, even though we had only just arrived there. I began making plans for us to move back to the more exciting urban area where we'd lived before Nat was born. I had not made many friends in our new neighborhood; I only had Merle and Ned. Merle, though a good friend, was absorbed with her own child and struggling with a full-time job while her husband finished law school. So most of the time, my main support was Ned. He was a cool rock for me to rest against, his own needs largely unrecognized. Ned did not mind my heavy emotional dependence on him. I had always depended on him that way, even before marriage. He did mind my perpetual sadness, though. He would say, "Just be happy, everything's really OK," as if that would help. I don't think I really saw *him* very much back then, just my own misery. I took up a lot of the emotional space in our relationship in those days, always more at ease with expressing my feelings than he was.

My mother also did her best to reassure me in those days, when I complained that Nat seemed to shy away from peers. "Just get Nat around other kids more," she said as we walked together on the beach near her house. "He just needs the experience."

My heart sank when she said this. Just getting him around other kids seemed only to make him withdraw, and I was less and less inclined to want to try it. "Mom, it just doesn't work," I ventured. "I don't know what it is." I felt like such a failure.

My mother had pounced on each of Nat's developmental stages like a hawk on meat. She would show up at our house with bags filled with toys, each geared to stimulate Nat's development. She was the first to bring him Play-Doh (he ignored it); the first to bring finger paints and toy trucks. My mother had an insatiable appetite for Nat. She was always pointing the camcorder and the camera at him. And she pursued Nat's attention with determination. Our house filled up with trucks of every size, boxes and boxes of crayons, an easel, toy figures, and puzzles, but he didn't show interest in any of them. Nat lit up when he saw my mother, but not because of the toys. What caught his interest was her animated face and her bright chatter.

Reaching Nat with Books

One winter's day, when Nat was around fourteen months old, we had a profound breakthrough. It had to do with a book my mother had bought Nat called *Corduroy's Day: A Counting Book*. We were snuggled on the couch together, Nat leaning against me, thumb in mouth, as I read the book once and then again. When I finished the second reading, he took the book from my hand and then gave it back to me, making the urgent sounds "Unh, unh, unh." He clearly wanted me to read it again, and I did. I felt a glimmer of what it must have been like for Anne Sullivan at that water pump, knowing without a doubt that she had gotten through to her student.

We had been reading to Nat for months and months, without him showing any sign of appreciation or understanding. Until now. Finally Nat began showing us how much he loved books, their predictability and comforting rhythm. Being read to from a book, with its logical progression from beginning to middle to end, seemed to make him feel safe. Every time I finished reading him the Corduroy book that day, he would make sure I knew that he wanted me to read it yet again. I must have read that little book twenty times, and I would have read it twenty more if he had asked me to. This was the first time we had done something together that he enjoyed. And he had found a way to tell me about it! My heart raced with excitement.

Corduroy's Day was a real turning point. It was momentous for us to realize that Nat could understand stories and be affected by them somehow. Something in his environment, something complex and with the potential to expand his world, was giving him pleasure. I had never felt before that we could give him anything he really wanted other than food or drink. And so we read to him constantly. Ned loved children's books, anyway, their perfect simplicity and beautiful illustrations, and was he always buying Nat new ones in addition to those my mother showered upon us. (One psychologist commented later that it was likely this saturation with literature that helped Nat grow any kind of vocabulary at all, given the degree of his autism.)

I soon realized that he liked books best when he was familiar with them, so in order to get him to listen to new books, I read them through quickly, then again, so that they would "catch" with him. This way, I could keep expanding his repertoire and maintain his interest.

By the time Nat was two, he loved books so much he had begun to memorize them. Our first conversations with him were mostly crafted out of lines from books: If I gave him strawberries, I'd say "Look, Nat, 'one-two-three-four strawberries,'" from a waterproof bathtub counting book. We began to play fill-in-the-blank with Nat, starting a sentence from a beloved book and waiting for him to finish it. When we played this way with him, he would reward us with happy book chatter and a wide smile. We found that we could use content from books to explain new concepts to him, too, a process that delighted and comforted him. For example, we used lines from the book *Corduroy Goes to the Doctor* to explain that he would have to get undressed, get weighed, and get a shot. "Do I get a shot?" asks Corduroy. "Yes," says the doctor. "We don't want you getting sick."

Though he mostly spoke by quoting books, his original

speech, rare as it was, was breathtaking in its expressive imagery. "Pejush-shush window," meaning "peanut butter and jelly sandwich window," was his way of describing a colorful stained glass window he had seen, for instance.

Before too many months had passed from the time of our breakthrough with *Corduroy*, he had memorized the *Velveteen Rabbit*, a rather long and complex children's book. There was even some excited talk among family members that he was going to be an early reader. Overlooking his eccentricities, we began to feel confident that he was actually gifted. A tiny seedling of hope unfurled within me.

By this time, however, doubts had sprung to life in Ned. In spite of Nat's success with books, there was something odd about the way he used language, and for once, Ned could not let it go.

"Have you noticed that Nat can't answer a yes-or-no question?" he asked me one day. We were at a restaurant near the ocean with Nat, the smell of french fries and milk shakes all around us. Ned underscored the point by asking Nat if he wanted a sandwich.

Nat said nothing.

Then I tried, saying, "Nat, want juice?"

Instead of an answer, he echoed back, "Want juice?" This, it seemed, was his way of answering "yes."

Ned looked at me gravely, with unaccustomed concern. *Aha*, I couldn't help but think. Something flared up inside me, reaching out toward Ned, but it wasn't yet strong enough to connect.

In the days that followed, I had a bad twinge of fear every time I thought about what Ned had shown me. Ned was right; Nat's language was sporadic, odd, and rote. At Nat's eighteen-month checkup and then again at two years, I brought this up with our new pediatrician, a young woman whom we'd chosen because her practice was close to our home.

"Oh, he's a little genius," she said adoringly, as Nat stood in her large, poster-filled examining room and prattled away for her, occasionally flashing his dazzling smile. She didn't do any testing or refer us to any specialists. She wasn't aware of the latest studies, tests, and resources. And so I let my misgivings go again for a little while, as did Ned. Which parents would not want to think their child was a genius? I wasn't fully convinced my worries were justified until I gave birth to Max.

Our Second Child Is Born

Although Nat's real name, Nathaniel, means "gift of God" in Hebrew, it was Max who felt like a gift to me. Though I didn't explain it to myself this way at the time, Max allowed me to enjoy motherhood for the first time because now I was parenting a normal child. It was like floating, like falling asleep, like breathing for the first time in a long while.

Unlike Nat, Max connected with me from the start, which made me feel confident that I was actually doing things right. Max was everything I had expected Nat to be but had not even dared to expect this time around. Max would look at me and look at me. We could not get enough of looking at each other. A big baby, he quickly caught up to Nat in size and abilities, even though he was two years younger. All this eventually helped clarify that the concerns I had been having about Nat were not about me—not a product of my own insecurities or lack of experience with children.

To Ned, Max seemed remarkably exuberant, happy, and outgoing. Although it was harder to have two children, and the lack of sleep was getting to Ned again, he felt buoyed by Max's obvious good nature. In spite of returning to antacids, Ned was optimistic about this new child. We could laugh about how absurdly hard it was, with a new baby and a difficult toddler. One morning, as we strapped Max into the Snugli baby carrier and took Nat and the stroller down three flights of stairs from our new top-floor condo (we had moved back to our old town, after all, several months before Max's birth), we made up a song together:

Family of four, family of four.
So much trouble just to get out the door.
We're always tired,
Please don't get fired,
Family of four.

This was the beginning of our positive collusion as parents in a difficult situation, of a playful us-against-them attitude that helped us turn to each other amidst the chaos and smile about how nuts it all was. Starting from this moment, I began to feel that Ned was joining me in dealing with the children, instead of standing apart and merely reassuring me.

With Max in the mix, I also felt for the first time that maybe I was not so bad at mothering, just that I had been inexperienced with Nat. Like many second children, Max made me feel like an expert. My new confidence probably also helped Ned; now that I could deal with our children better and didn't need so much from him emotionally, he was freed up to attend to other family issues, particularly Nat's development and his own feelings about it. Ned couldn't help but feel the contrast between his two sons, and more and more, he began to let himself see that things were not going well with Nat.

For my part, as my bond with Max strengthened daily, I could feel Nat slipping away. The voices in my head were getting louder. *Something is wrong with Nat,* they said. He started refusing to get out of the stroller to play in the neighborhood park, especially if there were other kids around—and there always were. If I tried to make him get out, he would have a tantrum, a new and excruciating behavior for us. He would not play with other children, ever, in the park or elsewhere. Their games were too complex for him, their words too fast. Their conversations swirled around him, confusing him and making him want to sit perfectly still and block them out or cry out to make them go away.

Why Does Nat Do That?

To me, it was like a bad dream. Our sunny, silent, compliant little boy was changing into a stormy, loud, difficult child. When I complained to Ned, he listened sympathetically. His questions focused on Nat's behavior rather than on my reactions to it, and my sense that Nat's problems were real got stronger, along with my constant dread of them.

One memorable afternoon, Merle came with Quinn to visit us, and Nat ran to hide in the bathroom. I could not get him to come out. He just sat there on the worn white bath mat, thumb in his mouth, immovable.

"Why is he in there?" asked Merle. Quinn was running around, pulling out all our toys as usual.

"Maybe Quinn scares him!" I said defensively.

Her face fell. In a tentative voice, she said, "Maybe the problem isn't Quinn."

My rage leapt up, fueled by all the months of anxiety. "Maybe if you could control Quinn, Nat wouldn't feel so scared. He's shy, you know! You always say so yourself."

Eyes downward, Merle said, "I know. Maybe he's too shy."

She had never said anything like this before, and we had been getting together nearly every week for months! "What do you mean? You know this is how he is. You're always going on about how you can't control Quinn! How Nat is the one with the manners!"

"Yeah. But I'm worried about him," she said softly, kindly.

"How can you put it on Nat? Why don't you take responsibility for your kid?" I countered angrily.

"I do, Sue. But look at Nat."

I looked at Nat, who didn't even seem to know we were there. He was focused on the bathmat, closing out the noise around him. All my defenses melted away as I looked at him doing nothing while Quinn played, destroyed, screamed with joy. "I don't know what to do," I said. "I've tried everything. You know I have. He doesn't like other kids! Is that so terrible?" I turned away from Merle and leaned my head against the wall, not knowing what else to do.

"I think you need to take him to your pediatrician and talk to her about this." Merle was no stranger to fighting with pediatricians. She was always trying to convince Quinn's doctor that Quinn had allergies and that those allergies affected everything about him, from his everyday behavior to his sleep patterns. I had always watched her do this at a distance, though, feeling a little sorry for her for not having as good a relationship with her pediatrician as I had with mine. My pediatrician knew my sister, was fun to talk to, and was young—she was a lot like me, and that had made me feel comfortable. I thought that her combination of qualities was ideal. Now, I was beginning to wonder.

"I've tried to talk to her!" I said to Merle. "She doesn't think there's anything wrong!"

Merle shrugged. "Well, *you* do."

After that conversation, I was so angry at Merle that I almost stopped being her friend. Ned agreed with me that Quinn was the probable reason for Nat's evasive behavior, and that Merle needed to rein him in. A part of me knew this wasn't quite right, but I was afraid to find out what was actually going on with Nat. All the while, my stomach hurt. I knew something bad was happening and I had to face it.

A Watershed Moment

The moment when everything crystallized came soon after, when we brought the boys to my aunt's house for the Passover seder, a large family gathering and festive holiday meal. Nat, who was two and a half at the time, was virtually unable to enter her house. Instead, he stood in the doorway, refusing to budge, crying insistently, "Go outside, go outside, go outside." To him, I now understand, it was a house full of people who were too loud and too big; he didn't understand why he was even there. He must have thought that staying outside would mean escaping from the confusion, crowd, and noise that were causing him misery.

We tried comforting him; we tried cajoling him; we tried firmness; we tried ignoring him. Everyone tried. People kept coming up to him, urging him to come inside. "Does he do this in other places?" my mother asked. Of course, he did! The playgroup had become nearly impossible for me. The exact same thing had happened there just the other week. Everyone at the seder was wondering, "What's wrong with Nat?" and "Have you tried . . . ?" or saying, "I'd just insist he come in . . ." or "It's the new baby. He's jealous." But we just could not get through to him. We could not find a way to stop his incessant crying, which went on for hours. He would not move from the doorway, either.

Nat's behavior cast a long shadow over the Passover dinner. I had to keep getting up from the table, checking on him by the front door. My grandmother chided me for paying too much attention to Max at the expense of Nat, reasoning that Nat was acting this way because of neglect. Suddenly everyone was looking at me, as if turning on me with pointed fingers. Across the long table, I recognized the contempt people have for a child who can't be controlled. Why did Nat do these things? Why couldn't I, his mother, make him stop?

Over the din of Nat's cries and everyone's questions, I looked at Ned for help, reassurance. But he was looking right back at me, an uncharacteristic helplessness and sadness in his eyes. The problem was real now, and we both knew it.

2

NOW WE KNOW

AFTER THE SCENE AT PASSOVER, my parents began making frequent solicitous phone calls to me, their voices filled with concern. The words "How's Nat?" seemed to begin every conversation. My sister gave me a book she had been assigned in a medical school class, *Caring for Your Baby and Young Child*, published by the American Academy of Pediatrics. She was probably beginning to draw sobering conclusions about Nat, but if so she didn't talk about them. I don't think she could have voiced her concerns then because of her blind love for Nat, and how hard it would be to tell me the truth about him.

The book my sister gave me described what a child should be able to accomplish in all areas of development up to age five. I turned with trepidation to the page that described a child of three. The description included many things Nat couldn't do, such as show interest in peers, build a tower, or respond verbally in simple, direct sentences. We made a list of all the things on the list that Nat couldn't do and brought it to our pediatrician. After reading it, she nodded quietly and gave us the name of a developmental pediatrician. *Oh my God,* I thought, my breath stopping in my throat. *She's not talking me out of it. She finally sees the same thing I see.*

Ned took this development stoically, shutting out the pain, one of his old reflexes. He accepted his fate grimly, like a soldier being sent to the front line.

We booked two hour-long appointments for an evaluation with Dr. E., a development specialist at a renowned children's hospital in our area. He would see us in January, just after New Year's. Having made the appointment, we didn't discuss it. We just waited.

The Horror of Validation

As we drove to the clinic for our appointment, we were unaware of how profoundly this evaluation would change our lives. Our world as we knew it was about to end. Of course, I was scared. This appointment was different; it was a new step for us. By taking Nat in for an evaluation, we were making a statement to ourselves that we actively believed there was something wrong. I knew we could come out of there with terrible news. But on another level I still had my defenses up. I figured any child of mine would have to be OK. Bad things happened to others, not us. I hoped, even expected, to hear more of what I'd heard for Nat's first three years: *He's fine. All kids mature at different paces. Einstein didn't talk until he was four. He'll grow out of it.*

Dr. E. interviewed us about my pregnancy, our family medical histories, my labor and delivery, and Nat's milestones. While we talked, he removed toys from a big black suitcase for Nat. There was a doll, some red and blue plastic blocks, a toy car or two, some picture cards. He performed some developmental tests with Nat, such as, and also tried to get Nat to play with him. Nat responded by smiling (something he did readily with many people), but that was all Nat did. After failing to get Nat to play with him, Dr. E. tried to get Nat to talk, eliciting a few of the repetitive memorizations Nat excelled at.

At the end of the appointment, Dr. E. told us he suspected something called PDD, pervasive developmental disorder, which, he told us, falls under the umbrella of autism. (Some doctors use PDD as a softer diagnosis than autism, which is what Dr. E. was doing. The term *autism spectrum disorder* was new then, and not many doctors were using it yet. Today, the terms *PDD* and *ASD* are often used interchangeably.)

Did he say "autism"? The word reverberated in my mind. Autism? How could it be? Maybe he was just unique. Or maybe he had a speech problem? Or he was developing in his own way, like Einstein? *Autism.* The brevity of the word conveyed all of its hopelessness: "aut," Greek for "self." The state of being unto one's self. I pictured images of fearsome devilish children. From the movie *Rain Man,* I recalled the mutterings, the isolation, the institutionalization. From the TV show *St. Elsewhere,* I remembered Dr. Westfall's autistic son, who wreaks daily havoc in the doctor's home. I thought of wild children banging their heads against the wall, flapping their hands, and spinning like little dervishes. But Nat didn't spin except when playing with us. Nat never banged his head. Nat did not mutter or flap.

But what about his repetitive quotations from books? Or his habit of lining up his toys? Or the way he endlessly twirled a piece of string in sunbeams that came in through the living-room window? Or his lack of interest in others, the pervasive self-absorption?

The diagnosis gave me a heavy, cold feeling; I instantly knew it was accurate. I sat there without much to say at first, while it began to sink into my consciousness. But this was only the beginning of a very long process of understanding, of letting autism settle itself into our midst.

The doctor informed us that day that autism was incurable, and that Nat would always need some sort of help. Inside, I went back and forth about it, knowing it was true, and not wanting it to be true. Why couldn't it be a language problem? Or that he was a late bloomer? *Please, please change your mind,* I begged the doctor silently. *This isn't happening.*

I asked whether I had caused Nat's autism by failing to love him properly in those early days of self-doubt and irrational fear.

"No, no," Dr. E. reassured me. "This is not your fault. No one believes that stuff anymore," he said, alluding to Bruno Bettelheim's debunked "refrigerator mother" theory, in which the mother is blamed for being so cold to her child, so rejecting, that she causes the child's autism. "It is probably because of all of the attention and love you've given him that he is as functional as he now is," the doctor told me. I brightened when he said that.

As for Ned, he told me later that he had felt mostly relief when he heard the diagnosis: relief that he finally knew what we were dealing with, so that now we could begin to work on it. But his relief was not very comfortable; it was like the relief that comes at the end of a long battery of doctor visits, where the doctor pronounces the chilling verdict:"We don't need any more tests because we know it's cancer." Ned didn't let on that his heart was breaking, if it was. More likely, he was thinking, "Better to look forward, not inward." Ned was not one to explore his pain.

Ned was frustrated, however, that the doctor didn't have any answers for us, except that we should find Nat the best education available. Unfortunately, there was disagreement in the field about which educational approaches worked best. Some people believed in one method, and others were equally wedded to an opposite approach, the doctor explained. In any case, he advised us to get in touch with our school department soon, in order to begin the process of getting Nat into a program.

"How will we know which program to pick," I asked,"if no one knows what the best kind is?"

The doctor replied that we would know within a few weeks of Nat's entering a program whether it was working for him. "You should see progress very quickly in the right program," he said.

Those words provided a glimmer of hope, the first one I had seen during this appointment. They told me that effective programs existed, and that one of them could help Nat. Those same words have come back to me many times in the last twelve years, guiding me as we make decisions about Nat's education. But I still don't know how either Ned or I was even able to listen at that moment, with all that was going on in our heads.

During the drive home, we talked intermittently, in a daze of information and feelings. I kept rerunning the doctor's words in my head. "So does this mean he's autistic?" I asked Ned. "Is that what he really said?" It was a stupid question, but I needed confirmation of what I had been told.

"Yep, that's what he said," Ned sighed. Looking very tired, he repeated the general information that Dr. E. had given us. I reached out and took Ned's hand. We were stopped at a light at a big intersection. I looked at the other cars rushing around us; it seemed that other peoples' lives continued smoothly on course, while we were suddenly so different.

"So what do we do?" I asked.

"About what?"

"Well, about telling people. Ugh! It's going to be so hard. Do I have to tell people?"

"Maybe. I don't know. Maybe we don't tell anyone just yet." Ned's tone of voice was measured, calm. I think he was shutting down because there had been so much to take in. He was trying to hold onto that sense of relief, but it was leaving him quickly. He needed to figure out just what this diagnosis meant for us before we started dealing with other people's reactions to it. In the end, it took months before he even told his own parents.

But, unlike Ned, as hard as it would be to talk about it, I had to release what I was feeling. I couldn't wait to unload some of this feeling onto someone else. Unlike Ned, I could not just sit with this quietly and privately. I came from a family of worriers and talkers—intense, analytical people who welcome detailed discussions of how and why things are the way they are. I called my sister as soon as we got home from the appointment.

"There's a cluster of symptoms that they look at, from three different categories: social interaction, social communication, and imagination," Laura explained carefully and clinically, surprising me with her equanimity. She must have thought that by handling the topic so abstractly, she could spare herself the pain of acknowledging Nat's situation.

"Do you think they're right about Nat?" I asked, cutting through her abstractions.

There was a long pause. Laura had just completed a psychiatry rotation. She must have recently understood what all the quirky things about her beloved nephew added up to. And she could no longer deny it to herself, much less to me. There was no getting around it, after all. Tearfully and softly, she said, "Yes."

Confronted with her pain, I could not stand it. I found I did not want to talk about Nat's autism, after all. I got off the phone quickly, needing to escape from Laura's pain, and my own.

The Rise of the Cult of Nat

I also called my parents that day. They didn't react as I had expected. I imagined tears, incredulity, questions, but they took in the news with remarkable calm. I think they were trying to control their pain to help me deal with my own. Or maybe the full meaning of my words had not yet completely sunk in. Later on, if pressed, my mother would tell me how sad they had been to hear the diagnosis, but mostly how sad she was not to be able to help me more because she lived three hours away from us. But at the time my parents almost seemed to be expecting the news. I suppose that, after Passover and especially after I had told them we were going for the evaluation, they had prepared themselves to hear something difficult. I asked them how they could be so calm, so OK about it. A part of me wondered, *Do they even get it? How can they not be screaming, crying in agony about this?* I found a way to ask them if they really understood what this meant, and if the diagnosis made them feel different about Nat (as I did—but couldn't admit then).

My father said simply, "Well, Sue, he's still our Nat." He seemed so certain and calm that, as the words sunk in, I felt some of my pain subside for the moment, even as I cried quietly into the phone.

My father's answer defined how he and my mother would always relate to Nat: with fierce loyalty, commitment, and ownership, mixed in with a little bit of denial of just how bad things were. Their flat-out refusal to see Nat as being very disabled can be both maddening (invalidating to me) and yet also, paradoxically, empowering. The same combination of commitment and denial has often provided me with just enough optimism to get through some very rough spots with Nat.

Over time we have found other people in our life who also see Nat in an all-positive light. These include both of our families and most of my friends. My own grandmother, who had chastised me at Passover for paying too much attention to newborn Max, and thereby causing Nat's abominable behavior that day, ended up being another fervent fan of Nat's. She refused to see anything wrong with him, except when she once referred to him as "a little slow," a remark that both annoyed and pleased me because it told me she admired Nat so much that she couldn't see his real problems.

She, our families, my close friends, and certain of his teachers all became part of what we called Nat's cult, people who believe that he is capable of much because that's what they want to believe. And yet because they do believe it, they often get a lot out of him. The Nat cult has been our lifeline. Its members defend Nat and see him as a delightful character. They chuckle over his spirit, his range of abilities in spite of his difficulty speaking. Instead of limitations, they see only his "vistful" smile, as my immigrant grandmother used to say. To them he was the boy who always did what he could, our Mini-Man who tried so hard. Members of the Nat cult help us get through some of our darkest times.

I trace the cult's beginnings to a conversation with my father back in the days before Nat's diagnosis. I was telling him about Nat's ability to memorize books. In spite of all Nat's problems, Dad said with the utmost confidence, "You're going to find he's gifted." I sometimes still draw on the hopeful certainty of those words to give me strength. Like my father, Ned and I told ourselves, "He's still our Nat."

Trying to Live Our Lives, A.D. (After Diagnosis)

Nevertheless, the pain in those days after diagnosis was almost unbearable for me. It was as if my baby had died and someone else had taken his place. I could not see him the same way anymore. I didn't know how to face this new life I had been given. I started going to a therapist twice a week. I went on Prozac temporarily, for my anxiety and depression. Needing company, I tried to go back to the neighborhood playgroup, but being there only made me feel worse. I tried to tell the mothers about Nat's diagnosis. For me it was a big moment, but none of the mothers seemed very shocked. The moment passed anticlimactically. No one knew what to say.

During this time I felt alone with my despair. Ned didn't talk about his very much, so I didn't want to bother him by talking about mine. I felt anxious, scared, sad. Angry, too. I was mad at Ned for having been wrong about Nat in the first place. I felt like an animal caught in a trap, wishing to chew off its own leg to get away.

How did I mother my children back then? I don't remember the details of those days. I see quick images of diaper changes, television, rides in the car, the drugstore, supermarket aisles. I called Ned at work way too much. I went to playgrounds and parks, where I unloaded Max—and Nat, if he would allow me to—and sat on a bench, watching them sadly. I was like a ghost mom—there, but not really there. I hated other women, with their perfect-seeming kids. Why did they get to have trouble-free lives? Why was Nat broken? When I looked at him, I felt ashamed, and sad, so very sad. *Where did you go?* I would think. He was so beautiful, with his serene look and blue leather sandals, that a friend used to call him Christopher Robin. Outwardly he was the perfect image of a boy. But his beauty belied a tragic secret.

Yet he didn't display any outward awareness of my state of mind. Instead, at least on good days, he ran around, prattling to himself and smiling at me. He didn't seem to mind Max's being in his life, either, despite what others had previously thought. But he was frequently difficult at the park. I didn't know it at the time, but I imagine now that as I wheeled him in and unstrapped him from the stroller, he probably had no idea what to do next. He saw children all around him, noisy and unpredictable, running around haphazardly, speaking what must have seemed like gibberish because it was too fast for him. Perhaps he would turn around, see my unsmiling face, hear my exasperated tone of voice. ("Mommy sad" is how he expresses it today.)

Looking back, I imagine him battered by frustration and confusion, and lacking the words to explain it to me. Sometimes he would simply sit in the stroller and suck his thumb, deriving primal comfort from that activity, as he always had. But there I would be, pulling at his arms, trying to extract him. He didn't know the word *why*, but he probably felt the pressure of it in his chest. Once out of the stroller, he would entertain himself in the ways that made sense to him: throwing wood chips or sand up in the air, and watching it shower down. The falling mulch or sand was a dependable and delightful cause-and-effect for him. He didn't notice other people's reaction until the inevitable yelling began: *Get that kid to stop throwing stuff!* People in the park must have thought Nat was a bad kid with a bad mother. I noticed the way they looked at me, and I heard them whispering. One day, a mother actually moved her kids away from us.

In those days, only Max could get through to me. He was the bright spot, bringing me a joy that helped keep me going.

SUGGESTIONS FOR GETTING THROUGH THE EARLY DAYS, AFTER DIAGNOSIS

- Try to keep to the same routines, such as going to the playground, nap time, and housework.
- Seek professional help. I went to a therapist and started a course of Prozac.
- Men often have more difficulty expressing their emotions than women. In the days after diagnosis, I talked to Ned often, but tried not to overwhelm him with my grief. (Visit *www.supportforfamilies.org/internetguide/index.html* for many helpful resources, including a link to the National Fathers' Network, a site designed for fathers of children with special needs.)
- Tell people slowly and deliberately. I didn't tell most people about Nat until I felt safe and ready to do so.
- Make a point of remembering what is still good in your life. I reminded myself of Max and of the lovely spring-time we were experiencing. These were just as real as Nat's diagnosis.
- For inspiration, read the short essay by Erma Bombeck in which she imagines how mothers "are chosen" for disabled children. It's posted on the Internet at *www.aboutautism.org.uk/reflections.htm.*

Finding a Way to Talk about It Together

Even though I didn't feel comfortable about constantly discussing my feelings with Ned, I simply could not control it. I would call him at work and cry while he listened in silence. I would suddenly start discussions just as we were falling asleep. I kept sending words his way, little missiles, hoping to break through his defenses. I really needed him to let me in, but he had little experience doing that. He was used to protecting me, not confronting his own pain.

But eventually my talk built a bridge between us. I slowly realized that it was up to me to get Ned to open up somehow. I had to be there for him, for once, instead of expecting him always to take care of me. I had to put more effort into watching him and figuring out what he was feeling.

As the old dependent, needy me shifted a little to make room for Ned's needs, he gradually started to express his feelings, quietly but in ways that I learned to recognize: sighing, telling me what he wished for—in phrases, not paragraphs. I had to learn to be quiet, to wait and listen, which was hard for me. Thus, we took turns being sad and reassuring each other. We could not both be sad at the same time because someone had to "mind the store." We never actually discussed this arrangement; it just happened. Some nights, Ned would rest his head against my shoulder, eyes watery, not saying much. Other nights—or days on the phone—it would be me crying, denying reality, unable to move forward. I was amazed at how differently we processed information, feelings, and ideas. I was so much faster, had so much more to say. But he would chime in when he disagreed with something I had said, so it was not simply a one-way conversation.

Talking about the problem in this way, facing up to it, was the best thing we could have done for our relationship.

The Excitement of Finding Helpful Books

Because I gave myself time to grieve, I was able to move effectively to the next stage: educating myself. After a few weeks, my despair began to boil off, replaced by a ravenous need for action. I was furious that I had doubted my concerns when Nat was a baby. I had a big chip on my shoulder about the people who had not seen, or had refused to see, his problem. But I was especially angry at myself for not believing what I had felt all along. All I could do now to atone for this terrible mistake was to learn everything I could about autism. It gave me a mission and a focus.

I walked to the library, settled into a carrel, and started with *The Diagnostic and Statistical Manual of Mental Disorders* (DSM IV). This cheerless book tells it to you straight, one way: the worst possible scenario. I read the book's definition of autism, and although I recognized bits and pieces of Nat in it, I did not believe it described him well. It was too bleak, too final. It said very few autistic adults can live independently, and most end up institutionalized. I wanted to kill the person who had written it. I wanted to kill myself.

In the end, I simply refused to believe it. *No way,* I thought. We would prove them wrong. I put the book down angrily, looked for other sources, but there was almost no other scientific information on autism to be found. What I did not know then was that this moment of angry disbelief was my first act of advocacy, the start of the new path we would blaze for Nat.

A book of a different sort soon caught my interest: *There's a Boy in Here* by Sean and Judy Barron, a memoir by a mother and her autistic son. Judy chronicles the events of Sean's life, while Sean comments periodically on how the same events felt to him. She describes the utter dearth of resources and educational opportunities available back in the 1960s, when Sean was little, and how she had to figure out the truth of her son's situation by herself. Judy is convinced that by never giving up on him and developing her own methods of engaging him, she pulled her son into normalcy and forced self-understanding upon him. Sean is a high-functioning adult today, and he and Judy believe he is cured of autism.

I was and still am skeptical that one can be cured of autism, but I do think an autistic person can improve with the right approach. However, you cannot argue with the Barrons' success. What grabbed me especially in their story was the courage, persistence, and *chutzpah* Judy showed in discovering what types of interventions were right for Sean in the face of a total lack of support—and in the face of downright blame. Judy Barron refused, point-blank, to accept what people told her and came up with her her own prognosis and her own approach for Sean—and succeeded.

I discussed the book with Ned, feeling the first tremors of excitement and hope; so did he. Judy Barron's pluck and ingenuity in the face of very few resources buoyed me. Ned felt excited and awakened by this story, too, and he was also relieved that I had done so much of the research for both of us. I could distill the pertinent stuff for him, leaving him free for a little while to escape into his work. But when he got home, I would lean on him. This division of labor suited us both. Doing research occupied me fully and gave me a sense of purpose. As for Ned, the information I had dug up gave him some peace, at last. I began to feel more peace of mind, too, as I understood better what we were dealing with and what I would have to do to help Nat.

Reaching Out

My next step was to locate other people like me, like Judy Barron. I called the local branch of the Department of Mental Retardation, which ran an autism support group at a nearby office. My first night at the autism support group felt to me like coming home. In this room full of strangers, I listened to story after story like mine. The mother whose child would not eat and for whom even the great Children's Hospital of Boston had no clear diagnosis, who had finally returned home to Venezuela only to hear from her old family doctor the word she had been fearing all along: *autism.* Or the father of twins, one normal, one disabled, who had been given multiple diagnoses but who kept hoping and emphasizing the positive, only to realize that all the diagnoses were euphemisms for autism. Or Sheila, whose son had just been examined because the doctors suspected a hearing loss. He had not spoken a word until he was three. Yet testing revealed that his hearing was perfect.

The more horrible the story, the better I felt. Hearing the stories enabled me to formulate a story of my own, an explanation for what had happened to us, and tell it to the group. It went like this: Nat's lack of interest in peers, toys, playing, all were clues if I had been strong enough to follow through. My pediatrician had also dropped the ball. If only she had known more about the early signs of autism! I should have trusted my gut. Because of the delay in diagnosing Nat, he had missed out on at least a year of potentially helpful therapies. What grim satisfaction I felt telling my story! It made me feel like a different person, cynical, hardened, and wise. I reveled in the eccentricity of the children discussed in the group; the collective misery we all felt was a balm to me. I found strength and relief being with people who had been wounded like me, who had lost the dream of perfect children, who understood how harsh this world can be.

I told Ned about the meeting, but going to support groups was not his thing. He had a hard time knowing what he was feeling at a given moment, let alone expressing it, especially to strangers, so he stayed home with Nat and Max while I went to the group. He took over giving them their baths, and loved sitting with them while they played in the bubbles. He read to them constantly, fervently. He also found comfort in making to-do lists. I would find little index cards scattered across his desk and dresser, with items on them like "Call school people" mixed in with "Talk to roofer."

After each support group meeting, I related what I had heard to Ned, recreating the session for him. It was the tender beginning of a shared experience that allowed us some distance from our grief. Together, we analyzed the people I had seen at the meetings, comparing their families to ours. Ned was my sounding board, my information synthesizer. But I think if he had gone with me to the support group, he would have broken down and cried as soon as he tried to speak. Instead, every now

> ### Beginning the Healing
> ### Process as a Couple
>
> - Share with each other whatever you've found that's given you hope and support. I talked to Ned about the books and information that inspired me, such as *There's a Boy in Here* and my local autism support center's "introduction to autism" packet.
> - Give your partner the space to share his or her feelings. I gently and persistently talked to Ned about my feelings, trying to let Ned talk more than me. Sometimes I had to will myself to be silent and listen.
> - Find a support group that at least one of you can attend. Visit *www.autism-society.org*, the website of the Autism Society of America. This site also offers information on different approaches to treating autism, chat rooms, and other valuable links.
> - Develop a way of making autism an acceptable and interesting topic to discuss. I told Ned stories from the support group, which helped us understand autism in a broader context and perspective than just what was happening to Nat.
> - In thinking about the future, think in terms of "we" instead of "I." What should *we* do?

and then, he would lie back on the couch and sigh, but he wouldn't say anything. He didn't have to.

A Helpful New Strategy: Crisis Storybooks

One breakthrough with Nat came even before his diagnosis, our first practical strategy for living with his autism came in the late fall, around Nat's third birthday. We were supposed to go to my aunt's for Thanksgiving, as we had for Passover. Visions of that last family gathering, with Nat standing in the doorway, refusing to come in, kept me up at night, nearly forcing me to cancel the visit to my aunt's. Unless something was changed, we knew without a doubt how he would behave there, and it was probably this clarity that inspired Ned and saved the holiday for us.

"There are no good Thanksgiving books out there," I remember grumbling to Ned the night before we were to leave. "Wouldn't it be great if there were a book that explained ex-

---

MAKING CRISIS STORYBOOKS FOR YOUR CHILD

- Determine the event that your child needs to be prepared for, such as Thanksgiving, a family trip, or the arrival of a new baby.
- Using simple sentences, write out a short story describing the event. Focus on aspects of the story that will interest your child and that are essential to his comprehension of it. For example, Nat's book about Thanksgiving had lines like, "Nat will sit at a big table. A lot of people will be there: Mommy, Daddy, Grandma . . . Nat will eat a piece of turkey, potatoes, and some cornbread. When everyone is finished eating, they will sit and talk a lot. Nat can watch a video quietly while he waits to go home."
- Be sure to explain not only what will happen, but how it will likely make your child feel. For example, "You might feel a little scared when you see all the people at Thanksgiving, but you will soon feel happy because they all love Nat and everything is all right." You can also take this opportunity to describe appropriate behavior.
- All stories should end with the most familiar, comforting

actly what to expect out of Thanksgiving? Like a step-by-step
account of 'here's what we do at Thanksgiving, here's who will
be there, here's how it will end'? So that a kid like Nat could
understand what it's all about? I mean, how many three-year-
olds need to understand about Pilgrims and Indians? Isn't the
real issue for little kids (especially Nat) the table full of people,
the food you have to eat, the traveling?"

"Why don't you make the book yourself?" Ned said. "Do it
exactly the way you just told me. Write it just for Nat."

By then, we both knew what kind of book Nat liked best,

---

continued

place or situation. Nat's Thanksgiving book ends, "When
everyone is finished talking, we will get back in the car
and go home." This gives a comforting sense of closure
and security. Once you've finished writing your story,
you can either handwrite each sentence or two onto
separate blank pages or create an electronic file on the
computer.
- To illustrate your story, gather photos to glue onto the
pages or draw pictures by hand. I even cut up some photos to fake the images I need, putting together different
people, places, and objects. If you're working on a computer, you can insert digital photos right into your text,
and, if you can't find the image you're looking for, you
can use clip art (there are many websites that offer free
clip art images, cataloged by subject).
- To bind the book, you can use tape or staples, or, to
make your book more durable, you can put it into a
plastic report cover (available at any office supply store).
- Read the book together many times until your child
has internalized the message.

and how the verbal repetition of simple facts sometimes helped him get through new experiences. If the book explained, one-two-three, the beginning, middle, and end of our particular Thanksgiving, complete with family pictures, maybe Nat would be able to walk all the way into the house this time.

That night I set about creating the book, gathering family photos that we didn't mind cutting up, along with magazine pictures of Thanksgiving food. I also wrote text that was simple and straightforward, just the kind that made an impression on Nat. It started something like this: "Nat's daddy just told him he would be going to celebrate Thanksgiving tomorrow." On the same page I attached a photo of Ned talking to Nat.

The text continued: "'What is Thanksgiving?' Nat asked Floppy Bunny, his friend," and so on. Making the book helped take our minds off the imminent evaluation appointment that hovered threateningly over us.

The book was a huge success. Nat insisted on hearing it over and over, thrilled to see a book about him and the rest of us. By the time we got to my aunt's house, he had memorized it, and to everyone's surprise and delight, he walked right into Aunt Rhoda's kitchen, quoting from the book. He knew, because the book had told him, how Thanksgiving would go and what it would feel like to be at Aunt Rhoda's, and this, I'm sure, gave him a sense of control.

After Thanksgiving, we made a book called *Nat's Christmas* because we were going to be having a large dinner with Ned's family, with equal potential for tantrums at the door. In one section of the book I wrote that Christmas is a holiday cele-brated by Christians. We learned just how closely Nat had fol-lowed the text when he looked around the Christmas table and loudly said, "Christians." Everyone burst out laughing, and Ned's cousin Rich looked around quickly in playful horror and said, "Where?" Nat's exclamation was so outrageous and also so momentous that everyone at the table could appreciate it.

We made great progress using these homemade books, which we called "Nat Books." Ned and I made them together and had fun doing it. It gave us a feeling of working toward a common goal, and more importantly, of having some control over a difficult problem in our lives. We divided our tasks in a way that felt natural: I wrote the text and gathered photos, and Ned helped with production. These crisis storybooks continued to play an important part in working with Nat after his diagnosis. We found that making these books gave us a purpose and distracted us from our pain, which was now beginning to become somewhat more bearable. Yet questions remained in the back of our minds. Our life as a family was stretching out before us, some of the path now clearly defined by autism. How were we going to walk that road with our two very different little boys, and where would we end up?

3

THE FIRST
SCHOOL PROGRAMS

T HE HAZE OF GRIEF WAS LIFTING, leaving us shaken and weak but able to see around us once more. I had a fledgling understanding of what we were dealing with, and a new sense of direction and purpose: we had to get Nat some help. Crying at the playground was no longer what I felt like doing with my days. We had lost so much time already, having failed to get him evaluated as soon as my first doubts arose. Now it was time to move ahead with the project of finding him a school program.

Before I contacted anyone, I recalled that the doctor who diagnosed Nat had warned me about dealing with the school system. He had said it could become adversarial. I decided I would try my hardest to keep that from happening. The school system would love us, especially Nat. I didn't realize then that their liking us would have no bearing on the way they would handle Nat's placement. If I could have seen our dealings with the school system as something less personal and more bureaucratic, I might have had an easier time expressing my concerns, and following my instincts, and I might have found Nat an appropriate placement earlier than I actually did.

I started the process by calling the school department. After speaking to a few different people, I hooked into the right offices (though it didn't help that our local phone book listed SPED, or special education, as "SPEB"!). I learned that what we wanted was a "core evaluation" for Nat, a series of evaluations that would lead to a team meeting with the evaluators, out of which we would create an individualized education plan (IEP) for him. (See the end of the book for a helpful glossary of terms used in the special education system.)

The Core Evaluation

The core evaluation began with home visits by the school psychologist and the speech language pathologist, which included a modicum of testing because, as had been the case with Dr. E., Nat was not able to follow through with the testing activities. They asked me a lot of questions about Nat, such as his level of competence with things like self-help, communication, and play. They seemed enthusiastic about his skills without giving me any indication of exactly which skills he lacked or what the school could do to help him acquire them. The specialists saw that Nat couldn't use language functionally, could not answer questions, used repetitive, script-like speech, and was not connected to anything we tried to do with him.

A few days later, a social worker called me and interviewed me over the phone about our home life. I had no idea why he was calling, and I should have asked him; now I understand that this kind of interview helps the school system form a picture of a child's development process and his home environment. If I had understood the purpose of this visit, I would have emphasized that we needed home-based support for Nat, to teach him things like toileting and play skills. If your family is struggling in any way, your child will also struggle, and school systems and other organizations (like your state department for mental re-

HELPFUL HINTS FOR HAVING
AN EFFECTIVE SCHOOL EVALUATION

- Don't be distracted by "happy talk," or positive, general comments. For example, "Oh, Nat is delightful. He's a very capable boy." While it's nice that they like your child, it's not enough. Instead, get those performing the evaluation to see your child's problems in detail. The more specific the evaluation, the better adapted the IEP goals will be to your child's needs.
- Be prepared to answer questions about your pregnancy and your child's skills and problem points in areas such as toilet training, dressing, pretend play, functional language, fine and gross motor skills.
- If a question occurs to you, ask it.
- Take notes. Get and keep names and phone numbers of all the people you speak with.
- For more helpful tips on school evaluations, visit the First Signs website at *www.firstsigns.org/treatment/schools.htm.*

tardation or the Association for Retarded Citizens) can help you by providing home-based support and respite care, among other valuable services.

I handled each encounter with the specialists as a separate, discrete event, not understanding the overall process, and I didn't have the preparation I would have needed to discuss Nat with them in an informed, proactive way. The resulting core evaluation seemed jumbled and confusing, leading to an ineffectual team meeting. I wish I had understood that the evaluators' data indicated substantial delays in communication, functional language, social ability, and even some cognitive deficits. While I understood that Nat had some form of autism and would need a special kind of education, I did not realize that the data from the school evaluation should have led to an education plan designed to target those areas with specific techniques and services (some of which I did not know about until later). I could have insisted on specific goals with measurable small steps that would demonstrate actual progress (or lack

---

How to Prepare for IEP (Individualized Education Plan) Meetings

- Familiarize yourself with the major available treatments and educational interventions for autism. See the appendix for a basic list to use as a starting point.
- Insist on setting measurable, quantifiable goals rather than agreeing to general descriptions as a way of determining progress. Some examples: (1) Accurate answering: Given the choice between objects for which he has strong likes or dislikes, the child will answer "yes" and "no" accurately eight out of ten times. Pickles are often offered to the child for this exercise. (2) Time on task: Using a timer and reward at the end of a designated time period, child will work at any IEP goal to extend the ability to work on demand. (3) Facility with money: Child will accurately identify types and amounts of different coins presented eight out of ten times.
- Be sure the goals cover everything you feel is necessary—such as pre-academics, socialization, play skills, attending skills, daily living skills.
- Make sure the service delivery (how much speech or physical therapy, for example) is frequent enough for your child's needs.
- Find out whether there are comparable peers for your child to be paired with and whether there are role mod-

thereof). Vague, merely descriptive evaluations can lead to vague, general, and ineffective IEPs. Avoid IEP goals that read "Child will improve his reading ability." The goal should be specific, for example, "Child will read Maurice Sendak's *Where the Wild Things Are* for content and comprehension. For a 'wh-' question such as 'Where did Max sail?' child will use the prompt, 'to where the . . .' when he does not have the answer."

---

continued

   els with better behavioral and communication skills in the classroom.

- Research all the programs in your area and their approaches, including those provided in-house, within your local school system. You may need to push your team facilitator for this information, but it is essential.
- Talk to trusted people outside the school system (specialists, support group buddies, doctors) about the different programs and understand their particular biases and favored approaches. Everyone's got one!
- Make a list of the features you would like to see in your child's program. The items on the list should answer the question "What does he need, and how is he going to get there?" But don't have unrealistic expectations about getting everything on the list. Prioritize—figure out what you can give up, if necessary. (An IEP meeting is a negotiation, after all.)
- If possible, arrange for a trusted specialist to attend the meeting with you as a support; a little of the "good cop, bad cop" routine can help parents get what they need.
- Visit the website of the Federation for Children with Special Needs (*www.fcsn.org*) and click on "education and special needs" for more valuable information.

The Team Meeting

The day of the team meeting with the school people was gray and snowy. Lugging Nat and Max, we trudged through sherbet-like slush to a conference room in Town Hall, which was filled with so many empty tables and chairs that I barely had enough room to put the boys down. While Nat scribbled on the blackboard, the team members gave cheerful reports, with everyone stressing how wonderful, charming, and engaging Nat was. The meeting gave us little useful information because the evaluations had not been very technical, avoiding labels and negatives and only describing what Nat could do, such as with language or during the cognitive testing. I didn't know what questions to ask, let alone how to determine whether the program being proposed for Nat was suitable for him.

Only later would I learn that public schools are notorious for shying away from labels or comparisons. Labels often come with their own set of recommended services, which cost the school system money and resources. Specific comparisons with other children are difficult because school personnel are obligated by law to protect children's confidentiality. So while it would have been helpful to know how Nat compared with other children, we couldn't find out.

I didn't know then that the meeting could have included a discussion of multiple placement options. No one on the team recommended we visit other schools or consult other professionals. Instead, the team agreed to a "diagnostic" placement of three months in a neighboring town, which would help us determine more precisely what Nat needed. Action, any action, sounded good to me, but three months seemed a long wait to see if progress had been made. After all, Nat was so far behind already! But I kept my concerns to myself, trusting the people around me—the same trap I'd fallen into before. My instincts were telling me to stop them, to ask questions, even ones that might make me unpopular. But that voice was still not strong enough.

We were sent by our team facilitator to observe the language-based special education classroom that Nat was to be placed in. It was staffed with teachers who spoke simply and repetitively, where distracting toys and games were covered with sheets, and where all other objects were labeled with small stick-figure images showing you their purpose. Some of the children there had feeding tubes, wheelchairs, blank stares, for this was a typical special-education classroom, meaning that it was devoted not only to autistic children, but to children with a variety of disabilities.

It changes you forever when you experience childhood contorted by disability or illness for the first time. It is like witnessing the distorted reflection of a heretofore perfect world. After a while, you get used to it and even come to appreciate the perspective it has given you, but I was not there yet. The images of childhood I had started to see in my life with Nat were different from those depicted by Brazelton, Leach, and Spock. Everywhere I looked, I saw so much ugliness and hopelessness. Max's world, by contrast, looked golden, filled with opportunities and possibilities. Nat's seemed like a dead end.

I suspected that the program I visited wasn't right for Nat. If a program treated Nat like a limited person, as I felt this program would, he would become a limited person. I also couldn't see how a classroom filled with such varying special needs would be right for my child's particular set of issues. But I didn't trust that I knew enough about the matter. The only way I managed to express myself was by complaining to Ned after the visit about the way the classroom looked, with so many different kinds of disabled kids who were not like Nat.

Ned didn't share my feelings. Instead, he believed that this classroom was a place where Nat could get help. "The kids in the program don't make him autistic," he argued with his usual logic. "The program will help him because he *is* autistic."

But I was so filled with anguish that I didn't even go with Ned to bring Nat to his first day at the program. I could not bear it. Still, I did not know of any alternative to the program in our area. After all, this was what the school was offering, and what did we know? We had to get him help. He had to go somewhere.

Nat's First Program

Nat cried a lot at school in his first days there. It made me too sad to see this, so in keeping with our new partnership style, Ned took charge of the school drop-off and even stayed at the school for a good portion of those first two days. The first day, Ned sat in the hallway outside the classroom, and Nat cried because he knew Ned was out there. The second day, Ned sat in the hallway upstairs, so that Nat would have to tough it out. This worked better, and by the third day Ned no longer had to stay at the school with him or even drop him off there.

Instead, Nat began to take the school bus (actually a van that accommodated the special needs kids). Ned felt particularly sad and nervous about this, however. He said to me, "How will it be for him, to go off on a van? We have to trust other people so much." I agreed, but I also noticed that Nat didn't seem to mind being on the bus at all; he probably enjoyed the monotony and predictability of the trip. We also found that his driver was a happy, kindly older woman who quickly bonded with Nat and made us feel that he was being given the best of care.

Over time, Ned relaxed and didn't agonize as much over the van issue, but some years later, we would both have new anxieties over the trustworthiness of van drivers. Once, when Nat was ten years old, a new driver took him to the wrong school, dropping Nat at the door and not waiting for anyone to collect him. Nat walked into the building and wandered the halls. Finally, an occupational therapist who traveled between school programs in the town recognized Nat, knowing immediately that he was in the wrong place. As she bent to talk to him, she heard him muttering something very, very quietly. He was whispering the name of his school over and over.

> ### HOW TO HANDLE THE INITIAL DAYS
> ### OF A PLACEMENT
>
> - Familiarize your child with the school and staff ahead of time. Construct a crisis storybook about the upcoming event. Visit the classroom prior to the first day and take pictures of the staff, space, and classmates (check first if the confidentiality policies of the school allow it). If possible, take a picture of the van (if the child is being transported) and the driver.
> - Visit the classroom with your child prior to the first day for added familiarity.
> - Determine what your child needs from you to ease his transition and whether you can stay in the classroom with him—or just outside—for the first few days.
> - Construct a daily update page that the teachers can use to check off activities from the IEP that your child participated in each day. List any activities you wish to hear about, such as "played pretend with . . ." or "interested in reading the following books." Some schools use notebooks for communication with parents, but you can design your own form if that suits your needs better.

In his first classroom Nat was a quiet little boy who made no trouble. He performed his school activities—including speech and occupational therapy, which he had three times a week—in the same docile manner he had exhibited at home. If he couldn't perform a classroom project, the teacher's aide would use the "hand-over-hand" technique, guiding his hands with hers to help him complete the task. As a result, when I saw the work he had done, I suspected that the teachers had really done most of it.

"He's able to participate in all the activities," they would proudly report.

"But does he understand them?" I asked. The Nat I knew still enjoyed twirling string in light beams and chewing on anything that wasn't food. As for finger painting and Play-Doh, better make sure he's had lunch first!

"Oh, we think so," they would say reassuringly. "He has really adjusted well to coming here."

Hearing this made my heart sink because I knew then that they did not get it. I knew all too well how easily Nat had separated from me after the initial difficult transition to school; I had no problem imagining him stoically enduring the long bus ride, sucking his thumb, staring into space. Because he was compliant, and smiled at the teachers occasionally, they assumed—incorrectly—that all was well.

Still, we kept Nat in that class not only for the entire three-month diagnostic period; we also kept him there for another year beyond that. Despite my misgivings, we let Nat languish in that classroom while my frustration grew. I was reluctant to raise objections. For one thing, I didn't know what else was out there. For another, I loved the head teacher, and so did Nat. He called her "Diane, you teacher." (Nat did not know how to use pronouns, and this remains a difficulty for him.) Diane, a lovely person, was very attentive to Nat, and she seemed to know a lot about autism.

But his responses in that classroom did not indicate strong progress. The doctor's words came back to haunt me: "You'll know within a few weeks if this is the right program for him." We were concerned that he was not improving rapidly or even measurably, but it was hard to prove because Nat's IEP goals then were too general and not sufficiently broken down into quantifiable objectives. Also, we both wanted to trust the IEP team. In doing so, however, we were unconsciously accepting a pessimistic view of Nat's potential, believing that perhaps this was all we could expect from him. And so Nat lost another year.

Having Doubts, Then Feeling Empowered

Later, in my autism support group I learned that my suspicions were correct, that it indeed was possible to get more out of our child and out of the special education system. One dad had set up exercises for his autistic daughter to do at home, to keep her engaged for as long as possible each day. He would insist that she play with her nonautistic twin, that she answer questions he posed to her, that she stay on task, whatever the task was. This little girl was the highest functioning of our group, and his reports sometimes made me jealous. I also learned from the twins' father the importance of a long school day, longer than Nat's school offered, and of one-on-one intense engagement, which Nat's school didn't offer, either. The idea that we needed to change Nat's placement began to take shape in my mind. I shared my feelings with Ned, who listened with an open mind, even though what I was suggesting would take a great deal of effort on our part.

Around this time I also read Temple Grandin's book *Emergence: Labeled Autistic*. Grandin was a real autistic person who could recount exactly *how* her parents had helped her! They had hired a governess to be with her nearly all day, a woman who would pop paper bags in young Temple's face to get her attention. They had realized that what their child needed was a way to keep her connected to others and as fully engaged as possible. Grandin, although still admittedly a person with autism, ultimately received a Ph.D. in animal husbandry and has earned the respect of cattle farmers worldwide for having invented a humane way to slaughter cattle. By this time I read her book, I knew enough about autism to appreciate the poignancy of this autistic woman's life: she was eternally puzzled by human feeling, yet so sensitive, somehow, to the feelings of cattle that she could come up with revolutionary ways to reduce their suffering.

What also struck me about Grandin's story was the parents' ability to figure out what their child needed. Just like the twins' father, they had a pioneering attitude, a kind of ingenuity that was effective and inspiring. The courage simply to make it up if it didn't exist and then stick with it was growing within me as I saw how other people grappled with problems like the ones I faced. They had all wrestled with the bleak realities of their situation, fighting for their children with little helpful information at their disposal, holding on tight to what they knew was true or could be true, and working toward their goal.

Grandin's book resonated with me, making me feel powerful and confident in my instincts. I felt new courage to do whatever I needed to do for Nat's sake. From models like Grandin's parents and the parents in my support group, I learned that if I were going to be a successful parent for Nat, I had to come up with my own particular approach to his education, something that might not be immediately obvious. The school professionals were not necessarily experts, not in who Nat was. *I* was becoming the expert, in fact, and after reading *Emergence,* I knew there had to be something better for him educationally than his current program. I could no longer wait for him to improve, nor could I wait for the initiative to come from the school.

I was beginning to understand that our dealings with the school system as a business relationship where both sides want something: The school district wants to provide an education program that follows the law—in other words, one that is as typical an educational experience as the disability will allow—and that addresses the child's needs, yet is also the most cost-effective. (Legally speaking, however, even though cost is *not* supposed to enter into the consideration of the school program, the reality is that it does. Parents need to understand this and still find a way to get what their child needs.) The parents, on the other hand, want the child to improve to the greatest degree possible, and they want the child eventually to be able to live as normal and productive a life as possible. The two sides are not necessarily at odds, but there are tensions inherent in these positions. For one thing, limited funding is a reality in public education, and for another, school systems have not, for the most part, caught up with the demand for quality autism programs, and so what they offer may not be up to the level that the parents deem necessary.

I was starting to realize that working successfully with the system is a delicate, strategic negotiation, like closing a business deal. What we wanted and what they wanted would not always overlap, but if Nat was going to get the help he required, there needed to be a working partnership, a collegial relationship.

As we learned more about autism and our doubts about Nat's placement grew, we decided to take him to some new specialists, people who worked outside the school system, to get more information on exactly what Nat needed. We saw a child psychologist at a renowned children's hospital whom we have kept in our lives as our trusted expert ever since. She was reluctant to confirm Dr. E.'s diagnosis of pervasive developmental disorder (PDD) because she saw so much potential in Nat and missed none of his engagement with the world, however erratic. "If you were to hold my feet to the fire, I'd say he had PDD," she said, "but I would rather say that he has an expressive language disorder with autism-like tendencies."

Of course, this still amounted to autism. There are many things you can call it, all many differing and interesting shades of the same basic diagnosis: pervasive developmental delay, autism spectrum, atypical development. But back then, this diagnosis gave me hope because it was so specific. She really seemed to understand Nat. We have always appreciated this psychologist's delicate calibration of diagnosis and evaluation. That is the sort of sensitivity we now look for in all our specialists. She also offered the additional benefit of connections: She knew everyone in the various private autism programs in our area, and she had an idea which programs would be good for Nat and which would not.

She also referred us to a neurologist, Dr. B., a celebrity in autism circles. The parents in my support group treated it as a status symbol that we were seeing such a prominent neurologist.

Dr. B. was one of the pioneers who had proven that autism was neurologically, rather than psychologically, based. By doing so, Dr. B. had helped exonerate the mothers of autistic children; she delivered us from being likened to refrigerators (as in Bettelheim's earlier theory).

Dr. B. did a full workup of Nat. She was the first to use the term "autism spectrum disorder" to describe his condition. Though she was not shy about using the word *autism*, she spoke about Nat optimistically, saying that with more of the right approach, kids like Nat can certainly improve. By the time we left her office, we knew that Nat needed a one-to-one student-teacher ratio; a very small class; some typically developing role models; and intensive, around-the-clock behavioral therapy. All in all, we felt strengthened by her assessment.

Shortly after Dr. B. delivered her recommendations, we politely informed the school system that we wanted to check out other autism programs because our specialists had told us Nat might require a different, more intensive program than the one they were currently offering him. They had to agree to our request and allow us to go through the proper procedures whereby the school district contacts the private program, sets up the parent visit, and sends the child's records to the school.

Visit to a New School

As part of our research into alternative placements, we visited a nearby school for the autistic. The director of this program reminded me of Albert Einstein, with his wild, frizzy gray hair. His perpetual grin told me that he loved his job, and his personal charisma energized his school. From him and his staff we learned about the relational approach to treating autism, which incorporates parts of Dr. Stanley Greenspan's popular Floortime method or DIR (Developmental Individualized Relationship-based method). The theory that underlies this approach is that children must be met at their individual developmental and cognitive levels; that their attention must be engaged spontaneously and naturally; and finally that, having been engaged, they can be led to higher and higher levels of development.

The approach used at this school appealed to us tremendously, but, inexplicably, Nat did not respond well to the director at the intake interview. Nat cried throughout the intake, and the director persisted in misunderstanding the reasons for Nat's distress. He had taken Nat's shoes and hidden them, as an experiment, to determine how well Nat could figure things out—a test in motor planning (many children with autism experience difficulties with motor planning). But we knew that Nat *could* see his shoes, and we believed he knew how to get them. We could tell that he was crying because he did not know that *he could simply go and get them,* and we were not supposed to help. The director let this go on and on, while we watched helplessly. It was tremendously frustrating: we became very angry at the director for this, and our initial positive impression of him faded quickly in the face of Nat's unhappiness.

For us, if not for Nat, the director's dogmatic personality was a problem. We simply could not come to any agreement with him about why Nat had responded so negatively to him at the intake interview. It felt to us like the director would not hear our side. His theories seemed to be based in something other than directly connecting to Nat, and so they seemed false to us. We had been through three years of people not hearing what we had to say about Nat, including nearly a year in which the personnel at Nat's school had failed to understand his needs. We were not about to waste any more time in a place where we weren't listened to. This was to be the first of many times when the two of us would be galvanized by a professional's lack of understanding of Nat. We simply do not accept it. We know that we, the parents, are in the driver's seat, and we know our kid best.

We next turned to a school that used behavior modification, a very different approach from that of the school we had just visited. The hallways of the second school were immaculate, with little or no kid art on the walls, giving it a coldly institutional appearance. Through the years we have been struck over and over again by the depressing, drab look of Nat's potential placements. Very few of them actually look like schools, full of creative learning opportunities and happy days. Max's schools have always been bright, messy, thronging places filled with children's projects, things hanging from the ceilings, off walls, poking out of the desks. Nat's schools, by contrast, look as if their equipment came from the reject pile, with a few battered toys, a few books, an outdated computer. We have to keep moving beyond the insult and the injury, the pinching injustice that our kid's not only autistic, but his school is also depressing. Ned helps by keeping his sense of humor, often bringing up the joke where the old couple on a cruise complains that the food is terrible and the portions are too small. We have to be brave, always pushing forward and trying to overlook the obstacles, including the unappealing look and second-rate resources of many schools for kids with autism.

The behavior-modification school had what is known as an inclusive classroom. This means there were typical (non-autistic) peers, at least at the preschool level. The typically developing peers served as role models in turn-taking and role-playing exercises. There was also a low student-to-teacher ratio as well as a highly structured, predictable day that Nat would be able to understand quickly. The approach there was clear: observe the behaviors that the child needs to change; set up his environment so that he understands rapidly what is expected and has ample opportunities to perform according to those expectations; reward him when he does; and repeat lessons frequently, taking small, achievable steps so as to maximize success and capitalize on the autistic child's predilection for repetition, predictability, and structure.

I worried that the personnel at this school took their methods a bit too seriously (sometimes I still do). They spoke in clinical terms, of prompts and cues, in jargon that sounded like it belonged in a lab, not a school. Viewing a child as a collection of behaviors can lead you to view him as a creature more than a person. But that method is that school's claim to fame. I have never enjoyed behaviorism as a way to raise children. My style as a parent is much more moment-by-moment, inconsistent but creative. Setting up a reward system to get a child to perform a task implies that the child will not understand the intrinsic value of the task and will perform it only after being bribed.

On the other hand, the approach does work for us, especially for teaching targeted behaviors and skills. I could see that this school would help Nat because it would focus on him, one-on-one, and work toward concrete goals like following instructions, making simple conversation, and playing with others. What I especially liked about the school, and what made it impossible not to send Nat there, was seeing the theory come to life in Nori, the head teacher. A towering, energetic woman, she looked as if she could convince anyone to do anything—even Nat. She showed us how the school's behavioral approach worked. She stood ten feet away from Nat, facing him.

"Nat, come here."

No response.

In a neutral, pleasant voice, Nori said, "Nat, this is 'come here.'" She went over to Nat and gently moved him bodily to where she wanted him to be. She then put him back where he had been, ten feet away. Nat was captivated by this strange maneuver.

"Nat, come here."

Nat moved back to Nori without a moment's hesitation. He had followed a verbal command, just like that! My heart leapt with joy.

"Great job, Nat!" She hugged him.

He smiled.

And I was sold.

Nat went to the new school the fall that he turned five, about six months after we visited. We had very little resistance from our team, probably because at the time our town chose to use out-of-district, private placements for the more complicated kids, rather than create their own programs. Also, it was fairly clear that Nat had not progressed too much, particularly after we had our report from Dr. B. The report stated that we ought to be giving him a far more intensive, one-on-one educational program that directly taught skills, rather than the classroom program he had been in, where skills were acquired more incidentally. But also, we had approached the matter through the proper process of letting the team know our every step and our thoughts, keeping the dialogue open and utilizing expert opinions that were respected by the school district. We had direct, mostly positive conversations with the school system's special education director about Nat's lack of visible progress, and we discussed our specialists' conclusions with her—that he needed the direct teaching and the specific behavior modification techniques of a school like the one where we were proposing to have him placed. There were some raised eyebrows, but in the end, they didn't argue with us. We had done our homework. We had observed Nat frequently in the school system's program, and along with observing the alternative programs, we had dutifully gone to look at the district's classroom proposed for the next year, finding it more of the same as what he'd been getting. We were determined to make this placement change for Nat, and the team knew it. We never caused them to feel attacked or defensive, however, because our attitude was that we all wanted what was best for Nat, and it was time to cut our losses. In the face of Dr. B.'s recommendations, the district's lack of a bona fide autism program, and our confidence, they could hardly refuse us.

When Nat began the new program, we found out, to our great pleasure, that Dr. E. had been right: Nat showed dramatic improvement within weeks. He quickly developed classroom skills such as attending (listening), participating with the group, and answering questions. He learned to take turns and actually played with Max for the first time (a game of Candyland). He began to be able to tolerate transitions. He even wore a costume and sang in a school play at the end of the year.

Nothing lasts forever, though, as I have discovered. Programs have their life cycles. Children's needs change, and staff members come and go. By the autumn of Nat's second year at the school, Nori had moved on. This was our first experience with the transient nature of the staffing of private special education schools. Generally the teachers are fresh from college, eager, enthusiastic, willing to take low pay in exchange for first-rate training in working with difficult special-needs cases. Then, once they have acquired some valuable experience, the public schools snap them up at higher pay rates, leaving this very vulnerable population of kids—kids who need stability and consistency for comfort—with new teachers every six months or so. Nat will still occasionally talk about teachers or bus drivers long gone from years before: "Elmer left. No more blue and gray van."

Nori's replacement had been trained in exactly the same way as Nori, and she got some fairly good results with Nat, but it wasn't the same. He continued to progress in his listening, social skills, answering, and beginning academics, like color and shape identification. But we began to be concerned about what we called his "silly talk," a disturbing new behavior where he would use nonsense language to stimulate himself and shut us out. In fact, we soon became mortified and alarmed by this new development. Silly talk was strange and embarrassing. Like us, the school disapproved of it and tried to teach Nat to stop it. It separated him from other people, making them notice that he was different, the teachers said. I desperately wanted to help him stop it, feeling that Nat had to pass for normal, as much as he could.

The school advised interrupting him, giving him things to say in place of his nonsense words—for example, "Nat, you can say, 'I'm bored. Let's play.'" This technique seemed to work, but it made me very uncomfortable. What if the words I was putting in his mouth didn't really represent what he wanted to do or say? And anyway what was *causing* this problem? His teachers didn't seem to know. All they could tell us was to continue to interrupt the "behavior," and it would lessen. Ned would shake his head. "I can't imagine that this is the right thing," he would say. I agreed. It was as if the school had only one solution for a given problem. So it was up to us to tell him what to say?

We were only beginning to realize that we had stumbled upon an immense and complex question: how much do we try to change his essential nature, to make him more of a person who can operate in the real world, and how much do we accept as inviolably him? It was a question that would plague us for years to come. Typical kids are allowed to have quirks. They're allowed to have hobbies, however odd. So why can't autistic kids? Most experts we have come into contact with, including that school staff, have assumed that when Nat does anything odd, it is the autism, and the odd behavior should be treated. But many of my friends and family members suggest that much of the behavior is just Nat being Nat, or Nat being a kid, a goofy kid.

Nat indulged in his silly talk more and more as he grew older, but in time I came to view it as an essential part of him. Yet it took me years to reach this understanding. My years of observing him—first as he uttered non sequiturs and incongruous sentences memorized from books, then as these utterances morphed into Nat's nonsensical words, and now, as he opens and shuts his hand in a rhythm that matches his utterances, as if he is working a hand puppet—have shown me that silly talk is far more to Nat than a strange behavior. It is a complicated and important act of self-affirmation, not something he can or should switch on and off.

He can modulate it, though, if I ask him to, something I do only if I must. "Nat," I might say, "quiet silly talk when we are in the store."

"Quiet silly talk in the store," he repeats, looking anxious, pulling on his lips. And he complies, at least until we leave the store, when he immediately goes back to the silly talk.

What does the silly talk mean to him? I have had to ask myself, observing his angst when he has to repress it. I believe now that he does it to comfort himself, and that it is a coping mechanism. Many of the experts we consult have said as much. But what is the silly talk helping him cope with? And what does it imply about Nat and his life? Could it be that simply being around other people, hearing but not comprehending them is often so difficult for Nat that he must make these everyday, seemingly harmless interactions more bearable by softly talking to himself, by creating around him the sounds he understands and therefore prefers? I've become more and more certain that the answer is yes. Nat has an absolute and basic need to do this, and I am increasingly determined to allow him this.

WHAT WE'VE LEARNED ABOUT SCHOOL PLACEMENTS

- No program, no single approach will be perfect for a given child. You have to accept some degree of disappointment with each placement.
- Programs have their life cycles; their success waxes and wanes with a child's development and changing needs. At each point in a child's development, one program will be more effective than another. Thus, you have to stay current about what's available and reevaluate frequently.
- A visit to the next year's classroom can convey a real understanding of whether the placement will continue to be an appropriate fit in terms of teacher quality and peer group.
- A positive visit to other programs can empower you to try something new. It's very important to see for yourself what else is out there.
- At the same time, of course, transitions are hard for the child. It's important to ask yourself if it is worth making a change.

We began to break away from his behavioral school during that second year, largely over the silly talk dilemma and the school's simplistic view that the problem was strictly behavioral. Though we didn't understand the silly-talk yet, we knew we disagreed with school's approach, and it felt like an important philosophical disagreement. In addition, we didn't like the classroom the school was offering to Nat for the following year, which was no longer inclusive, meaning that Nat would no longer be exposed to typical kids as role models. Finally, Nat was getting the behavioral approach eight hours a day—sometimes at home, too—and I wondered if it was what he needed at that point. Though we were sad to see Nat leaving what had been a wonderful placement for a while, we wondered whether all the rigidity was good for him and also whether he could do with less intensity, now that he had improved so much.

When we met with the team that spring, the district's early-childhood social worker picked up on our ambivalence toward Nat's program. She offered us another avenue: a pre-K classroom in our town, which had a top-notch teacher and three support staff (aides). Nat would do his kindergarten year in this pre-K. Nat was doing well enough at the behavioral school, but maybe it was time to try a "less restrictive environment"—language the social worker took from the federal law concerning students with disabilities (the Individuals with Disabilities in Education Act, or IDEA). The law calls for children to be educated, whenever possible, with "typical" peers.

I loved the thought of Nat going to school in our own town. Our town has an excellent school system, and I was so proud that the team thought he could make it there. There's a kind of machismo in autism circles about inclusion: Parents whose children succeed in regular classrooms crow about it, and who can blame them? Schools enforce this attitude by claiming that their programs are so effective, you can't even tell which students are disabled and which are not. Having a kid who can "pass" for normal seems to be the goal of many parents of autistic children, and although that is understandable, it can also set you up for a feeling of failure when you have a child who simply can't, as I was to discover.

The agonizing choice between inclusion and seclusion, between a challenging program and a safe but stagnant program, was to plague us often. I have always wanted to see Nat as more capable, more successful, less affected by autism than perhaps he actually is. My denial, like that of my parents, manifests itself as hope, sometimes realistic, sometimes not. I have often been the one in our marriage to push the envelope, to try Nat at the new activity, the more typical school setting. I feel that you never know, maybe it will work out, and then you'll have something great: a higher-functioning kid. But Ned always says, "Why? Why does he have to be in our school system? Why do we need to see if he's going to fall on his face or not? Just sending him to a regular classroom, someplace that might be beyond him, doesn't make him capable of being there."

Yes, but we had to try. Not trying, to me, meant giving up on him.

The Inclusion Experiment

Even though there were no children remotely like Nat in the proposed classroom, and the level of instruction seemed over his head (the teacher actually used the word *oviparous* in a lesson about eggs with her prekindergarteners), we chose the inclusive placement because it appealed to our desires for Nat. It spoke to what he might become, rather than what he could actually do. Almost immediately, though, I had misgivings about this experiment. I watched Nat enter the basement classroom, in a daze from all of the chaos of a public school. I felt buffeted by the whir of children all around us as we entered the building. I hated the din, this noise of normalcy, because I knew how overstimulated it would leave Nat. And sure enough, he was already shutting down. I saw him walk wordlessly by his teacher, past student after student as they greeted him. And then watched as no one tried to make him respond. At this new

school, they all just let him be, with a slightly baffled resignation. My blood started to boil. *Nat could have answered you, you
just have to make him do it!* I wanted to yell at them. *Touch him on
the shoulder, make him look at you!* Didn't they know that he
needed follow-through and reinforcement? Almost right away,
I knew this setting was wrong for him. I panicked, thinking of
all the time he had already lost: missing out on early intervention and then his first, inadequate "classroom."

"Oh my God, they're so lax!" I screamed into the phone on
the second day of school. "He's going to regress! We have to get
him out of there. Right away!"

"Sue, calm down," Ned said sharply. He'd been through *this*
before, my panicking. He knew how I could get and how difficult it was to fight me when it came to Nat. And somewhere
inside, I suspect, he also knew I was probably right, for my instincts had proven right so many times before. Still, he doggedly
pushed back, his part in a now-familiar dynamic that usually
gave our marriage strength as we dealt with all the challenges
autism brings. "We don't have to do it right away. Maybe we
can work with them," he said.

"No!" I snarled. "I can tell they just don't get it. Why should
we wait? He is already so far behind! Don't you remember
what the neurologist told us: 'You'll know very quickly if a program is right for him or not.'"

"Sue, this is very soon to be making a change. You know
that's what they are going to say ..."

"I don't care what they say! We're the parents, and we
know!"

"Let's just give it a few weeks, that's all I'm saying. Let him
settle in."

What was making me so adamant was that this time, I
knew how long it would take to get a new placement. All the
people involved would have to agree: the team, the special education administrators, and the new school he would go to.
There had to be an opening, as well. I just was not ready to do
all that work yet.

So instead, the second week of the placement, I complained to the program director, who, as Ned had predicted, counseled me to give Nat's new classroom time. Time. Who had time? I felt certain Nat would lose all he had gained, very quickly, and it made me nearly crazy.

By December we called a team meeting to discuss what to do about Nat's progress. I had gotten hold of a kindergarten checklist, which listed the skills that our school system's kindergarteners were supposed to work on. Using the list, and with Ned's help, I drew up a new IEP for Nat, with activities that would promote each of these skills, using the choices and areas that were offered in his particular classroom. For example, during work time, Nat could be encouraged to use games and puzzles and other manipulatives to help him gain facility with letters and number recognition. During break time, he could go to the playhouse area, but there the aide would provide him with scripts for role-playing with the other children. Another goal for Nat to work on was computer and pre-literacy skills, using the computer and library areas. When he was in the library area, the aide would teach him reading, not simply let him flip through a book mindlessly, as the staff had been doing since the start of school. He also needed to be drilled several times a day, as he had been at his behavioral school, on pure language skills, with repetitive grammar lessons.

During the December meeting, Ned and I explained this new IEP, and the team appeared to understand and accept it. We presented our case cogently, using concrete examples they could easily grasp. They could see our frustration, and they shared our desire to make Nat's placement work out. Before the meeting ended, the team agreed to our new plan—and to assign one of the three aides directly to him—and the school followed the plan for the rest of a very successful year. Even though we felt pretty certain that we would have to find a new placement for next year—there was no classroom in the next grade up that could be adapted in the same manner as Nat's current classroom—we were very satisfied with how the staff worked with Nat for the rest of the year, using the new plan we had drawn up for them.

We now felt we had a pretty good idea of how to work the school end of things. With three placements under our belts and a detailed picture of what Nat needed in a program, we had the freedom to consider another question: What was next for us as a family?

4

LIFE WITH OUR
TWO SMALL BOYS

In HIS EARLY YEARS, Max followed Nat around everywhere, usually smiling, sure of his welcome, even though Nat mostly ignored him. When Nat walked into a room, toddler Max would exclaim, "Nah!" and joyfully point to Nat, delighted once again to have discovered he had a big brother. But over time, Max, whose face registered every emotion, looked puzzled by his brother's unresponsiveness.

I knew we couldn't go on acting as if they had a typical relationship. We needed to help Max. The sooner he understood about Nat, the better, I reasoned, so that he would not blame himself for the difficulty between them, as siblings of autistic children sometimes do. But a direct lecture about Nat's disability made no sense at this stage. Instead, I would need to look for occasions that naturally called for explanations of the awkward interactions that left Max bewildered.

I began to discuss with Max the things that transpired between him and Nat, describing aloud to him what I imagined Max was feeling. I believed this would help him get a clearer idea of his situation, and maybe it would lessen the pain of being chronically ignored. If his feelings were clear to him, they would be easier to deal with—or so I hoped. Max was a very perceptive, bright little boy whose skill with language seemed beyond his young years. It seemed to me, as he listened intently to my words, that he understood what I was getting at: that Nat's responses were about Nat, and not about him. And certainly because he never exhibited signs of anything other than normal anger or sadness, I was inclined to believe he had internalized my message. Openly acknowledging and discussing what was happening became a key element in our family life after diagnosis.

Ned and I also believed that by talking to Nat about the emotional and social dynamics between him and Max, we could improve Nat's understanding of relationships and feelings. I hoped that the more Nat heard descriptions of social interactions and the emotions that accompany them, the more emotional vocabulary he would acquire, and the better he would understand social interactions in general. Back then I knew that one of the tools I had for dealing with Nat was repetition. Why not repeat to him simple descriptions of the emotional/social interactions between him and Max (e.g., "When you hit Max, it makes Max sad. Look, Max is crying. Max is sad.")?

Nat did seem to understand what we were saying to him, and unfortunately this was most evident when he would smile after we pointed out that he had upset Max. We began to realize that Nat was drawn to intense emotions, particularly those that were predictable. We wondered if Nat preferred the drama of strong emotions because they were easier for him to notice and understand. For Nat, angering people was a predictable and easy way to interact. From his perspective, making someone happy was more complicated and not always as satisfying, especially when you compare a smile's impact to that of a sharp cry.

Sometimes we felt our approach backfired, but we also understood on some level that it was a good thing that he could make the connection between his behavior and Max's response; we understood that making connections between cause and effect could be very difficult for people with autism. We were just at a loss as to how to help Nat seek out positive interactions.

Finding Shared Activities for the Brothers

At about this time, when the boys were around five and three, Nat and Max discovered videos. They especially loved the Disney Sing-Alongs, which they watched repeatedly. And the more they watched a given video, the more Nat liked it: in his case, familiarity breeds enjoyment. The winter Nat was five was filled with "Heigh-Ho" and "Spoon Full of Sugar." The predictability of these videos must have appealed to him, as well as the brevity of these sing-alongs and the fact that they didn't have any confusing plot for him to follow. The music helped, too. Nat has always liked music. In fact, I know now that many autistic children love music videos, especially those by Disney, with their obvious emotions. In a Disney production, you know who is good and who is bad; what is sad and what is happy. No guessing needed.

Nat still loves music; any radio station will do. But he can't bear it when we change the station—it's always too abrupt a transition for him. He puts our CDs in the player and listens to certain tracks repeatedly. He happens to enjoy the Allman Brothers and R.E.M. as much as Jiminy Cricket, Snow White, or Ariel. As Nat and Max have grown older, Nat has remained a Disney fan and finds it difficult to appreciate the new, age-appropriate movies that Max enjoys. They no longer watch as many videos together; but our youngest son, Ben, eight years Nat's junior, now watches those old Disney videos. Nat loves watching the videos with Ben. When Ben asks to watch one, Nat will leap to his feet and say, "YES!" Sometimes, by the end of the worn-out old video, Max will have wandered in to watch with them, attracted by the comfort of the familiar and the desire, perhaps, to be able to share a moment with both of his brothers.

Just about the only other activity that Max and Nat could share at this point was going to the park. But this held limited enjoyment for Nat, and for me. Even though Nat was now in his first special education program, he hadn't learned what to do in the playground. Thus, I spent a lot of energy trying to get Nat to play with the actual playground equipment instead of throwing sand and wood chips. It wasn't until Nat began attending the behavioral school program that I learned how to get him to play on the slide or the swings. What it came down to was forcing him to slide a given number of times before rewarding him with his preferred activity, such as pacing the perimeter of the sandbox. For a while, we followed that dynamic: I forced him to try a desired activity, let him know when he could stop, and rewarded him for the effort. My interactions with him during this era were fraught with boring repetition and minimal progress. But if I did not ask anything of him during our playground visits, he would learn nothing new and remain completely in his own world.

I knew that this was no way to raise children and be happy. Sure, I wanted to help Nat improve his play skills, but the days of drawn-out trials, rewards, and struggles stretched out before me like a prison sentence. I told myself that I would only do a little bit during each playground visit, and that it was OK to let Nat be for the rest of the time—a reward system for me. Anyway, I needed the time to play with Max, who needed me just as much as Nat did.

Things started to get better after I began going to the park with Sheila, a friend from my support group. Sheila had an attitude toward life, and especially toward her son Sam's autism, that was new to me. She approached everything—from her children's mischief, to literary discussions, to marriage—without surprise and with the same jaundiced eye and wry half-smile. Sheila accepted it all with equanimity, calm, and dry laughter, and this was both startling and soothing to me. In the playground she would turn Sam loose, rolling her eyes and hoping for the best, while her older child, a daughter, would play with Max, even though she was three years older. They found things in common, especially because Max has always been old for his age. A quick study and a sensitive little kid, Max could stretch himself to play with whomever was around; in this case, he found some common ground with Elizabeth in their shared love for animals. They played animal games with Beanie Babies or pretended to be animals themselves. While they played, we could focus on Nat and Sam, or just talk to each other. Sam, a year younger than Nat, needed a lot of supervision. He was always trying to leave the park or do dangerous things like climbing fences or trees. Sheila and I enjoyed helping each other with our boys' problems: Nat with his tantrums, isolation, and throwing; Sam with his bolting and climbing. We could laugh at our children together, and this made us feel as if our lives and the autism were manageable and not so bad after all.

Traveling with Nat and Max

Over time, because we felt we had cleared some of the initial hurdles of autism (we had begun to figure out how to live day to day with it), our confidence as a family of four grew. We decided to take some new risks, planning two vacations the year that Nat was five. That January, we went to Florida, staying at Disney World. In preparation, I created *Nat and Max Go to Disney World,* a book that included pasted-in pictures cut from the Disney hotel brochure to illustrate where we would be spending our time. It also emphasized the long time we would be spending at the airport, on the airplane, and in the taxis.

The book helped make our trip fairly smooth, but I was still not prepared for how difficult Nat's silly talk would be for others on the airplane. When he got loud, as he sometimes did, other passengers would look over at us, and some of them would stare angrily. What could I say to them? Was I supposed to explain to strangers, who hadn't even asked a question, that my child was autistic and couldn't help it? Would such an explanation help or hurt? It was on this trip that I came up with a good method for dealing with Nat in public: I would show them without telling them. On the way home from Florida, as Nat got on the plane, I said in a fairly loud, schoolteacher voice, "Nat, you'll be sitting there, next to Mommy. There. That's right. Good boy." This way, I indicated to those around us that Nat needed more coaching than a normal child; that there was something unusual about him, but that I had it well under control. This technique seemed to work. I got appreciative smiles from the surrounding passengers, rather than judgmental frowns or raised eyebrows.

At Disney World, I decided reluctantly to use the autism to our advantage, showing the people at the ticket booth a note from our doctor that detailed Nat's disorder, including his inability to wait in lines. Why not, Ned asked me? We pay enough for this problem in all the other parts of our life; why not take a break when we can?

After reading our doctor's note, the ticket booth attendant gave us a handicapped pass that allowed us to cut to the head of lines for the attractions. At the Dumbo ride, we encountered hostility from the other people in a very long line. I heard someone say, "Hey!" when we were allowed to cut ahead. Others just stared at us, doubtless trying to understand why we were getting on the ride so far ahead of them. After all, none of us was in a wheelchair, and Nat was behaving perfectly.

We found that at Disney World, as corny as it sounds, dreams really do come true: Nat learned how to use the toilet for bowel movements, which was a miracle to us. When we got to the hotel room, I showed him where he would sleep and where the bathroom was. I also showed him the Cadbury chocolate cream egg he would get if he pooped in there (reward system dutifully set up). To my surprise, he went right into the bathroom and did it! We could not get over it. One entire year of messy accidents, disgusting laundry, growing despair, and all it took was a trip to Disney World!

Later that day, while walking down Main Street U.S.A., I caught sight of none other than Jiminy Cricket. By then Nat and Max were very familiar with the whole Disney canon and all the Disney characters from having watched the sing-alongs. This familiarity, in fact, was one of the reasons we had chosen Disney World in the first place. We were already beginning to understand that the more things in a new environment that Nat could relate to a previous experience, the more comfortable he'd be there. Because we'd told him we were going on a vacation where Pinocchio and Snow White live, Nat was set up for success.

There was only one problem: Jiminy Cricket was surrounded by children clamoring to hug him. Nat would probably withdraw from their noise, or not even notice Jiminy. My instinct was to pull him and Max back until the crowd cleared, but I was afraid we would miss Jiminy altogether if we held back too long. And we could not afford to miss this opportunity: this was Jiminy Cricket, from *Pinocchio,* Nat's favorite movie!

Then Max caught sight of him; there'd be no hanging back now. And as we moved closer, Nat saw him, too. Nat's eyes widened, and he marched right up to Jiminy Cricket, past all the other kids, yet somehow, nobody protested. I had never before seen Nat so assertive about something that he wanted, especially if other kids were in the way!

As Ned and I watched, holding our breath, Nat said, with giddy happiness, "Hello, Pinocchio! It's Pinocchio!"

Debonair as always, and not missing a beat, Jiminy Cricket reached out toward Nat, and they shook hands like old friends. The encounter left Nat beaming.

Our Disney vacation would turn out to be an emotional roller coaster ride, though, with burning disappointments and then, right around the bend, heady triumphs like the meeting with Jiminy Cricket. We were building up our toughness during that vacation, learning to regroup quickly after each unexpected difficulty. One low point came on Pleasure Island, where a colorful little fountain burbled up at unpredictable intervals, accompanied by a song from *The Little Mermaid* called "Part of That World." I found myself listening to the words: "I want to go where the people go. I want to see them dancing, laughing . . . wandering free . . . wish I could be part of that world."

Looking at Nat, who appeared to be listening intently to the music, which he knew from his Sing-Alongs, I was suddenly paralyzed by a grief that came out of nowhere and hit me with such force that it left me speechless. My breath caught in my throat, and I began to cry quietly. I was crying for Nat, who

---

WHAT MADE OUR FIRST VACATION A SUCCESS

- I created a crisis storybook to prepare both boys.
- I thoroughly researched our destination in several guidebooks in order to make our days more predictable.
- I prepared a travel bag with snacks to distract or reward, as appropriate.
- On the airplane, I tried to enlist fellow passengers' empathy by displaying my confidence and control (even if I had to manufacture them.)
- I normalized the hotel room, making it a home-away-from-home. I set up an area for toys. I put Floppy Bunny on Nat's bed. I showed him where we could eat snacks and watch television. I showed Nat the bathroom and his reward for using the toilet.
- I used a handicapped pass to make our visit to Disney World more bearable.
- I allowed myself my moment of grief when it overtook me.

knew the words but was not really part of this world. Did he want to be? Did he know what he was missing? It was a possibility I hadn't considered until then. What if Nat understood he was different but didn't understand why? How could I comfort him? How could I ever explain it to him if his language abilities were so impaired? For a few moments I struggled helplessly with my sorrow. Then Max called me, wanting to move on to another attraction. I shook my emotions off; I had to. I ran to meet Max, taking Nat's hand.

Summer Vacation

We were becoming a crack little family, full of strategy and purpose, yet no matter what we did, or how well we prepared for each new event, we still could not prevent or predict the little spasms of sadness that would seize us from time to time. But we didn't let this stop us from taking a vacation on Cape Cod that summer, when Nat was five and Max was three. My parents had rented a lovely house near the bay, with enough beds for the six of us, and a loft space for my sister and her husband. It was wonderful having my parents there as extra support. It enabled Ned and me to go out to dinner by ourselves several times, which felt like a luxury, even if it was to roadside clam bars and lobster shacks.

My parents are very active grandparents, and they enjoyed being our hosts. My father was determined to bond with Nat, to overlook his autism, and to act as if nothing was really wrong with him at all. This attitude worked well. During that vacation, my father got Nat to do things that others couldn't, such as take walks and pick up fallen twigs from the yard. My father's stubborn optimism seemed to be just the thing for getting Nat's attention and commanding his best behavior.

I had prepared for this vacation by putting together a book called *Nat and Max Take a Summer Vacation,* which described the daily routine of breakfast, beach, picnic lunch, bath, dinner out, and bedtime. I made some of the text into silly little songs, which got through to Nat even better than straight prose. He and Max seemed to enjoy the songs and quickly learned them:

> We're going to a restaurant, restaurant, restaurant.
> We're going to a restaurant: chicken, hot dogs, fish!

But Nat had difficulty on that vacation in a way that we hadn't foreseen. When you don't play with beach toys and can't swim, being at the beach is boring. Every day we would go there, lugging the shovels, the buckets, the trucks, the sifter, but only Max and Ned would dig in the sand; Nat refused to. The most he would do was to take a bucket, fill it with water, and systematically wet section after section of the sand at his feet. At times, just like at the playground, we tried to teach him "beach skills." We had Nat fill up buckets with sand using a shovel for a certain number of minutes, and then we rewarded him for this activity by letting him be, or giving him a sweet snack. But it frustrated both Ned and me that although we could teach Nat to play with shovels and buckets, we couldn't get him to enjoy it.

After a few attempts at building up Nat's beach skills, we let it go, choosing instead to manage his behavior and to focus on Max and on having a good time ourselves. Ned had perfected the art of building sand cars, realistic-looking automobiles made of packed and sculpted sand, for Max to play in (something Ned's own father had done with him on the beach). Ned would try to engage Nat in making these—and had to keep him from wrecking them. Sometimes he built structures specifically for Nat to wreck, but it was hard to limit his destruction to only those. Our attention shifted from trying to engage a bored Nat in beach play to discouraging a mischievous Nat from spoiling other people's sand castles, sand cars, buckets full of beach treasures.

One strategy we began to employ at the beach was the five-minute warning. We would tell Nat, "Five minutes of bucket play, and then you'll try swimming." Or "Five minutes in the water, and then you can eat." My sister once laughed, "God, Sue, with you guys it's always 'five minutes this, five minutes that!'" But the five-minute system actually helped. Nat and Max both benefited from the structure and the cushion the warnings gave them. It was during unstructured play time that Nat would become most mischievous and destructive.

Our beach days were a mixture of great fun and dreary effort. We had to find ways to protect Max's feelings as much as we had to work with Nat. Ignore and redirect were the strategies we had found so far. We would try to respond neutrally to Nat's mischief so that we didn't reinforce it. (Responding angrily would excite Nat and possibly lead him to do it again, just for the strong, predictable response.) We would also model positive beach behavior to him and give him ideas of other things to do. But because he wasn't interested in typical beach activities, this strategy didn't work too well. And so our new emphasis became empowering Max instead.

Our approach was to help Max by letting him in on what we knew about Nat's mischief. We would educate him, and give him strategies to deal with his brother. We explained that Nat was doing bad things to get our attention or to get a big reaction. We explained that when we ignore Nat's behavior, we're teaching him not to try to get our attention that way. "Try not to let him see that it bothers you," I would say. Max seemed to understand us, but as a three-year-old he had a hard time feeling good about this solution. What Max really wanted was for me to punish Nat, or better yet, for me to force Nat to rebuild the things he'd wrecked. But we didn't know how to get him to do that. We thought we had a better chance of getting Max to adjust his response. It wasn't until much later, when we understood much more about Nat's motivations, that we got better at taking control of such situations.

Fortunately Max's gentle, understanding temperament was a perfect foil for Nat's difficult one. But I worried about Max, about his psychological well-being and his emotional safety. I was determined not to let anyone take advantage of Max—including Ned and me—and so I was always sure to talk to Max about his feelings concerning Nat and validate them. I learned to say, "I know it's not fair when he wrecks your things. I know you hate it when he laughs at you. Mommy and Daddy are working hard to teach him how not to do that." And Max soon did pick up on the art of ignoring, coming to me with his feelings rather than sharing them with Nat.

When Nat tired of wrecking our sand structures, he would pace the beach, talking his silly talk and turning heads as he went. We had to watch him constantly, or else he would wander off, walking far away from us. I felt sure that people who saw him walking by himself were thinking: "Whose kid is that?" How I wanted him to be someone else's! I knew intellectually that I had no reason to be ashamed of him, but I was ashamed. I felt responsible for who he was. I knew that most people had no real understanding of autism, no awareness that these kinds of bizarre behaviors could be part of a developmental disability. I couldn't help thinking how much easier it would have been if his disability were manifested with a wheelchair or hearing aid.

In his beach mischief, Nat sometimes targeted people beyond our family group. Once he pushed a little girl to the ground. He would laugh loudly at anyone crying. Once, he even poured a bucket of water into a stranger's handbag while she was sunbathing.

"What? What's the meaning of this?" she sputtered, jumping to her feet, outraged. She towered murderously over Nat.

My husband stumbled over as fast as he could, shamefaced and guilty, and blurted out apologetically, "Well, it's no excuse, but he's autistic . . ."

Her entire demeanor changed instantly. She waved her hand, stopping Ned. "Oh, well," she said kindly, sitting back down on her wet blanket. "Well, it's going to be a process, you know." She must have had some familiarity with autism—and we were grateful for it.

Tips For Surviving Beach Vacations

- Arrange the trip so that you can go home easily if you want to. We stayed with my parents so that we would not have to invest money in a trip that might not work out. We gave ourselves the option of going home at any time and kept our expectations low. This way, when we made it to the end of the vacation week, we felt victorious.
- As much as possible, make the vacation predictable. We constructed crisis storybooks and made up songs to explain what our vacation would be like, activity by activity.
- Give your child ideas on how to spend time at the beach, like blowing bubbles, filling buckets, and playfully running away from the water. We reminded Nat of the positive things he could do, like spilling water out of his own buckets. We also made sand structures that he was allowed to wreck.
- Bring along rewards. We brought his favorite treat (fudge) to the beach to reward him for good behavior.
- Prepare for transitions. We gave the boys five-minute warnings before changing activities.
- Try to maintain the upper hand. We cut our beach time short when Nat's behavior became too difficult, but rather than leaving immediately after a bad incident, we announced to the children that we would be leaving in five minutes. Leaving immediately after a bad incident reinforces the acting out, sending the message that if Nat acts badly he can get out of a situation he doesn't like.
- When necessary or appropriate, be honest and direct with those around you about your child's issues.
- Don't go it alone. We got others to join us at the beach so that we would have support.

We despaired over ever being able to enjoy ourselves wholeheartedly at the beach. Nat's behavior was stressful. We didn't know why he had to act out, why he had to use his little bit of connection with the world to annoy other people. All we could do sometimes was grit our teeth and get through an hour at a time. Nat seemed immune to reasoning, and we didn't feel we could punish him for mischief because we feared that would escalate it and feed into it. He wasn't attached to possessions the way that other kids were, so we couldn't threaten him with taking something away if he misbehaved. Anyway, Nat didn't have the cognitive ability to understand threats. The anguish of the question *Why did he do that?* would remain a defining, potent force in our lives for some time to come. But even if we didn't understand Nat's motivation yet, we were beginning to anticipate and grapple with some of his difficult behaviors, enough to have some confidence that we'd enjoy ourselves when we went away.

Home Becomes a School for Nat

Through young childhood so far, Max and Nat hadn't developed much of a friendship. Aside from watching videos with Max, Nat didn't show much positive interest in anything Max did. I had thought we would be able to foster better interaction between them, and that Nat would have developed better communication skills by now. Not knowing where to go for help, I started to fantasize about pulling Nat out of school altogether and teaching him myself. I proposed this to Ned, arguing that I had learned so much about autism and about Nat that no one was better equipped to teach him.

But Ned responded, "If you're so sure about wanting to teach him, why don't you do it while he's home after school? You know, supplement what he's learning?"

I didn't know what to say to that because we both knew the truth was that I couldn't do much more than I was already doing to interact with Nat or play with the two boys when Nat was home. I had too much to do just running the household and being their mom. I dropped the subject with Ned, but I kept turning it over in my mind, hoping I could turn my impulse into a workable plan.

During a walk with my parents a few weeks later, I complained about the shortcomings of Nat's placement in the prekindergarten, as well as his former behavioral school program. I could tell they understood my desire to teach Nat myself. They asked questions that conveyed their support. They sympathized with my fear that Nat was going to regress, and they agreed that I knew him best and was probably qualified to teach him. They were excited by my enthusiasm to take Nat out of a setting where the expectations of him were low so that I could shape him into his fully realized self. Their fiery enthusiasm for Nat's potential further ignited me, making me feel that anything was possible, including homeschooling him. But they also worried about me becoming overloaded and overwhelmed, and somehow their concerns got through to me where Ned's had not.

During that walk the homeschool scheme was transformed in my mind into a more realizable plan: an after-school homeschool, just as Ned had suggested, but with the details now fleshed out in my mind: I would develop the curriculum, educational goals, and activities suited to home life and leisure time, but rather than trying to do the teaching myself, I would hire a tutor. I set about creating a mini-school in Nat's room, and I wrote out a list of goals along with ideas for for how Nat could reach them. I bought special toys and games for this purpose, and a notebook where the tutor I would hire could record the day's activities, successes, and problems. I already had someone in mind for the job: my neighbor's nanny, Liz.

Our first foray into a tailor-made, home after-school program for Nat worked very well. Liz was young, enthusiastic, and bursting with love for Nat (and Max). Her presence added something to our home life that I had forgotten about: relaxation. While she worked with Nat on playing the games, singing songs, and basic interaction, I could take a deep breath and go to the store or simply to another part of the house and not think about Nat for a while. Her mission was to keep him "with" her; to make sure he always answered her questions, even if he had to be given the answer, just as Temple Grandin had been made to respond to her governess. Liz did not have any behavioral training behind her, but she did have the desire to understand children like Nat, and the compassion needed for the job (she wanted to go into teaching one day).

Liz would spend the two hours getting Nat to sing with her and Max, joining them in Play-Doh activities, taking them to the park and getting Nat to play on the slide or the swings instead of sifting the sand. It was a wonderful situation for us that worked for about a half year, until Liz moved on. I quickly replaced Liz first with Teresa, a teacher from Nat's former behavioral school, and then with Karen, a student from a nearby college.

Moving to a New Home

When Nat was nearly six, we decided it was time to leave our condo and buy a house we could expand into. At our new house we had a small yard. In our urban town, most houses didn't have much outdoor space, so this little green postage stamp felt like a luxury. I dreamed of the small cottage garden I would plant out there, where there was room for a tiny play structure and a couple of café chairs and a table. This house represented a new era for me and my family: one where we would have room to entertain, hold family cookouts, and have a place for the boys to play safely outside without having to go to a park. The little yard satisfied my desire to avoid the curious eyes of other mothers. By now I had come a long way in terms of my ability to function well with a child like Nat. Yet taking Nat to playgrounds and parks was still difficult for me, and I was glad to have the option of playing at home, and to get a break from his difficult behavior around others.

HOW TO SET UP TUTORING
SESSIONS IN YOUR HOME

- Advertise at local colleges or in local newspapers for someone who has patience, creativity, a sense of humor, and the desire to work with a disabled child. Be prepared to pay more than for typical childcare. We tried to pay as much as we possibly could, reasoning that we wanted a highly motivated person.
- Interview each candidate and observe each of them interacting with your child before hiring them.
- Get a notebook with dividers, one divider for each goal the tutor is to work on. We jotted down ideas about how to work on the goals and what materials/toys to use for each.
- Get your child comfortable with the whole idea of homeschool by starting slowly, an hour at a time, with breaks and rewards. See my website, *www.susansenator.com*, for more ideas and inspiration.
- Encourage the tutors to take notes on their progress. These notes will help you understand your child better and may come in handy at an IEP meeting when discussing his skills and motivations.
- Encourage the tutors to branch out and come up with their own ideas for goals and methods. Some of ours brought their own materials such as papier mâché, beads to string, and bags of treats for rewards.
- If you are considering actual homeschooling, the MassPAC website has a homeschooling resource link at *www.masspac.org* (MASSPAC is a Massachusetts-based parent organization, but the site is helpful to anyone.)

The house was wonderful, and I lost no time painting every room and fixing up a bedroom for Nat and Max. I painted their walls a creamy white with a periwinkle blue border that depicted the "Hey, Diddle, Diddle" nursery rhyme. It was a comforting, pleasing environment. We had to make the move as comfortable for Nat and Max as possible because transitions were hard for both of them. Like Nat, Max would become very attached to familiar things and places—at age twelve, he still keeps his tattered baby blanket in his bed—and he would need to see that this new place was going to be OK and hopefully better than what we'd had before. Having bunk beds and getting to sleep on the top bunk would help him with that.

Nat, too, would have to get used to new routines and new walls, but I was not as confident that I would know how to reach and comfort him. We would have to guess at what he needed. I suspected that he would like the bunk beds too, and wouldn't mind sharing the room with Max. I wanted to give them every opportunity to bond, even if all it amounted to was just breathing the same air at night. Maybe the habit of being together would help them develop a silent communication with each other, and a loyalty. This was a dream that I indulged in because I didn't want to give up on their having a relationship of some sort. I was afraid that soon Max would not want one since they didn't play together and because of the way Nat broke his things. And so I was glad to find that Max still wanted to room with Nat.

To make the transition to our new home smoother, we walked through the new house before moving day with the boys and took pictures of all the rooms, with the boys in them. We used these photos to make a book about the move to help both Nat and Max to visualize what was going to happen. During the move, we made a point of following the narrative of our book, saying "goodbye" to our old house when we left it and "hello" to the new one when we got there. I set up the boys' room as quickly as possible, with the exciting new feature of the bunk bed to make it all feel like a wonderful adventure.

Taking Risks

The spring that Nat was seven and a half, my father and Ned taught him how to ride a bike. At first we were uncertain whether Nat would understand braking. We couldn't take for granted that he would know when and how to stop. But he did. Painstakingly, in several afternoons over the spring and summer, my father taught Nat by holding onto the bike in the back, just the way you'd teach any kid, and just the way he had taught me when I was seven. He was determined to continue to find things in common with Nat, to have a relationship with him, and because he was an avid cyclist and outdoorsman, he found a connection with Nat, who is also naturally athletic. (Gross motor skills have never been a problem for Nat.) When my father was not around, Ned would follow through with the bike lessons, teaching Nat in the middle of our street on Sundays.

Nat loved the freedom the bike gave him. He quickly saw it as a way to be a little "naughty," a way to get away from our supervision. As soon as we got the bike out and attached his helmet, he would ride off beyond our line of sight. One day, he tried to escape from us long enough to ride around the block, on the sidewalk, the way he did when one of us accompanied him. When I realized he had taken off, I ran after him, watching him from several yards back, running hard to keep up but not overtaking him. I wanted to give him some space to see whether he could be trusted. I had a strong feeling he would be all right, that all he wanted was to go off by himself without permission. I figured that Nat, a creature of habit, wouldn't want to go off the path he was accustomed to. He just wanted to make the loop alone, to feel the exhilaration of going off without us.

When he approached the halfway mark, I watched as, sure enough, he turned right to continue in the full circle toward home. Then I ran back the other way, to watch him come down our hill toward us. We all cheered him as he appeared around the corner. He had done the ride safely, and he had done it well. My heart swelled with pride. He was a bike-riding boy, just like any seven-year-old.

Our contentment in those days was often still dampened by Nat's destructive outbursts, but we were getting used to them. I was learning to live with a restive happiness, fleeting moments of joy that flared up and warmed me, often taking me by surprise. I tried not to dwell on the absence of the kind of easy, enduring happiness that I imagined others with typically developing children must be experiencing. I brought those feelings to my therapist. I looked forward to my sessions with her, where I freely dealt with my grief so that it didn't disable me in other parts of my life.

One of the best things about our new neighborhood was that there were other children around. Although none of them became an actual friend to Nat, they certainly got to know him and accepted him, which felt very good to us. For Nat's seventh birthday we had his whole class over for the party, and many of the neighborhood kids ended up coming as well. We hired a petting zoo with bunnies, hens, and a pony ride, something I figured Nat would enjoy because he'd ridden a pony at another child's birthday party, a few weeks earlier.

Nat did enjoy the pony ride, but so did the entire block of children, the classmates, and the siblings of the classmates whom their parents had brought along. All told, there must have been more than twenty children at the party, most of whom followed us back inside for birthday cake. In retrospect, I guess you can't expect to have a spectacle like a pony ride in a crowded little neighborhood without all the children within a one-mile radius running over for their turn. But Nat couldn't handle large groups at the time. He spent most of the party upstairs, away from everyone, while Ned and I entertained twenty kids on his behalf. We were as pleasant as could be to our guests, but I was hurting for Nat, upstairs alone and out of it. What I didn't realize until later was that we should have been doing this kind of event all along because it brought children into our home and broke the ice for them with Nat, and it also did a lot of good for Max, who enjoyed the party as he enjoyed all things that were meant for Nat. He must have thought he was the luckiest little boy in the world, for a little while anyway, for he always had exclusive access to his older brother's brand new presents. The Nerf footballs, the Playmobil castle, the "make your own solar system" mobile—all birthday presents meant for Nat ended up in Max's room either right away or eventually.

Max and Nat, of course, only rarely played together. But a great opportunity materialized for them where I least expected it. at Nat's occupational therapy sessions. I used to take Max to the twice-weekly sessions, and the therapist ended up working with Max as much as Nat. We came to approach it as a group session, thinking Nat would benefit from being able to work with Max. Although Max was younger, he served as the presence of a typically developing peer whom Nat could imitate in playing and taking turns. For his part, Max loved the ball pit, the swinging, the giant Physio balls, the roller boards, and the sessions on the computer.

I hoped these family O.T. sessions would help the boys forge some sort of bond. Looking back on those days when Nat was five, six, and seven, I suppose I had visions of Max taking on the role of Nat's play therapist, enthusiastically teaching him to play Power Rangers or mold stuff out of Play-Doh. Though that didn't happen, and was neither appropriate nor realistic, Max and Nat enjoyed a largely positive relationship, with a lot of happy parallel play. Although Max has never managed to teach Nat play skills—in fact, very few people, even those with a lot more expertise, have succeeded in that area—Nat has certainly benefited from being around Max. Max is a great role model for Nat, an ideal peer: a child close to his own age who has great empathy and patience, who can show him how to do things when he's ready.

As for Max, he also has benefited from having been thrown together with Nat so early in life. He developed tremendous self-confidence—he could always do so many things that his older brother couldn't. At the same time, Max's self-confidence is tempered by a compassion that he might not have acquired so early in life had he not grown up with a brother with disabilities. Max's easy tolerance and good-natured acceptance of the family and its limitations have been part of him from his earliest days. These aspects of his personality would become more evident as he became a teenager and was called upon to be a support to Nat, to Ned, and to me.

5

HITTING BOTTOM

The Challenges that Led Us to New Solutions

JUST WHEN WE WERE AT A POINT where we had a functional family unit and some pretty good strategies up our sleeves, I began to feel restless and to cast about for something to take us beyond where we were, something new; something that would enrich us further. I started feeling that I wanted another baby. As always, my role in the family was that of catalyst and instigator.

But if I was the change agent, Ned was the rock. I traced this difference between us to our differing natures: mine more outwardly emotional and active and Ned's more thoughtful and reactive. But my therapist challenged me with the question: What happens when Ned needs to make changes? Do I ever get to be the rock? I had to admit it was difficult to switch roles. When Ned spoke of his feelings about Nat, I would have to remind myself to be quiet and just listen. The pauses between his sentences, the gaps between his thoughts were often twice as long as my own gaps and pauses. I had to use all of my powers of concentration to figure out the emotional subtext of his words, the underlying discomfort that had led him to talk to me at a given moment. This dynamic has not changed, except that I now have a clearer idea of what to do when he needs me in this way.

The Sleep Problems

Even before Ned and I began talking seriously about having a third baby, our family had trouble remaining at rest. Stasis has always been elusive for us, but that's probably a good thing. Somehow our turmoil has always brought change, often for the better. Frustration and the drive for improvement fueled all of the changes we had made in Nat's school programs so far, for example. Similarly, my discontent and the desire to see more improvement in Nat led me to create our home tutoring program. The same dynamic played out again when Nat's emerging sleep disorder propelled us into a new series of changes and eventually to the decision to try medicating him. But unfortunately, getting to that point was a long, arduous process.

When he was seven, Nat began waking up in the middle of the night, laughing hysterically. Sleep disturbances are not all that unusual for children with autism, and plenty of children without developmental disorders go through phases of poor sleeping. Complaints about children who don't sleep well or won't stay in bed are part of the standard conversations among mothers. Max had had sleep issues, too. When he was three, he had gone through a period of waking up with night terrors. He would sit up, shrieking in fear, eyes wide open, but he didn't seem to hear anything we said to him and could not be comforted by us. A quick look into Richard Ferber's best-seller *Solve Your Child's Sleep Problems* confirmed that Max was having night terrors and gave us some helpful instructions to follow. We learned that night terrors are common in young children and, though disturbing, are harmless. Ferber's instructions were not to try and calm him by talking to him, holding him, or waking him (though he seemed awake, he wasn't). Instead, we were to coolly and calmly lay him back down and leave the room as soon as possible. Because I knew Max's sleep disturbances were normal and wouldn't last forever, I was willing to follow Ferber's instructions, though they went against my instinctual desire to hold Max until he calmed down. Ferber's advice did indeed work for Max, and his night terrors passed.

So when Nat started having trouble sleeping, we turned to Ferber again, but his techniques did not work for Nat. Nothing did. According to the Ferber, I was to close the door on Nat every time he laughed, to demonstrate that this was not appropriate behavior at three o'clock in the morning. But Nat didn't like having the door closed, and so he would get out of bed and try to push it open while I quietly held it closed from the other side. Ferber's book instructed me not to talk to him, other than to say in a neutral tone: "Get in bed, Nat." If I said anything else or showed emotion, I risked reinforcing his behavior. But being neutral and silent was the last thing I felt like doing during those moments.

Night after night, I would stand on the other side of the door, holding it closed. Nat would say, "You be good" (his way of saying, "I'll be good") and get back into bed. Then I would let go of the door and get back into bed myself. Soon after, Nat would once again be giggling like a madman. Before long, I began to hate his laugh. "We had to go and give him the middle name 'Isaac,'" joked Ned. (In Hebrew, Isaac means "laughter.") The laughter went on for weeks, not every night but often enough so that Ned and I never caught up on our sleep.

Eventually, I tried another tack: I created a book called *Good Night, Nat*. It began by introducing Nat as the main character—this was a good way to get Nat's attention—and then listed all the good things that happened to Nat as he prepared for sleep: "Nat sleeps in his own room. He listens quietly to a story. Mommy sings him 'You Are My Sunshine.' Then the lights are turned out." The rest was about how Nat is supposed to sleep when it's dark, what he might dream about (the ocean, ice cream), and how the whole house is dark, calm, and quiet.

Unlike most of the Nat Books, this one didn't work. Nat's sleeping problem was beyond the reach of things like behavior modification or the comforting and clarifying descriptions of the Nat Books. He continued to wake up during the night. We tried a new room for Nat, his own room without Max. It had pale blue walls and silver stars and moons as a ceiling border. We put in snowy white curtains and got him a fluffy white comforter. The room breathed tranquillity. But this too had no effect on Nat.

We took him to the pediatrician, who suggested melatonin, a natural sleep aid that is available over the counter. We crushed a melatonin tablet into the cream filling of an Oreo, because we didn't think Nat could swallow pills, and gave him that before bedtime. Sometimes it worked, but just as frequently, it didn't.

The uncertainty over whether we'd get a good night's sleep on any given night settled heavily over us, weighing us down as much as our exhaustion. My fatigue made me feel anxious and physically uncomfortable. I was permanently exhausted, and I was very angry about this problem. It seemed that we should be able to solve it easily, but the usual solutions didn't work. I felt a new cold distance from Nat, seeing him as a stranger whom I couldn't figure out, someone who was out to get us. When he woke and started laughing, I felt he was laughing at us, at our vulnerability, our need for sleep. Our lives had hit a new low.

The sleep deprivation did not affect Ned quite as badly as it did me, for a change. Ned had a remarkable equanimity during this time. This was most likely because of his recent success in his career. Ned has always loved his work; writing software is both his job and his hobby. During this latest sleep crisis, he was working on an important, highly rewarding project; his boss and his coworkers were a great team to work with, and the project was falling into place. In fact, it was his best work experience ever, and so he was riding a wave of career success that couldn't be dampened by exhaustion. I also enjoyed these coworkers, and we became friends with some of them, which added a pleasant new dimension to our lives. Those happy circumstances probably helped soften the harsh reality of what was going on at home, but for Ned far more than for me.

I, of course, had no place to go to escape Nat's problems. My older son had now begun to feel like a terrible weight that would always be with me, one that no one else could carry. One afternoon, the pent-up misery got to be too much for me. On top of the ongoing, daily challenges we faced, the uncertainty of getting a good night's sleep was making me crazy. I felt like screaming, crying, kicking something. I felt so desperate that I packed a suitcase to leave. Standing at the base of the stairs by our front door, I told Ned that I just couldn't take it anymore. I had to go. Either that or I wanted to die, to escape this life that had caught me by the throat. Nat came downstairs and watched us intently. Through my tears, I tried to tell Nat that I needed sleep—he just had to stop waking up. I couldn't stand it anymore.

I left the house and got as far as our porch steps. I couldn't leave my family. I put down my suitcase and looked across the street and saw my neighbor sitting on her porch and impulsively ran over to her. She invited me to sit and talk with her. She was a maternal woman around my mother's age, and I felt comfortable confiding in her. I told her everything. She comforted me, telling me about what she went through as a young mother, when her older child had severe asthma that required frequent trips to the emergency room. Hearing about her vulnerability and the relentless fear for her child made me feel less alone and more normal.

Up until then I had tried not to let the neighbors see us sweat, believing that they would only like and accept us if we appeared to be doing well. But it wasn't until I opened up to our neighbors about what we were really going through that we found a strong community of support on our street. Until then, I hadn't realized just how ashamed I'd been of Nat. My suffering back then was really twofold: the problems Nat's autism brought and the strain of hiding our struggles from the world.

After talking with my neighbor on her porch that day, it became easier to connect with other neighbors, who offered support in their own ways. Two neighbors had dogs the boys could play with; another was understanding and kind when Nat made mischief in her yard (riding his bike through her garden or turning over her flowerpots). Our whole family was always welcome at neighborhood parties, and everyone at these events was pleasant to Nat, even when he overturned bowls of salsa or licked the salt off all the chips before returning them to the bowl. Eventually we helped most of the neighbors to understand and care about Nat. They came to appreciate our unusual situation and cheered us on when Nat showed signs of progress.

It Is Always Darkest Before the Dawn

With autism, every new challenge is made more difficult by the anxiety of not knowing why it is happening or its expected duration. We never know, and didn't know then, what in Nat is a normal developmental phase and what is autism. During Nat's difficult phases, we live as if under siege, trying to defend ourselves and waiting wearily for the phase to end. But it is also in those darkest moments of not knowing what to do and wanting to give up that we frequently have breakthroughs. There is no doubt that with Nat it is always darkest before the dawn. The trick is not letting the darkness engulf us.

As Nat's sleeping problems persisted, our own lack of sleep, along with the tension of waiting to be woken up at night and the uncertainty about when this would all end, were quickly becoming too much for us to handle without help. I complained to my sister, who by now had a flourishing pediatrics practice in Florida. We had reached a point in our relationship where we frequently traded information with each other about autism. She would ask me advice about how to break the news to parents that they needed to get their child evaluated—there were more and more of them each year—and I would ask her medical questions when I couldn't reach my own pediatrician.

When I first told her about Nat's problems at night, she said, "Our nurse practitioner just told me about a drug called Clonidine for sleep problems in kids." Clonidine is primarily used for treating high blood pressure in adults, but it also acts as a sedative and is used for treating a range of illnesses, including attention deficit disorder, Tourette syndrome, and panic disorders in children.

But medicating Nat seemed too drastic a step to me and Ned. Nat was so young; barely seven. Back then (in the mid 1990s), it was far less common to give children psychoactive medication than it is now. Our attitude changed one afternoon, when we were sitting with my Aunt Rhoda and Uncle Sree, who had hosted that fateful Passover dinner five years before where we all finally understood that Nat needed help. This extended family of mine had since become a strong support for us and invited us over every summer for a swim or a family dinner.

My uncle, a doctor, listened attentively as we described Nat's sleep problems. After thinking it over for a few moments, he said, "Don't be afraid of medication. It will help." *Afraid of medication?* We realized that indeed, we were. Yet if Nat had had a heart condition or diabetes, we would not have hesitated to give him the right medicines. Why should autism be any different?

We went back to Dr. E., who had diagnosed Nat, asking him to prescribe Clonidine. To my astonishment, Dr. E. refused. "You need to Ferberize him," he said, grinning. "This is not a medication issue. You're letting him get away with it, that's all."

I wanted to slap him. He was implying that this was a parenting failure—that it was *our* fault that Nat was waking up in the middle of the night.

I said, "We already tried Ferber; it isn't about setting limits. This is something else. We just need relief."

"Well, then I recommend Benadryl. That makes kids go to sleep."

We tried the Benadryl. It only worsened Nat's problems, leaving him more wired than we had ever seen him.

Next, we asked our pediatrician to prescribe the Clonidine. "No, you mean Klonopin," she said. "That sometimes works for this."

I trusted my sister's advice and knew our pediatrician was mistaken. Klonopin is in a different class of drugs (benzodiazepines) and is used to treat seizures and panic disorders. Still we gave it a try, and it did nothing. This failure to treat Nat's problem adequately and to take our input seriously caused us to lose faith in our pediatrician. We resolved to find a new one who would listen to us and see us as experts when it came to autism. We also realized that for a problem this persistent, we needed a specialist who knew the latest research about medication and autism, who specializes in psychiatry or psychopharmacology. I got a referral to a child psychiatrist from one of our doctors. He prescribed Clonidine without hesitation. The first night we gave Nat the Clonidine, he slept through the night. We crossed our fingers, hoping it would continue to work, and it did, night after night. This was our first encounter with a miracle drug. We slept, and we felt like newly released prisoners. To this day, Nat still takes Clonidine. Without it, his sleep problems come back.

Establishing a relationship with a psychopharmacologist opened up an entirely new avenue of possibilities for us. Once we experienced the positive results of the Clonidine, it was only natural for us (for me, really, as the agent of change in the family) to explore the use of medications that might help with other problems. Our psychopharmacologist was glad to help, but unfortunately he did not go about this process methodically. He would recommend a drug found to have some positive results with self-stimulatory or aggressive behavior. We'd try it for a few days and see some negative changes in Nat, which we'd ascribe immediately (and often incorrectly) to the new drug. The doctor would respond to our concerns by immediately taking him off the drug and putting him on some-

DECIDING WHETHER TO USE MEDICATION

- Start by educating yourself. Though the idea of using medication was scary to us, we tried not to let fear and ignorance influence our decision. The following website is a good place to begin learning about medicines that are commonly used to treat autistic symptoms and behaviors: *http://autism.about.com/cs/medications/a/commonmeds.htm.*
- Ask for referrals to a psychopharmacologist from sources you trust, such as another parent of an autistic child or a local parent advisory council (PAC) Listserv, like *Masspac@yahoogroups.com,* a Massachusetts-based alliance of public school parent advisory councils with helpful links no matter where you live.
- Understand the expected result of the medication you're going to try. Medications can't cure autism, but they can alleviate certain symptoms.
- Be sure that you understand the potential side effects— many drugs have them—and ask if there are any interactions with other medications or foods.
- Find out whether any lab tests are needed before taking the medication or during the course of treatment.
- Create a controlled trial period for any new medication, during which you refrain from making any other changes in medications or routines. This will give you the clearest sense of what effects this medicine has on your child.
- Get a twenty-four-hour phone or pager number from the doctor who prescribes the medication so you can always reach help if there's a problem.
- Inform your primary care physician, education team, and school program when any medication has been prescribed for your child.
- Follow up regularly with the doctor who prescribed the medication.

thing else. Consequently, we never could learn definitively what affected him and why.

Although regular sleep was now restored to our family, Nat's main problems—perseveration (repetitious behavior), sporadic aggression and destruction directed at Max, and generally being tuned out—were still not improving. But it was difficult for us to know for sure which of these problems could be ameliorated (with medication or otherwise) and which we would simply have to accept as part of who Nat is.

Our approach began to shift toward accepting some of Nat's less attractive attributes and selecting which problems to put our effort into. We saw that Nat's behaviors were the result of a combination of elements: his personality, growth factors (such as hormonal changes), and his autism. There is no way we could "fix" it all—no way to make him completely acceptable to the world. But, we decided, what we can improve, we will, and medication offered opportunities for improvement. Even after our misadventures with the first psychopharmacologist, Nat's success with Clonidine continued to spur our interest in trying other medications, an interest that eventually led us to a new doctor and a new class of drugs.

We Discover the Benefits of Zoloft for Nat

While discussing Nat's issues with his psychologist, she said, "You know, there are some doctors I know of who have begun to study using Prozac in autistic children." She offered to refer us to one of these doctors, Dr. K.

Prozac is the best-known medicine in the class of drugs known as selective serotonin reuptake inhibitors (SSRIs) and has been proven effective in treating anxiety, obsessive-compulsive disorder, and depression in adults. We took Nat to see Dr. K., and he was willing to start Nat immediately on a miniscule dosage of Zoloft, a drug related to Prozac.

I was very taken with Dr. K., a young, smart, and handsome man with a serious manner but a ready smile for kids.

MANAGING THE SPECIALISTS

- Stay organized. I keep a folder called "Nat's Resources" in which I store all referrals, names, phone numbers, and leads on any new ideas of things to try: medications we have heard about, support organizations, and new doctors.
- Trust your instincts. I pay attention to how I feel with a given specialist. If the dynamic with him or her doesn't feel right, I change doctors. There are enough of them out there that it doesn't make sense to stick with one you don't feel you can trust.
- Keep current with the latest treatments and watch others' progress with them. You'll notice that some trends in autism treatment have more staying power than others. Right now, there's a lot of interest in the role of diet. A few years ago there was a lot of talk about the use of the hormone secretin in treating autism. I try a new treatment only if several respected sources have recommended it *and* it is affordable (or covered by insurance).
- Be assertive. If necessary, I have pleaded, insisted, and cajoled to get an appointment.

He was delighted by both Nat and Max. He clearly enjoyed being around children, and affectionately called his patients "kiddo." Anytime Nat answered a question of his, Dr. K. would beam with pride. He told us he'd been seeing some excellent results with Zoloft, and that we should expect to see something, although no one knew quite what, within two to four weeks.

Dr. K., we would discover, was extremely careful and deliberate about altering Nat's treatment and dosages. With him we could feel sure that someone knowledgeable was keeping track of the medications and their effects in a systematic way, keeping an eye on the entire picture of Nat and how different medications affected him and his cycles of behavior.

A month or two after Nat started Zoloft, we started seeing things in him that I thought I never would. First of all, he began to talk more. He would come up to us and comment on things in complete sentences. He would see an airplane and say, "The airplane is going to Florida," which was in his experience the only place planes ever went. He seemed to understand more of what we were saying to him. I imagined the medication somehow loosening up Nat's brain, making his rigid mind more supple and flowing. It also seemed to me that he was now more comfortable physically, more relaxed, and he had become more capable of accepting new information, possibly even better able to filter out some of the noise and excess information that normally assaulted him. It was as if he could now tune into the more important information and filter out the rest. So finally, after years and years of learning the alphabet and memorizing the shapes of certain words he saw around the classroom and in favorite books, he was ready to make the greatest leap yet: to reading.

At the same time as Nat was starting out on Zoloft, we hired Sara, a college junior who was interested in working with children with special needs once she graduated. A tall, sturdy young woman with wheat-colored hair and a quiet voice, Sara was exactly what we needed. Granted, I had had doubts about her at first because she seemed understated, almost meek, but then I saw her go right up to Nat and quietly start talking to him without self-consciousness or fear. Right then, I knew that rejection was not an option with her, that she would persist with Nat in that quiet, certain way of hers until she had connected with him.

During the time she worked with Nat, I got to know her better, learning that she came from a strict but loving Midwestern family and didn't go in for the usual college life of parties, late nights, and self-absorbed self-discovery. She was kind-hearted, unflappable, and centered, and she seemed genuinely taken with Nat, impressed with what he could do rather than by what he could not do. If he began to pull her hair during a lesson, she would simply remove his hand and continue teaching him. Because she was so calm with him and so respectful of his abilities, he was generally calm and respectful with her, too.

We set Sara up with our tutoring curriculum, which by now was pretty well developed. For reading preparation, I thought she should use Spell-A-Puzzle, by Battat, which my mother had picked up for us. By now Nat liked jigsaw puzzles, especially simple ones, and Spell-A-Puzzle had only four or five pieces that, when put together, spelled a simple word like "C-A-T" or "W-H-A-L-E," and also depicted the object or animal denoted by the word.

Day after day, Sara sat with Nat, helping him put together the little puzzles and having him repeat what each one spelled. He seemed to like this activity and was paying attention. Then one evening, in a restaurant, there was a picture of a whale on the wall next to our table, with the word *whale* underneath it. Suddenly Nat pointed to the word, going letter by letter, saying, "W-H-A-L-E spells whale!" He had generalized from the puzzles, an incredible achievement for someone with autism.

After that, he began spelling out loud wherever he went, particularly food and animal words. Soon he started to open children's dictionary-type books and spell words he found in them. He also began to read stories from *Bob Books,* short, extremely simple stories like this one: "Dot. Mat. Dot and Mat. Dot sat on Mat. Mat sat on Dot."

Reading became a favored activity for Nat, which was not surprising, considering how much he had loved being read to as a baby. Sometimes he would take out books from his bookcase or from the coffee table, which was piled high with them (always ones that he was familiar with) and read aloud, pausing along the way to spell a favorite word. He loved books that categorized things, like colors or food. Reading a book about colors, he would turn each thick cardboard page (it was a baby book) and point to each letter of each word: "O-R-A-N-G-E spells orange! R-E-D spells red!" He read the entire book over and over, in a self-stimulatory manner, but I didn't care. He was strengthening his reading skills and his love for reading, and entertaining himself in a fairly normal way, so what was the harm? His gangly body bent over the tiny baby book, his reverential whisper as he spelled, his obvious pleasure in his pursuit were wonderful and poignant, and I would think to myself proudly, *My big little boy.*

The Zoloft period coincided with Nat's beginning to tell jokes. Nat's jokes usually took the form of purposefully making an error and then waiting, with a big grin, while we corrected him, or while we played along. For instance, he would point at Max and say, "It's Daddy. Yes!"

And I would say something like "Hello, Daddy!" to Max. Then I would wait, and Nat would be smiling, waiting for me to say, "No, it's not Daddy! Who is it, Nat?"

Nat would answer, "Max." Then he would walk away, unsmiling, as if the exchange had never occurred. It seemed as if that small bout of happy interaction with us had been so intense for him that he had had to turn it right off. But although the interaction had been brief, it generated a lot of joy for us.

Max in particular appreciated the beginnings of Nat's sense of humor. The boys and I were in a hardware store, and Max and I became separated from Nat by one aisle. Over the Tupperware and the detergents came Nat's voice, spelling, but this time, he was spelling nonsense words. We paused and listened, not sure what he was doing but hearing him shout, at the top of his lungs, "P-X-O-B-S-T-L-I-Y." This was the start of a long chain of letters that went on and on until: "W-A-T-X-V-L spells: BM!" Max and I dissolved in laughter. At the age of eight, Nat had finally discovered toilet humor, and it had never been so welcome to a mother's—or brother's—ears. More than six years later, Max still talks about this incident, and we end up laughing.

Negative Effects Emerge

The Zoloft seemed to reduce Nat's inhibitions, granting new abilities to communicate and an increased willingness to try activities without advance preparation. But this loss of inhibition had a serious downside. Nat sometimes became "manic," in Dr. K.'s words, though I don't think he was using this term in the clinical sense. Nat's desire to tangle with people became a more disconcerting problem than ever before. After a long period of mostly positive gains—other than the sleep issues—Nat's difficult side emerged again, and the problems, including aggression and acute destructiveness, made us increasingly worried about how to control him. In addition to breaking Max's Lego sculptures, Nat would rip Max's drawings and books, tear up houseplants, urinate on the bathroom floor, and then laugh giddily just thinking about what he had done. As Nat continued to misbehave, we shifted into what we call "siege mode." In siege mode, we're just barely functioning, always bracing ourselves for the next incident, hyperalert to any signs of trouble, focusing on damage control. Our expectations become very low and we become very tense.

When we're in siege mode, the mere sound of Nat running is not a good thing. It usually means he has just destroyed something or made a big mess and is leaving the scene of the "crime." It means that when I realize that Nat is no longer downstairs with us I have to run upstairs, to see what he's doing. Sometimes he has urinated on the bathroom floor, probably to provoke a dramatic reaction from us. Another favorite activity is pouring out the contents of all the containers in the medicine cabinet.

Once, a few years ago when under siege, I heard Nat running around upstairs, and I scrambled to find him running from his bathroom into our bathroom, his hands wet and full of feces, with toilet paper sticking to his fingers.

"What are you doing?" I yelled. I watched, aghast, as he plunged his hands into our toilet.

"WHAT ARE YOU DOING?" I yelled, this time really loud, in a way that made it clear that I didn't require any answer. He pulled his waste-filled hands out of our toilet, ran back to his bathroom, and deposited the feces in that toilet, then flushed.

"You . . . you're washing your hands [I'm washing my hands]," he said nervously, as he began washing his hands.

My heart was pumping fast as I thought about other families I knew whose autistic children habitually smeared feces on the wall or on themselves. Were we now going to have *that* in our lives, too?

But no. I suddenly understood what Nat had been doing, and my anger evaporated. His toilet wasn't working properly. Nat had tried to use it, but it would not flush, so he had carried his feces into our bathroom, to flush them down our toilet. Being Nat, he just had to see everything get flushed. To him it was better to carry his feces in his hands than have an incomplete, unsatisfying flush.

When we are under siege, Nat gets blamed even for things he hasn't done. Siege mode severs our connections because we become too wary and mistrusting of him. Nat senses this and becomes more anxious and more prone to disruptive behavior. We now know it is up to us to stop the cycle of anxiety and fear, but it takes a lot of fortitude—and a willingness to be unpleasantly surprised. But we didn't understand this at the time.

One night, while the family was in siege mode, I came into my bedroom and found a pile of feces on the floor.

"Nat! Get in here!" I cried.

Nat looked at the excrement at my feet. He said nothing.

"Nat. You can't do this stuff," I said, trying to be calm. "You must . . . you have to use the toilet. Where does BM go?" And so on.

Finally, I bent to clean the thing up. It wiggled like Jell-O.

What the—? I touched it, gingerly. It sprung back into shape. It was Max's fake poop from the joke shop.

"Max! Get in here!"

He explained that his friend Andrew had put it there and he had forgotten about it.

I went to find Nat in his room. He looked at me and said, "Sorry I yelled at you."

"Oh, Nat," I whispered, nearly in tears. "I really am."

Even if we sometimes blame him for things he didn't do, Nat still does create a lot of mischief. When I smell my expensive perfume wafting up from a sink drain, I have to push down the anger that rises into my throat, the desire to scream at someone. I have become a hostage to my child. It is difficult not to drift into a morose state of resignation and sorrow. *Why do I have to live with this?* I ask myself. Sometimes I do scream. I yell at Nat. I feel better for a minute, and then I feel terrible, remembering that this child is so differently wired. The only way he can feel happy is to do predictable things that other people find irritating or trivial. There is so little I can do for him that I enjoy and that will also make him happy, and so many things he wants to do that I and other people don't want him to do.

He loves to watch liquid pour out of containers. He loves to squeeze bottles, especially bottles filled with stuff we need, like shampoo and toothpaste, for he also loves the predictability of my angry response. It makes me so sad to think of how limited his happiness is; it is far more constrained than the limits he puts on what I can keep in my bathroom.

At some point under siege, we started to buy the cheapest shampoo available, six bottles at a time, leaving the bottles half-hidden in the bathroom closet, where he could discover them and think he had stumbled upon a gold mine. Little did he know these were plants, decoys. He was free to squeeze all the cheap shampoo he wanted. When I would see the big empty bottle, bought just that morning, I would act a little miffed, just enough to satisfy him. And I *was* a little miffed, because his behavior was still wasteful and irritating. But I still understood that this small annoyance was better than the bigger tragedy that would befall us if, for example, he discovered bleach.

During sieges, when Ned and I were too tired to check on Nat ourselves, we sometimes enlisted Max's aid. "Max! Time for a stealth mission," Ned would whisper conspiratorially. "Go see what Nat's up to and report back."

"Yes, sir!" Max would creep away to spy on Nat. This light-hearted play—about something that is, of course, rather frightening—would help us feel better about the situation because we were talking about it, joking about it, acknowledging it.

New Strategies

During the first siege, we didn't want to take Nat off Zoloft, even though things had gotten so rough. We loved his progress, his talking; we just needed to control his excesses. We asked our team for help at home. The special education director agreed that we should hire a behavioral therapist. We checked with one of our parent networks and found one with a background in autism education and child psychology, to help us come up with strategies to combat Nat's misbehavior. The behaviorist observed Nat and then instructed us to act neutral when Nat misbehaved. He confirmed for us what we had already observed on our own: that charged responses were rewarding for Nat because they were easy for him to understand and they were predictable. All Nat needed was the memory of just one intense reaction to a negative behavior, and he would commit the act again and again just to relive the pleasure of the predictability and intensity.

The behaviorist also suggested that we try to think up activities to keep Nat busy, a technique he called "chaining," which was essentially a list that Nat could check with, which would give his time at home some structure. We were to take pictures of Nat engaging in these activities, and put together a small album of them so that Nat could help choose the order of his activity chain. For example, a chain could be lunch, clear table, computer, read, ice cream, fold laundry, video. We constructed a laminated Velcro schedule board with written descriptions of activities that could be rearranged at will. Rewards, like ice cream or video breaks, were also velcroed in between, as needed. The behaviorist also suggested creating a "ripping box" filled with old paper and magazines for Nat to rip as much as he wanted; or constructing a behavior chart that reminded Nat of things he was not allowed to do and what rewards he would get if he didn't do them.

These strategies had mixed results. For us, the problem with schedule boards, however great they are in theory, is that there are never enough enjoyable activities for Nat to do in a long day at home, and thus there are bound to be struggles and downtime. It's during unstructured time that Nat is most mischievous. And so, because our home life is so variable and spontaneous, I would often wind up upsetting Nat by rearranging his activities halfway through the day.

By contrast, the behavior charts worked fairly well, because of the certainty of the reward or treat at the end of the morning, or whatever time period we had set up. Nat also enjoyed reading the chart over and over, looking at me after reading each rule to make sure he had read it right. I was delighted by this little interaction, and so my response was highly charged and highly positive, as Nat could see. This was probably what ensured our success, perhaps even more than the ice cream after lunch.

Like the schedule board, the ripping boxes didn't really work, because Nat didn't want to rip things he was allowed to rip. What he got out of ripping things was the anguished response from Max or me. I couldn't get him to appreciate our positive reactions nearly as much.

During this difficult time we consulted a different behaviorist to get some fresh ideas. This one told us about the uses of nonviolent punishment. His theory was that by making Nat aware of possible undesirable consequences to some of his actions, we could control his behavior more easily than by waiting for good behavior and reinforcing it with rewards. He talked about the use of a quick squirt of water in the face, much the same technique people use to discourage cats from walking on kitchen counters; it is harmless, but it quickly gets the point across.

This suggestion seemed extreme, but we appreciated this man's "outside-the-box" approach to Nat's behaviors. We tried to find another punishment to threaten Nat with (a nonviolent one, of course) and came up with removing his socks as a possibility. We knew he felt uncomfortable with his socks off, unless he was in the shower or in bed. Going around without his socks on seemed incomplete and somehow wrong to him. Nat is someone who has always needed closure in every sense of the word. For Nat, doors must be either wide open or firmly shut; videos snapped away in their boxes; glasses full to overflowing with water or completely dumped out. And socks and shoes must be on feet.

And so removing his socks upset him and produced some positive results. We removed his socks when he hurt someone or broke something, and it would stop him. He would become upset and say "Want the socks," but it was effective. The problem came when we needed him to remove his socks for something unrelated to bad behavior, like walking on the beach. On those occasions, the suggestion that he remove his socks made him feel as if he were being punished. It is always the unpredictable, the exception, the gray area, that causes Nat to become bewildered and confused.

During this time when Nat's behavior first spiraled out of control, we began to despair of ever getting our lives back. Ned and I spent a lot of time talking about Nat and how to gain some leverage over him, but we came up with nothing more than sock removal, behavior lists, rewards, and ripping boxes. Nat seemed always to be laughing at us, which made it very difficult to remain detached and not reinforce his misbehavior. He could sense our tension, our wariness, and our mistrust of him, and those feelings probably made him more anxious and overstimulated, and thus more prone to bad behavior.

One evening, though, Ned had a stroke of genius. Nat had run upstairs and purposefully destroyed something of ours. Drawing from our behaviorist's suggestion—that we find something startling and unpleasant, like a cold squirt of water in the face, to get Nat's attention—Ned thought of the alcohol pads in the bathroom and remembered Nat's anxiety over doctor visits and getting shots. Without really thinking about it, Ned ran into the bathroom and got one. He tore open the tiny foil packet and put it right under Nat's nose, releasing its sharp, clean smell. I was nearby, watching curiously.

Nat's pupils often dilate when he becomes aggressive or destructive. Smelling the pad, his eyes quickly changed from black back to deep blue. Something in the air shifted, and the tension broke. The siege was over, and we all knew it.

Nat's behavior once again became tolerable, all because of a smell and a negative association. Days later, when he got that mischievous smile on his face again and started to run toward Max's room, we only had to show him a foil envelope to get him to stop. Nat was quite impressed with the alcohol pad. He began to talk about it to us. "You get the akeehol pad." He knew that if he misbehaved, he might have to smell that alcohol. Who knew whether an injection would follow? In short, we had to be cruel to be kind; we had to let Nat think something frightening but false to get him to stop the siege.

I have very mixed feelings about this technique. It still makes me sad that we had to use it. Even at the time, it seemed somehow abusive to play on Nat's fears in this way. On the other hand, we felt we had little choice. I kept thinking, *Let Department of Social Services come and judge my life. If they know of some better method, I want to know about it.* My bravado, of course, was superficial; I was terrified of what professionals, friends, or neighbors would think of us if they learned how we were keeping our son under control. But I also knew that in the scheme of things, our new technique was really harmless and almost bizarrely funny.

While it lasted, this first siege was extremely frustrating. In raising Nat I find that when I can get past my tiredness and fear and just manifest my optimism, I can bond with him—and when Nat and I bond, I can get him to do just about anything. But when his aggression and mischief first appeared, I couldn't always be so emotionally vigilant and connected to him, and so the roller coaster of good and bad behavior, of Nat being stoic and then manic, continued.

I had to wonder if the hard work and harsh realities of autism would ever abate. Yet overall this was not as dark a time for us as the sleepless period had been. First of all, we were get-

---

⌇ RESOURCES FOR GETTING THROUGH ⌇
"SIEGE MODE"

- Try using schedule boards that list your child's activities for the day and offer some choices. Go to *www.mayer -johnson.com*. Mayer-Johnson is a company that produces graphics about daily activities, all of which have easily recognizable drawings of stick figures performing tasks and so forth. These small images can be printed out, laminated, cut up, and velcroed onto a schedule board.
- Implement a reward system. We used a picture of ice cream on Nat's schedule and on the refrigerator door, to give him lots of reminders of what he would earn if he did what was expected of him. An image of an ice-cream cone or any such reward can be placed on the schedule after the child has completed a series of desired activities.
- Use visual reminders of what you consider desirable and undesirable behavior. We had a list that had "Do" and "Don't" columns, with the given activity and a drawing next to it, such as "Do use your words to get help; Don't pee on the floor."
- Find a nonviolent punishment that will get your child's

---

ting regular, reliable rest, which helped us to cope. Also, Nat's personality was emerging. He may have been mischievous, but he was *there*. We could get to know him. This was wondrous, like the first spring day after a hard winter. We were endlessly tickled by our discovery of Nat's nuances. I went around with a bubble of joy in my throat, ready to burst into laughter at any moment. I began to see that Nat was the kind of kid who challenged authority, tested people, liked pissing them off. Yes, he teased Max by ripping Max's books and drawings, but what older brother did not bug a younger sibling sometimes? And Max seemed to be handling it well.

---

continued

attention. For Nat, we tried removing his socks and then discovered the alcohol pad. The Autism Home Page is an autism website that has a distinct, and perhaps helpful, point of view on interventions for challenging behaviors: *http://groups.msn.com/TheAutismHomePage/ behaviormanagement1.msnw*

- Scale back your expectations of your child, and of each other. By thinking of a rough phase as "siege mode," we were expressing our sense of being overwhelmed, and the need to acknowledge, once again, just how challenging a disability autism is. This was not a time for travel or starting Nat in new activities. Rather, our focus turned toward problem-solving together, and taking each crisis one step at a time.
- Give your child controlled ways to misbehave, such as offering "ripping boxes" filled with paper he or she is allowed to tear. I also bought cheap shampoo for Nat to squeeze down the drain.
- Remember that nothing lasts forever, including sieges.

I actually didn't feel as desperate at this time as I had in the early days when Nat couldn't be reached and didn't seem to notice I was there. Even though Nat had become a handful, we could handle it—if it didn't get any worse. As long as the alcohol pad kept working. Ultimately, this, too lost its efficacy, but by then his behavior was not so acutely difficult.

Our feelings about Nat's determination to get to people were complex. We wanted to connect with Nat, and we sensed by his misbehaving that in his own way he was reaching out to connect with us. After trying for so many years in his early life to establish a connection with him, we welcomed Nat's becoming more of a presence in the family.

Over time, we learned to live with the uncertainty of autism. Of course I still had moments when I asked myself (or Ned) why we didn't get to have a settled, peaceful home life free from worry about how much worse this or that new behavior would get. Even so, a feeling of competence came to permeate our experiments with managing the disorder. We enjoyed tinkering with rules and seeing that our "let's wing it" style was working. We took pride in our strength as a couple, and our ability to keep our sense of humor. Sometimes we would make up our own silly talk, a way of gently poking fun at Nat's self-stimulatory verbalizations. We would sometimes even imitate Nat in his presence, to see what he would do: "Nat, what's 'feem-ssh?'" He would look at me with disgust and say, "No feem-ssh!" (Nat's version of "Cut it out, Mom!") We loved getting a reaction out of him; anything was better than autistic, stony silence. Our lives together would never be perfect, but by now we were also beginning to realize that no one else's family was perfect either, and that ours, though quirky, seemed to be working.

6

A NEW BABY
IN THE FAMILY

W HY WOULD WE CHOOSE to shake things up further, when life had already thrown us such a curve ball? Crazy though it was—our hands were full to overflowing—I let my thoughts about another baby develop into full-blown yearning. I told Ned there was another sweet soul waiting in the wings. I also began to feel that if we had another normal baby, like Max, it would strengthen the family, lessening our sadness and doubling our joy. Our lives would consist of more normal experiences, and the autism would dominate us less.

Ned opposed the idea, feeling we were already struggling enough with the two boys, which of course we were. And we had heard some scary stories about families who had had more than one autistic kid. I didn't want to adopt a child, though. I wanted to relive the entire experience of motherhood: the excitement of a positive pregnancy test, hearing the fetal heartbeat, feeling the baby move for the first time, giving birth. I wanted the baby to look like us. There were *a lot* of things I wanted, but I also understood that there was also a very real possibility of getting things I didn't want. So I tried to repress my yearning, for a while.

The desire for another baby came back to me again shortly before Nat's sleep problems surfaced, when our college friends Paul and Nancy had a third baby. Their first two children were twin boys. When we first met the twins, Peter was a precocious one-year-old who followed Max around everywhere, but Henry was uninterested in any of us, wanting only to play with a toy motorcycle that had flashing lights and a siren. He pressed the toy's buttons over and over, mesmerized by the display.

"That's all he ever does," complained our friends. As I kept glancing at Henry sitting in a corner with the flashing toy, I felt a familiar dread settle in my stomach. I had highly developed autism radar by this time, and I often conducted secret mini-evaluations when friends or neighbors brought new babies to visit.

When Nancy left the room, Paul talked to me earnestly, asking how we had gotten Nat diagnosed and telling me how worried he was about Henry. Worried, but not doing much about it because Nancy didn't like it when he talked about the differences between the two boys. I tried to tell him gently that I thought they should look into Henry's behavior, that just looking into it couldn't hurt.

Soon after, Paul and Nancy did get Henry evaluated, and sure enough he was autistic. Nancy has since become an autism expert and a great resource for me, because she is constantly looking into alternative treatments for Henry, the success or failure of which she readily discusses.

So Paul and Nancy's third child was big news to me. Like us, they had already had their hands full, and I had some idea about the genetic roulette you play when you make such a move. Yet the third child had turned out just fine; Nancy told me she had known this immediately, and I believed her. In my irrational desire for a baby, I imagined that if it could work out for her, it could for me.

My therapist urged Ned and me to continue our conversation about having a third child until we both felt we had reached a resolution. I wondered how that could happen. It seemed to me that someone was bound to win or lose. My therapist disagreed, however; she thought that if we talked the decision through, it would not have to feel that way.

And so we restarted our conversation about the third baby, and it took on more urgent, serious tones. I kept feeling that there was another person who had to be added to the family, and I was certain that if we could just pull off normal, we would be exponentially happier. Max would have a normal sibling experience, something I wanted for him above all else. I wanted him to understand how special he was, not just in contrast to his brother, and how much joy he had brought to us, so much so that we wanted to have more, and to give him someone to share everything with.

Once Nat's sleep issues seemed well resolved, I began taking prenatal vitamins and started to wean myself from Prozac, even though Ned and I had not yet agreed that we were having another baby. I did this, though, because I wanted to be prepared months in advance in case we did agree in the end. My own psychopharmacologist assured me that Prozac would not harm a fetus, but I wasn't taking any chances. He also told me that I'd made so much progress with my therapy that the odds were fairly good that I wouldn't ever need to go back on Prozac. I was continuing weekly therapy, a safety net in case I felt more anxious without the drug.

I got Ned to agree to go to a geneticist. Without stating explicitly to ourselves that we were thinking about having another baby, we both felt we should know more about our genetics so that we could offer any relevant information to Max, such as whether he was at risk for having autistic children. I also felt we should get some testing to rule out disorders like Fragile X syndrome, which presents similarly to autism. If they tested me, we could learn whether I carried the genetic possibility, but we would not have to test Nat. I did not want to have to stick him with a needle if I didn't have to.

We made an appointment with a geneticist at a nearby city hospital where Max had been born. The geneticist asked us questions about all the health problems in both our families, seeming particularly interested in the anxiety and depression on my side of the family and the fact that Ned had a cousin with schizophrenia. She told us about the links between autism and mood disorders like obsessive-compulsive disorder and depression. Scientists had not yet isolated the genes involved, but she felt she knew enough to be able to tell us that our chance of having another child with an autism spectrum disorder (that is, some form of autism, from mild social issues to severe developmental delays) was one in twenty. By contrast, the odds of having an autistic child in the general population were thought, at that time, to be about one in one thousand (today the incidence has increased to one in 166, according to the National Alliance for Autism Research). The doctor also told us that, unlike for Down's syndrome, there was no DNA test that could be done during pregnancy to let us know if our new baby was autistic (there is no DNA test for autism at any stage of life). In short, if I were to become pregnant, I realized I would be just as ignorant as we had been during my first two pregnancies.

One in twenty. The numbers rang in my head and made me dizzy. How could I possibly push for another baby now, knowing the odds? Yet sometimes these odds seemed pretty good to me: they meant if we had twenty more kids, only one would be autistic. Max had stood the same chance of being autistic, and look at him; he was fine!

And what about this baby that I somehow felt was waiting in the wings? Autism or not, I couldn't get this child out of my head. My heart sagged at the thought that I was finished having children. Finally, Ned and I talked about it more and something shifted for him. Instead of putting up obstacles to the idea of having another baby, he would simply laugh and say, "What are we, nuts?" Even in more serious moments, it no longer seemed as if his mind was completely made up against the idea. He would halfheartedly point out our need for a new car, or complain that we would have to convert the guest room into a nursery for the new child. Minor stuff to me, though not to him. Ned is a pragmatist who focuses on the real and the tangible. I gloss over the details, and then later they take me by surprise. Ned also asked about losing time to ourselves and the lack of sleep. But there was one thing he never asked: "What if we have another autistic kid?"

So I asked it out loud for him, and answered it myself: "I want another baby so badly, I think I could even handle it if the baby had autism. I don't think I could handle a *new* disorder, like Down's, but I know what I'm doing with autism!" Anyway, somehow I was convinced that it wouldn't happen to us again, that lightning wouldn't strike us twice. I don't know why, but suddenly, the air cleared, and Ned stopped resisting. The tide had turned, and it was bringing us a baby.

The chance to start anew. A clean slate. The opportunity to get it all right this time; to experience the bliss of motherhood as it should be. I had lost my chance with Nat because I had been in such turmoil wondering what was wrong with him. And I'd also lost some time of happiness with Max because I'd been coping with the emerging fact of Nat's autism. The calm with which I approached this third pregnancy demonstrated my certainty that this new child would bring balance to our family and to my universe.

It was as if I was looking for the hand of God to scoop us up, cradle us, and set our family down in a new direction. Being Jewish, I decided that if this baby were a boy, we would call him Benjamin, Hebrew for "hand of God." At this point, my relationship with God became very personal: I nagged him and bargained with him. I told him that I would take care of my physical well-being as well as the family's, scrupulously watching my diet and carefully preparing the boys. But God was going to have to hold up his end, too, by making the new baby normal. He'd sent me Max, a child so sweet and kind, and so in need of a sibling who responded to him. But I feared that Max would drift into a quiet, unreachable sadness if he had to cope with yet another brother who wasn't really there, who took pleasure in wrecking his things, who gave him so little. Max was not one to explode in anger or lash out at us in pain; he would just become dimmer.

Back then, I didn't appreciate the value of Nat's presence in our family. In reality, he was shaping us all in important and positive ways, helping us to become flexible and accepting. Though I didn't realize it at the time, Nat, too, had been a gift to us. But back then I was still angry about Nat's condition. How in hell had it happened? How could God allow such children to be born, children who are so poorly equipped to handle life? Nat would always have it rough. He'd always have to depend on others.

Well, now he'd have *two* others. This would be particularly important for him when Ned and I were gone. Oh, how I hated to think about that. But there it was. I did not want Max to be alone in this.

First Glimpse of Ben

Benji's birth was the easiest yet. When the doctor handed him to me, I grasped him in my arms and immediately looked deeply into his intense, dark, steely eyes. And he looked right at me, unabashedly and directly, though seeming a little perturbed about what he'd just been through. That was Ben. From the start, he had to have things exactly so, or we would hear about it. Yet that one look made me feel that he was OK, not autistic. I cried and laughed, while he yelled louder than any baby I'd ever heard. "Littlest, Loudest" was his first nickname, given to him on the night he was born.

An hour after Ben was born, my parents brought Max and Nat into the room to meet him. Nat scampered away from the baby and was more interested in the red "sharps" container, unfortunately. But what had I expected? That Nat was suddenly

PREPARING YOUR CHILD FOR
THE ARRIVAL OF A NEW BABY

- Talk with your child about the new baby as much as possible. We showed our sons the nursery, the crib, the tiny clothes that waited in the drawers.
- Read books together about it. We liked *The Berenstain Bear's New Baby* by Stan and Jan Berenstain, *Baby's First Year* by Debbie MacKinnon, *101 Things to Do with a Baby* by Jan Omerod, and *Baby's Book of the Body* by Roger Priddy.
- Make a book for your child about the new baby. I made a crisis storybook for both of my boys, so that they could more concretely imagine themselves with the baby. I faked new baby pictures by using photos of baby Max, which I then cut and pasted in with shots of Max and Nat so that it would look like Max and Nat with a new baby. The book told them things like, "The new baby will cry a lot," and "Grandma will be staying with us to help. You can help, too." It also told them that Mommy and Daddy still loved them even though they also loved the new baby.
- Offer your child chances to practice being around a new baby. We bought our boys a lifelike baby doll to familiarize them with the concept of handling a baby safely.
- If possible, have your child attend a "siblings class" like those offered by many hospitals to prepare children for the arrival of a new baby. We took our sons to a siblings class at the hospital where I would be giving birth. The class included a tour of the newborn nursery. Seeing the tiny babies and the physical location of the maternity wing helped give Nat an idea of what was to come.

going to be capable of understanding the momentousness of Ben's birth? Still, the disappointment flickered through me as I barked at Nat to get away from there.

Meanwhile, six-year-old Max was holding Ben, instantaneously becoming a big kid. I felt so strange when I looked at this boy holding my newest baby, and a pang hit my heart and stayed there like a bruise. Max had changed irrevocably; he was no longer my little baby. None of my careful planning and anticipation had prepared me for this.

I left the hospital the very next day, eager to begin at home. In our haste to check out we forgot to bring a winter blanket to wrap Ben in. We wrapped him in Ned's large fleece ski mask instead, so that Ben's face peeped out of the facial opening and the rest of his tiny body lay shielded in the mask's warm felt. We were proud of our ingenuity, which we would come to see as symbolic of our style with Ben, of winging it and creating whatever we needed—indicative of the free-spirited attitude we were developing.

In our first few days at home, everything appeared to be going smoothly. I was having no trouble nursing Ben. (Although that didn't mean much, since the other two boys had nursed well for the first few days, too. It was when the soreness set in that I had given up both times.) When we arrived home from the hospital, I sat down in the living room to nurse Ben. Max and Nat watched curiously for a moment as I awkwardly attached Ben to my breast, and then they quickly turned away. "I'm feeding him," I explained, more interested than they were. But in just a few weeks Max became very good at anticipating Ben's feedings and fetching me my nursing pillow. He would do the bottle feeding, too, which I had quickly introduced to get Max involved with Ben as soon as possible. As for Nat, he remained uninterested in the feedings, but he enjoyed Ben's growly cries and once exclaimed, "Wah-hhhhh! Noise like a baby," which delighted us because, of course, he didn't usually comment on anything and also because it was so apt.

On Alert about Ben

Max was beginning to read at this point, beginner books like *Sir Small and the Dragonfly* and *Danny and the Dinosaur,* and he would read to Ben, sitting on the couch with tiny Ben propped up on a throw pillow against the arm of the couch. Ben's metallic eyes would focus intensely on Max. In some ways, Ben's delicate features and slim frame (as opposed to Max's sturdy body) reminded me of infant Nat. He also startled now and then and threw his arms in the air. The first time I no ticed this, I felt a mild cramp in my stomach. I was not out of the woods. I was going to have to watch Ben, after all. No matter what I thought I had arranged with God, there was something subtly Nat-like here—or maybe it was just a different kind of normal than Max's normal.

So I was on guard. Although I was very happy, very satisfied with what I had been given, Ben would be the subject of occasional worry. The worries had started long before his birth, with our discussions about the genetic possibilities, and they continued during the pregnancy when I had to go to the emergency room twice because of some minor bleeding. Each time they did an ultrasound, and in one of them I could swear his profile showed him grinning mischievously, "Ha, ha! Gotcha!" Ned and I still refer to him as the Ha Ha Kid, our own Nelson Muntz, the character from *The Simpsons* who thumbs his nose at everyone. Ben seemed to be the kind of person who gets in trouble and enjoys the chaos he creates.

I enjoyed my days with Ben, nursing him in the backyard in the unusually warm April sun. I couldn't believe it was me, lying there in a plastic blue lawn chair, so at ease with a baby. Nursing was something I had wanted to do with each baby. I had taken those classes with La Leche League to learn to do something I didn't really get to do until eight years later. With Ben, I was able to see a lactation consultant and I was able to get past the soreness and the feelings of inadequacy that had stopped me before.

He was a passionate baby who took to everything we showed him with great enthusiasm. On the other hand, he was also very demanding. I could get into quite a sweat trying to give him what he needed without attracting a lot of attention. Once I was struggling to nurse him in my room, with house painters on the other side of the wall, painting the back of the house. In between Benji's cries I heard one of them say, with an Irish lilt, "Ahngry bahby." My laughter broke up my tension.

During this time, as I adjusted to life with three children, I had to scale back my expectations of what I could accomplish in a day: just feed Ben, feed the boys, keep them safe, get them to school. The boys watched a bit too much television at this time, but it gave me a needed break. And this time I called my pediatrician as much as I needed to: no more hesitating or doubting myself.

The Five of Us

> Family of five, family of five,
> So much trouble trying to stay alive,
> We're always tired,
> Please don't get fired,
> Family of five.
> —song our family came up with
> after Ben was born

Ben fit very well into the family dynamics. He was an adaptable baby, once even allowing us to carry him in a school backpack to go apple picking when we forgot to bring his baby carrier. He was game for anything, an attitude that fit in well with our spontaneous, anything-can-happen lifestyle. He was more outspoken about his feelings than Max had been, a bit tempestuous even as an infant, but still very manageable for me. And he couldn't wait to catch up to Max, the benevolent giant in his life.

In Ben's early days, Nat treated Ben the way he had treated Max, generally avoiding him and, once in a while, pinching him when he was frustrated about something. Nat's attacks on Ben terrified me. I could not let them continue. We became hyper-vigilant, always watching over Ben, an activity that wore us out, physically and emotionally, especially because we were already so tired from caring for our newborn around the clock. In the end, Nat attacked Ben only a few times; I swooped in so fast in my horrified anger that I scared him out of it for the most part. Behaviorists would have said that my response was the kind that, in the end, reinforces bad behavior. But there was no way I could treat Nat's aggression toward Ben neutrally. I was determined to win this one. I would get the upper hand by making Nat fear my anger and my yelling. I would not let him turn this into a ploy for attention. I even threatened to remove him from the house. My heart clenched as I told him, in words he would understand, "If you hurt people, a man will take you away. You will not be able to live in Mommy's house." His pupils dilated to black, and I knew what I said was having an impact on him. But my threat, tossed out in anger, probably upset me as much as Nat because at that moment I realized it was actually plausible: We *could* send him to live in a residential program. I felt miserable just considering sending him away, even though plenty of parents with similar kids did just that. For me, sending Nat away would have felt like giving up on him.

For the first few months after Benji's arrival, Max would occasionally regress, wanting to be a baby again. "Will you cuddle wif me?" he would ask in his little kindergartener's voice. But I felt impatient for him to be the big boy, which I still regret. Back then, I didn't understand that by going through this needy, clinging phase, he was honestly and openly expressing his feelings. I told him, "Yes, you can be my baby now, but it's also great being a big boy."

I hated the sour taste of my mixed feelings, of guilt, sadness, and loss combined with the heady joy of having a new baby. I talked to my friend Ann about it, who also had a new baby and an older child. Ann was a tall, striking, auburn-haired woman, a former dancer given to wearing boots and black miniskirts. She was a tough-talking chick who was soft on the inside. I confided in her during one of our visits that I feared I was pushing Max away when he needed me, that he wanted to be babied, while I wanted him to be the cool kid he was.

"*She* wants to be a baby, too!" said Ann, referring to her older daughter. "What am I supposed to do?" Then we both laughed. It felt good knowing that she was experiencing the same thing. Maybe it was fairly common behavior for older siblings, we reasoned.

Max's metamorphosis to big kid happened soon enough, as he became more used to his new role in the family structure, still in need of his mom sometimes but also able to help out and show Ben the way. As soon as Ben was old enough to know anything, he knew he loved Max best of anyone in the world. Max quickly responded by becoming the highly competent brother Ben thought he was. Max read to Ben, helped bathe and dress him, took toys to him, and helped feed him solid food for the first time. Max was delighted with the way Ben pushed the food out with his tongue, and he wanted to know all about why babies did that.

As I recall the giddy happiness that Max felt with Ben, I feel again and again that I had been right: Having Ben did make Max happier. Ben's existence helped us all feel happier, in fact. If we paid a little less attention to Nat because of Ben, that was probably OK for all of us, including Nat, who certainly did not appear to mind being left to himself a little bit more. Having Ben in our family quieted down some of the noise around Nat since we now had something else to focus on.

Still Worried about Little Ben

With baby Ben, I felt all the radiant happiness of a new mother. Sometimes it felt as if Ben was my first—this was the way I had imagined motherhood from the beginning. In other ways, though, because I had so much experience under my belt, I enjoyed him like a third baby: a relatively easy though tiring addition to the family. When he was six months old, I signed us up for mother-and-baby music class. It was the first time I'd taken a class with one of my boys since the terrible swim class with Nat years before. But Ben was a little odd compared to the other children in the class, growling at them at first, and then acting fearful and withdrawn. I was not going to quit this time, however, and I persevered until he felt comfortable with the other babies. A little panic arose in the back of my mind but it stayed back there, not blowing up on me until Ben was two.

My fears about Ben began to grow sometime during his second year, as he occasionally struggled to answer a simple yes-or-no question, or refused to do something I asked of him with more tenacity than I had ever experienced with Max. And then one day, he pointed up at the grille in the bathroom ceiling, an ornate Victorian iron vent cover, and said, "Rabbits!" I looked hard at the thing, and suddenly, with Rorschach-like clarity, the shape of rabbits appeared in relief against the abstract pattern. I flashed back to an autism support group story told by Linda, who had been walking with her son Josh down a school corridor when he suddenly exclaimed, "Green!" After looking and looking, Linda finally saw what he had seen: a miniscule green dot of paint amidst a sea of colors, papers, and art projects. The knack of picking out the irrelevant, or the off-topic, is a very common autistic trait.

Even though I had so much evidence of normal development in Ben, his seeing rabbits where most others merely saw a swirly design made the hair on the back of my neck stand up. All I knew was autism: that was the filter through which I looked at the world. I now think of this event as a example of Ben's creative, artistic sensibility, but then I feared it was a sign of autism. Today I sometimes think of Ben as being "dusted" with autism spectrum disorder, a light, fairy's sprinkling, just enough to make him extremely focused, wildly creative, and an early reader, but not enough for a psychologist to detect, or to cause learning problems in school.

But toddler Ben just did one too many unusual things for me to say, "Oh, never mind." Besides, I had made that mistake before. I found myself in a miserable déjà vu, crying over the phone to Nat's psychologist that I not only needed a three-year evaluation for Nat's school program; I also wanted her to see Ben. I had to know for certain what, if anything, was wrong with Ben. So we took Ben to the psychologist, who put him through a thorough battery of tests while we waited in dread of what she might say. I could not keep from crying and trembling with relief when she told us, smiling, that Ben was "normal but stubborn" and congratulated us on what a "unique little guy" he was.

Her theory was that Ned's and my personalities had contributed to Ben's strong-willed, highly focused demeanor, because we, like Ben, are very intense, not all that gregarious, and are very driven by our hobbies and pursuits. In addition to recommending a language-saturated preschool program and perhaps a little speech therapy, she also suggested that we engage in more interactive play with him and not leave him to play by himself as much. But she said this knowing full well that we could only change so much, and she made clear her feeling that ultimately he would be fine even if we did nothing. I knew enough by then to be able to tell when a doctor understood my child, and our psychologist certainly did. Thus, her diagnosis cleared away a lot of my doubts.

The "Puppies"

As the boys grew older, Max didn't always choose to play with Ben, certainly not if one of his own friends was around, but at the end of the day, when he couldn't bear any more television and he didn't want to read, that's when he'd remember he had Ben to play with. When he would call to Ben, my heart would beat a little faster. Was this fair-weather friendship or the imperfect reality of siblings many years apart? Whatever it was, I was enormously proud of the way they played together. *Yay*, I would think, *the family's working!* I called them "the puppies" because of the way they would wrestle around together, building forts out of couch cushions and afghans in the living room.

"Makth! Let *me* have the big pillow on my head! Makth!" Ben would yell in his full voice (still "Littlest, Loudest").

"No, I've got it right now," Max would yell back possessively.

Then, "Ow! Ben!"

I would come into the room and find them on different couches, both sulking. They were having a fight with all of the pettiness and button-pushing of sibling squabbles. But it was easy to get them back together. I would sink into the middle of the altercation with a delicious sigh. Here, I knew what to do. I could help. This was the stuff I'd read about, learned about from therapy, thought about, discussed with friends who had normal kids. De-escalate, express it, validate it, get them to think about how to resolve, move on.

"What's going on?" I would ask them, and get each of them to tell the other what he wanted to happen and how he felt. As soon as they would get the words out, their anger would melt away, and they would resume their playing. This fighting, this intense interaction and mess, this is what I had craved when I first dared to imagine a family with three children. Maybe one day I'll despise the fighting, take it for granted, or grow bored with it, but somehow I doubt that. The fighting is good because it's normal. And it shows how much they care about each other.

7

BUILDING A STRONG MARRIAGE WITHIN AUTISM'S TURMOIL

F RIENDS HAVE OFTEN REMARKED that Ned and I have "such a good marriage." They say we're lucky, even knowing what we're living with. I do think that luck has something to do with our marital success, but conscious behavioral changes and our dedication to working on problems are more important factors. So are our obsessive, endless conversations about the same old topics, our willingness to fight with each other, and a determination to follow up with kindness and apologies.

What we have today as a couple is not what we began with. I don't know if the Sue and Ned who met at the University of Pennsylvania and started dating at nineteen would have stayed together knowing what was to come. Taking a step back from all the emotions and changes we've gone through, I can single out a few key commitments that have helped us to keep our marriage strong.

The Sweetie Treaty

Ned has told me that over the years he's seen a recurring pattern in me, where I get upset about a situation and then feel guilty about being upset. Nothing changes or gets fixed; I just go into a tailspin of bad feeling. For example, I go on and on about how guilty I feel about all of the time I spent being sad and worried about Nat without doing something about it. Then I apologize for being such a downer! When Ned first pointed out this pattern of mine, early in our relationship, he named it "feeling bad about feeling bad." I really laughed when he said that; I was surprised and a little embarrassed, but I knew he was right. My emotional wheel-spinning sapped us both of our energy and time. Early on, he tried to break me of this pattern with an agreement between us that he called the Sweetie Treaty. The original provision of the Sweetie Treaty was "no feeling bad about feeling bad." Instead, we agreed to experience our feelings, whatever they were, without judging them. This idea was a revelation to me: that I would be best served by really feeling it, whatever it was, and then letting it go. With my obsessive personality, as well as my own family's culture, I liked putting things under the microscope, which often made letting go difficult. But what also struck me was the fact that my husband was turning out to be very astute about human nature, despite his outward appearance as a bespectacled computer scientist. And the playful nature of the treaty made the idea of change into something nonthreatening.

The Sweetie Treaty was the first thing in our marriage that made me feel we could invent new ways of being, new family institutions that were ours alone. Other provisions of the treaty have since been added in our twenty years together. Though less important than the original provision, they increase our enjoyment of each other. One later provision is "no moving heavy furniture without first asking Ned for help" (if he hasn't responded in twenty-four hours, I can then go ahead and do it myself). That provision came in response to my impulsive decorating. Ned would come home to a newly pink living room with all the furniture pushed together in the middle of the floor, covered by a sheet; the next day, the room would be white again. He worried about how this was affecting my back (and the condition of our floors). Though he wisely understood that he couldn't prevent me from painting a room, he could keep me from injuring myself by moving heavy objects by myself. These sorts of agreements give us our "couple culture," separate and inviolate from the children and the rest of the world.

The treaty has served us well when times got rough. One night not too long ago, I went to bed depressed, remorseful about having taken on a new pursuit that was becoming so draining and stressful for me that I hadn't been able to read with Nat for an entire week. I began the downward spiral of despair "I just can't seem to get my priorities straight," I cried to Ned as I lay sleepless in bed. Long after Ned had implored me to let him go to sleep, I kept tormenting myself—and Ned—with a list of my crimes. In addition to not having read to Nat, I couldn't even remember the last meaningful conversation I had had with Max, and I had a vague memory of having told Ben I'd be with him right away and then having forgotten all about him. What had he wanted me to help him with, was it something related to Chutes and Ladders? It was all one sad jumble in my head.

But desperate to sleep and to stop this familiar emotional descent, Ned cut right into my thoughts and said bluntly, "Sue, you're in violation of the Sweetie Treaty. Just do one of those things with one of the boys tomorrow, and you'll be better off than you were today."

And that's all it took for the fog to clear. I found myself smiling instead of crying, and soon enough, I fell asleep.

Anniversaries of Tradition and Invention

Anniversaries are important to both of us. We celebrate the standard anniversaries, of course, like our wedding anniversary, but we also celebrate things like the day we started dating. One summer, when our wedding anniversary came around, it seemed important to celebrate it in a special way. This was the summer of Nat's first year of school, when he was four. Although his school program would prove insufficient to meet his needs, we saw that we had passed from being a family in crisis, unsure of what to do, to being a competent family following a reasonable course of action, a family that had developed helpful routines around Nat's school day and around baby Max. Our youthful innocence, so shaken at first by the trauma of Nat's autism, was now hardening into something stronger and less vulnerable. Along with our two boys, Ned and I were growing up, for better or worse. In exchange for no longer being young, fresh-faced parents, we had gained new confidence and equanimity as a couple.

That same summer, Ned and I were finishing our ninth year of marriage, and I got the idea of renewing our vows. I found myself daydreaming over how I would do a wedding now as opposed to the way we had done it almost a decade ago (a very traditional and large Jewish wedding organized mostly by my mother and grandmother). The soap operas I watched while Max napped filled my head with images of over-the-top weddings where the characters renewed their vows dressed as Cinderella and Prince Charming, or in full Victorian regalia, with white horses and buggies. I thought about a white gown and lots of tulle, and before I had even gotten Ned to agree to a second wedding, I found myself shopping for a special dress, one perfectly suited to such an occasion. I went downtown in a kind of starry-eyed mood, and before I knew it, I had bought yards of pastel tulle in a fabric store to festoon the ceilings of our condo. I then checked flower prices at the supermarket— which had a fairly bountiful selection—imagining calla lilies and white roses in a bouquet.

The fact that I could start to dream again was evidence of how much I had healed. Decorating, planning, going out into the world and buying things had become a part of my life once more, as they had been when I was first married. I felt a kind of surprised happiness that once again there was something more to me than sharp grief and routine childcare. I was learning to compartmentalize my grief, to put it away at times, and this was allowing me to move on.

The women at the playground were looking at me differently now that I had something positive and fun to talk about. Since the diagnosis, which had come the year before, I had been like a ghost haunting the playground, there but not much a part of things. Being able to talk about our anticipated second wedding brought me back to life in a way, and suddenly gave me a bit of elevated status (that of a happy, indulged wife) among the other mothers, which I badly needed then. The playground mothers were intrigued by our plan. They wanted to know the details of our ceremony and where we were going to go for the "honeymoon."

As Ned noticed the change in me, we talked about it. We didn't consciously admit that we were passing out of a stage of mourning; we may not even have realized it at the time. We only felt a kind of lightness, a sense that it was OK to do a frivolous, whimsical thing like our planned celebration. Even though we knew it was unusual to renew vows on a ninth anniversary, rather than some round or greater number of years, we both understood that this particular anniversary marked something momentous for us: survival of our son's diagnosis of autism.

And so the plan began to take shape. It would be just the two of us. We would play our favorite music in the background as we talked to each other about how we felt about our lives and our marriage, about where we were at the time, and our hopes and dream for the future. We would renew our vows, and then my parents would take care of the boys while we had dinner in a favorite restaurant and spent a night away for the first time, at the Fairmont Copley Plaza, a grand old Boston hotel that I loved for its Victorian architecture and the cream-and-gold splendor of its decor.

The morning of our second wedding, which was July 4, a convenient date for my parents, even with Ned and the kids around, I prepared with the joy and abandon of a new bride, hanging the candy-colored tulle from the living room and hallway moldings and pinning flowers to the corner moldings. I put on the new ivory-colored dress I had bought and looked from the bedroom doorway, down the hall at all the decorations around me. Everything looked and felt just right, exactly as I had imagined.

When my parents arrived, they took the boys downstairs and into the yard. I walked from the bedroom down the long hallway, toward Ned, who waited in the living room. When I got there, we laughed and kissed. Then I read a Bible passage I had chosen from the Song of Songs: "... I am my beloved's and my beloved is mine." After my reading, I promised Ned "to listen more and talk less."

Once he decided to go along with the idea of a second wedding, Ned put his whole heart into it. He composed two poems for the occasion that described me, the boys, and our life together in deft and funny rhyme. In one, he calls me a "Collector of lace, endowed of face" and "Mother of boys, shepherd of toys." In the other, he describes his love for me in dreamlike verse, asking me to "dance with [his] bliss." I had rarely seen this side of Ned before, and it was breathtaking. I felt as though I was falling in love with him all over again, but it wasn't the kind of heart-stopping crush I had felt for him during our college days. That sort of love, an inebriating emotional flood, had passed for me; my heart and mind were steadier now. I had found the cooler refreshment of mature love, of knowing each other so well, thinking of one another, and making a life together.

Ned had polished our wedding rings for the occasion, and in the restaurant, the maître d' remarked that we must be newlyweds because of our bright new rings. After the meal we strode out to Storrow Drive, which was closed for the Fourth of July celebration, and with the crowds of happy Bostonians, we watched the fireworks over the Charles River, something we had not done since before having children.

Our ninth anniversary celebration marked the start of a new era in our lives, though we scarcely knew it then. It helped us to see ourselves as a happy couple and a successful family despite our challenges, and it bolstered our commitment to one another, giving us a powerful memory to refer to and relive, both in conversation and by watching the video we made of that day.

Encouraging Each Other to Grow and Change

With our heads above the turbulent water of the immediate post-diagnosis years, I felt some peace at last. I found that I wanted to start writing again, after having stopped for some time. Ned had always championed my writing, from the day we took a walk together, newly married, and I complained to him how unfulfilled I was with my job as a research assistant for the local historical society. What I really wanted to do, I told him, was write books.

"So write," he said.

"And quit my job?" I was dumbfounded. I had been raised by two education professionals whose careers had followed a strict path of college, grad school, and then work in increasingly important positions. My father, having paid his dues, as he was fond of pointing out, was at that time the principal of an excellent high school. My mother was a K–12 library curriculum coordinator. My sister was a pediatrician. One did not simply decide to become a *novelist*. Not with a master's degree in history! I was expected to teach or do research, and work my way into a respectable position. As much as I loved my parents and sister, I didn't end up following this pattern at all.

"Yeah, just write," Ned said to me that day, his eyes twinkling. His words were like a benediction, setting me free to follow my vocation. He knew, I'm sure, that I was thinking of all the reasons not to do it. He also knew how badly I wanted to do it.

Ned has been the catalyst for all my career growth, and his upbringing helped him play this role for me. On the surface Ned's family appeared to be quiet and ordinary, but Ned had a highly unconventional childhood. His mother and father had divorced just three years after their third child was born (Ned and his sister Sarai were twins; his brother Patrick was younger by seventeen months). Ned's mother, Eleanor, went on to have many different careers: starting a women's bookstore, becoming a Japanese language scholar, and working as a computer scientist long before many women had entered the field. A feminist and lesbian, she raised her children to be creative and independent, and to question social convention. She shrank from traditional labels or roles, making it clear to her children that, as much as she loved them, she wasn't about to act like a typical mother, and they could take it or leave it. So Ned learned very early that, for better or worse, he was responsible for his own life.

Whether he wanted to or not, he had a lot of independence even as a small child. One day when he was in third grade, his twin sister forgot about him and left for home after school, taking his subway tokens with her. It never occurred to Ned to call home for help. Instead, at eight years old, he figured out how to get home on his own, walking six miles through the streets of New York City.

"When I got home, Mom let me know she was happy to see me," Ned says, "and then she got out a map, and together we traced my route." No doubt she had been worried, but what she showed him, what he remembers most about that afternoon, was how impressed she was with what he had done. When I first heard this story, I thought of it as a tragic account of a child who had learned to rely on himself because no one else was there for him. But over time I have come to see that Ned benefited from his upbringing. His childhood circumstances, which forced him to take care of himself and others around him, helped make him into the grounded, nurturing person he is today. Ned understood early that wherever you find yourself in life, there is always a way to get where you need to go. You just need to use your wits to find it.

And so I listened to him about writing. For five years I wrote my books, and I had never felt so happy as when I sat down with a new plot or character. Then Nat and the diagnosis put a halt to all that. But by the time Max was almost five, the desire to move beyond house and home seized me once more.

It was at that time, at my mother-in-law's suggestion, that I submitted my first article to *Exceptional Parent* (a magazine for parents of children with disabilities) about our Nat Books. Eleanor and I were not close, and yet she had appreciated my work enough to encourage me to do something with it. The article, which was accepted for publication, drew positive attention, spurring me to write more articles about other strategies that had worked for us.

Approaching Parenting as a Unit

Nat Books have remained a valuable tool for us. On a recent trip to Woodstock, Vermont, where we spent a weekend with my friend Ann and her family, we had a sudden, unexpected crisis. We had become so accustomed to traveling to Cape Cod for weekends that we did not realize that visiting a different place would be very disorienting for Nat. For a while, things went well. We arrived in time for a barbecued dinner of chicken, corn, and grilled vegetables. Nat and everyone else ate heartily, sitting in candlelight around a long table, surrounded by the happy chatter of friends who had not seen each other for some time. The problems didn't start until the next day. After breakfast, we all began talking about possible activities: perhaps a trip to a glassblowing factory, a few hours' play in the river that ran behind Ann's farmhouse, a drive to a country fair. Right on the town green there was a show of antique cars. Why not go there for half an hour?

"Nat, let's go see the antique cars," said Ned, as we all started to look for shoes, keys, and wallets.

"No antique cars," Nat said defiantly. The activity around us came to a stop. I could feel the energy start to drain from the room.

"C'mon, Nat, it'll be fun," Ned cajoled.

Before we knew it, Nat had lunged for Justin, Ann's husband, pinching him on the arm. I swung into action, taking Nat aside and patiently explaining, again and again, our planned excursion: beginning, middle, and end. Nat, wide-eyed, listened raptly, but I could still feel his tension. He was breathing rapidly and there was a desperate look in his eyes. After telling him how short the visit to the antique cars would be and promising him that if he were calm, he could have a cookie when we got back, I thought I had covered all he needed to know. Why should this be different from any other spur-of-the-moment excursion, I wondered, glossing over the fact that Ann's house was new to him; that her family, though he knew them, wasn't one he'd ever spent long periods of time with; and that to him their routines were unfamiliar.

"Yes, yes. OK, yes," Nat repeated. But his eyes still looked wild.

And then he lunged for Ben. We pried him off Ben with minimal injury, but Ben's arm was red from being pinched, his lips were pressed together, and he was glaring at Nat, his eyes burning like coals.

So it was time out for Nat, sitting cross-legged on the floor, while everyone watched in uncomfortable silence.

"It's OK, Sue, we don't have to go," offered Ann. This is what people naturally do when Nat acts out. Everyone wants to help, to excuse his behavior, to make it go away; I, more than anyone. But Ned and I knew that now, especially now, we had to go. Nat had to do some of what we had asked of him, or else he would have learned a terrible lesson: that aggression pays.

"Nat, you're going for a little while," Ned said in a tight and low-pitched voice. "We are going to the green."

"Sweetheart," I told Nat, hoping to reconnect to him, to make his misbehavior stop. "It will be all right."

"Yes, yes. OK, yes," Nat whispered. Then he walked away from us, and lunged at Ann, clawing at her hair repeatedly.

"No, no! Stop!" Ann cried out, covering her head with her hands. I wanted to die. I had never seen him attack other adults before. I was scared, and so, I'm sure, was everyone else.

Everyone but Ned, that is. "Nat. Let's go," he ordered, taking Nat outside, by the arm. They were going to the green alone. None of the rest of us followed them; I guess we were all feeling instead like waiting to see how it went for them. But Nat and Ned would be all right, I could tell, because of the way Ned had simply and resolutely taken Nat with him, conveying to us all that he had this completely under control. Nat probably could feel Ned's determination to win, no matter what, and this strong confidence would serve as a boundary for Nat, and calm him down. He would now understand that going to the green was the consequence of his disruptive behavior.

Seeing them go, I felt sure Ned would succeed. Ned does not mind being pinched, and he always wins struggles with Nat, though not by much. It's Ned's determination that wins the day. That, and his confidence, which reaches out and pulls Nat in.

While Ned and Nat were at the green, I got to work making sure there would be no other episodes. I got out Ben's markers and paper and quickly constructed *Nat in Vermont*. I made it seven pages long, with drawings and brief sentences describing what we were going to do that day: (1) a glassblowing factory trip, where Nat would be calm; (2) if he was calm, he would eat ice cream and watch a video when we got back to the house; (3) dinner at the long table; (4) sleep in the beds with Max and Ben; (5) go home on Sunday, after breakfast.

Ann and I talked about going to the local farmers' market once Ned got back. I had to get away from the heavy, fearful atmosphere that Nat had created in the house, which was threatening to spoil our weekend. When Ned and Nat returned, about ten minutes later, I could see Nat was calm again. He was doing silly talk, a sure sign of his being relaxed. I checked with

Ned, who agreed that I could go with Ann. I'm sure Ned understood my need to get away. Of course, he was being the strong one for me, but I had helped out, too, by constructing a good Nat Book while he had been out. Two hours later, when I got back from the farmer's market with Ann, I felt better, having eaten some delicious cheese and enjoyed a good hour of deeply satisfying conversation. My spirits lifted further when Ned told us, "We're going to the glassblowing factory now. Nat's fine with it."

"Really? How do you know?" I said.

"He read it in the book. Just ask him."

I found Nat lying on a couch in the living room. "Nat, are we going to the glassblowing factory?"

Nat raised his head, looking tired and soft-eyed. "Yes."

He was mine again, but only because Ned and I had thrown ourselves into action together and figured out how to win this one.

Snapping into action as a team has been the key to solving our biggest problems. This was especially true at the beginning of Nat's orthodontic treatment. Nat had sucked his thumb constantly throughout early childhood and showed no signs of stopping. When his adult teeth emerged, we could see they were going to be a big problem. At age eight, his teeth were coming in like Bugs Bunny's. We clearly had our work cut out for us: talking to dentists and orthodontists, getting second opinions, and figuring out what Nat could and could not bear.

As was typical for me, as soon as Nat's adult teeth began emerging, I wanted to take action right away.

"No, it's too soon," said his dentist, a kindly man with a kid-friendly practice. My boys loved his office, from the brilliantly colored murals on the walls, to the Polaroid snapshots the dentist took of each child at their first checkup, to the ten flavors of toothpaste kids could choose from. This dental practice was especially good for Nat because the dentist and his assistants were consistent, methodical, and gave the children simple, clear explanations and choices. Nat starting getting his dental care here early enough in his life that checkups were now a comfortable routine for him. He knew exactly what to expect.

Quietly adamant, Nat's dentist explained to me that until all of Nat's adult teeth were in, there was nothing we could do. But Nat's buckteeth and his autism made a powerful, negative combination that was probably harder for me than for anyone else, including Nat. When I looked at him in those days, my heart twisted in pity. Now I was going to have to contend with his being stared at for something else, in addition to his autistic behavior. Nat probably didn't even notice the stares, and if he did, I doubt he understood why people were staring at him. I noticed, though, and I talked with Ned about it.

"Why can't the dentist do a little something now, and the rest later?" I complained.

"I don't know, Sue, because he says it's too early." While he knew that Nat's teeth were a problem, he felt that lots of kids had goofy teeth. "You've got to ignore what other people think."

If I could do that, I wouldn't be me! I thought glumly. Nat's good looks were a gift, something that probably helped him with teachers and others. After all, the world responded to physical beauty. I wanted to give Nat any possible edge. "Can we talk to another dentist?" I asked.

Ned thought about it. "I guess so, but that'll be more work."

He was right, of course. We would have to ask around for referrals, prepare Nat for an appointment at a new office, and get him accustomed to the new person. Ned would have to take time from work because something of this magnitude required two parental heads rather than one.

But we went ahead with it, because Nat's appearance was important to me. Sitting with us in the new dentist's office, Nat seemed edgy and bored. We hoped that the dentist would call our name soon and that he would offer us a treatment plan we could live with, one that didn't involve waiting several years to start fixing Nat's teeth.

"Well," said the dentist, a tall man with a cool smile, when we finally got into his examination room. "I wouldn't call this a world-record overbite, but it is definitely Olympic class. We have a few options. First, he has to stop sucking his thumb. After that, you can surgically remove some of the back teeth, and then go with traditional braces. Or you can wait a few years and go through headgear, braces, retainers. You can . . ."

The other options remain a mystery to me. I stopped listening after the thumb-and-surgery part. Nat was not going to stop sucking his thumb anytime soon, and the proposed surgery seemed extreme.

So Ned and I agreed that this guy was out. He wasn't warm, and he didn't seem to understand what we were up against with Nat. We'd take our chances with our regular and his cautious appraisal of the situation. But that meant waiting. For now, I would just have to get used to Nat's teeth.

"C'mon, he's still cute anyway," a friend said to me once. I would have to try to see him that way, too.

Eventually I did grow more accustomed to Nat's gawky preteen look. By the time he was eleven, his face had filled out, and the teeth didn't appear quite as fanglike as they had. Still, they were remarkably crooked, with big spaces between them, and they stuck out far over his bottom lip. Nat's pediatrician even remarked that they could break easily or hurt his lip if he fell forward.

The more Ned and I discussed it, the more clearly we saw what we needed to do when the time came. As I told Ned, "All I want is for his teeth to be somewhat better, not perfect. Perfect is too hard for him." Soon after that discussion, the dentist told us Nat was ready. After four years of waiting, of longing for my boy to be handsome again, we could talk to an orthodontist and discuss the options.

Dr. L. was a woman around my age, who smiled a lot and tried talking to Nat, even after we explained that he didn't really talk to people.

"How are you, buddy?" she asked.

"Good," he said, sucking his thumb.

"So we're going to fix those teeth, huh?"

"OK, yes." This was the way Nat usually talked, and so he seemed to understand some of what she said.

After the examination, Dr. L. told us Nat could start with braces; later she'd use headgear to correct his lower jaw problems. Apparently Nat's awkward look was caused not only by a tremendous overbite but also by a lower jaw that was too short.

"You know," I said haltingly, "we don't have to make him perfect."

Dr. L. looked at me with curiosity.

"I mean, all we're looking for is an improvement. We can't do everything. In an ideal situation, we would, but this isn't an ideal situation. He may not stop sucking his thumb. He may not tolerate headgear. So what's the minimum we can get away with?"

Dr. L. probably was not accustomed to this sort of discussion. Usually, parents and patients had the recommended work done. "Well, I guess we could get creative," she said. "It would be better if he didn't suck his thumb, but there are other things we could try instead of the headgear. For now, let's just do the braces and see."

That day, Nat went to school with little rubber-band spacers between his teeth, to get them ready for the braces, which would come in a few days. Within hours, some of the spacers had fallen out—or been taken out by Nat. I nervously called the orthodontist's office, feeling as if we were now in trouble, as if Nat had done something terribly wrong. And then I caught myself. I took a deep breath and said, "He took the bands out. But you know, if we are going to do braces for Nat, there are going to be things like this that we don't foresee, and we'll need to wing it a little bit. Do you think you can deal with that? If you can't, tell me now, and we won't go any further."

Dr. L. paused a moment, and then said cheerfully, "Of course, we can deal with that! Don't worry about the rubber bands. We'll work around it. I'll see you in a few days."

The braces went on successfully, but even though Dr. L. now understood the situation she faced with Nat, Ned found that he had to educate her staff, which he did the first time he went back with Nat.

"Parents don't come in when we do the exams," the assistant told Ned that day, taking Nat by the hand and gesturing for him to lie down in the chair.

"Well, he's not going to be able to answer your questions," Ned warned her, and then went out and sat in the waiting room. In just a few minutes the assistant came out to get him. "We need your help interpreting," she said quietly. Later Ned and I had a good laugh over that: "interpreting." Soon, we had developed an easy orthodontic routine because we knew that the office now understood Nat. Either Ned or I brought Nat for his braces appointments, which were always the office's first appointment of the day. Nat would go for his fifteen-minute visit, choose the color of the new ligatures, ride home (in our accustomed silence) with one or the other of us, and then get a treat before the bus came to get him for school.

Two years after Nat's first appointment, Dr. L. greeted us one morning by saying, "Hey, he's almost done. I mean, just look at how great he looks!" She went and got the "before" pictures, and I gasped. Nat's teeth had been monstrous back then, and now they were even and beautiful. The lower jaw was no longer an issue, because Dr. L. had indeed been very creative: instead of intrusive, uncomfortable headgear, she had attached little rubber bands to Nat's top and bottom braces to exert the right pressure on his jaws, and over a long period this had greatly improved the alignment of his mouth. "Funny thing is, before Nat, I had been doubting that rubber bands could work this way. Now I know that my other patients are lying!" She laughed. "I mean, they tell me they wear them, and yet they come in, and nothing's improved. But with Nat, I can see that the rubber bands work because he really wears them!"

She was right about that. He wore them because we told him he had to and because he was so accustomed to dental work by then that he easily accommodated each new treatment. Also because the office was so good with him, so kind

Tips on Successful Dental or Doctor's Office Visits

- Read books to your child about the upcoming experience. I recommend *Corduroy Goes to the Doctor* for very young children. *The Berenstain Bears Visit the Dentist* and *Barney Goes to the Dentist* are also good bets.
- Construct a crisis storybook for your child, explaining what to expect, whom he will see at the appointment, how he might feel during the appointment, why he does not have to be scared, and what he will get at the end.
- Discuss your child's needs with the dentist, doctor, or orthodontist ahead of time. Find out if you can get the first or very last appointment of the day, and if you can break up long visits into a few shorter ones.
- Discuss compromise treatment options if the recommendations are too arduous for your child. We refused to give Nat "perfect" teeth that would require too much of him, opting instead for improved teeth.
- Establish a familiar office routine, at the same time of day, with the same treat at the end.

and tolerant. But mostly because of Nat's conscientiousness. Even though he is autistic, he often tries hard to do the right thing—my Mini-Man still does what he can.

"Nat, you're my model patient!" Dr. L. exclaimed, and she really meant it.

We both smiled proudly at Nat, who said, "Yes, OK, yes."

Our Shifting Needs and Roles

A year after publishing my first article, I began to write a regular column for the local newspaper called "Schools of

Thought," which looked at special education, school politics, and parenting. Until Max started kindergarten, most of my school experience had been with special needs programs. In Nat's schools the families come from different towns, and they're not so easy to get to know because of the distance and the emotional circumstances of their lives. But when Max began kindergarten, an entire world opened up for us: the world of the Parent-Teacher Organization. Through the PTO, we got to know other families, and we began to socialize with some of them, getting invited to parties and eventually even going away on vacations together.

We also started attending school events such as plays and concerts. These didn't always go well because Nat, who sat in the audience with us, might be talking to himself, laughing out loud, or having a tantrum, and eventually one of us would have to take him out into the hall. The other parents would tell me to relax, it didn't matter, look at the babies who made noise, but I felt Nat's behavior wasn't really OK. Nat was not a baby; he was a big kid. Once or twice we brought a sitter along to deal with Nat, but mostly we just left him home. The first few times we did that, we felt sad about it, but after a while we saw that it made sense. It freed us to enjoy the new life we had discovered through Max's, and later Ben's, school days.

With all the material I was gathering thanks to my kids' school experiences, I found it easy to write the seven hundred word newspaper columns, and the feedback I got was mostly positive. The more attention I attracted with my pieces about special education, the more convinced I became of the need for SPED advocacy in town. It angered me, for instance, that there were no programs for Nat in our wonderful neighborhood school, which was housed in a beautiful brick and slate building, designed to blend in with the grand old Victorian houses that surrounded it. It seemed that Nat would never have a chance to go to such a school. Nor was there a program for Nat at any other school in our town; we always had to look elsewhere.

Granted, our town sent most of its severely challenged special needs children to expensive private placements, where they could get comprehensive care (one-to-one teacher-student ratios, home-based consultations, parent training opportunities). By contrast, parents in other towns struggled with administrators and received only minimal services. But I loved our town's schools and grieved that Nat couldn't be a part of them. Max's school gave him every opportunity to shine. He sang in the school's nationally renowned chorus; he was invited, along with us, to parent-child book talks with authors; he was exposed to curricula for gifted children; he joined the math league, helping his school's team win a trophy.

Because of Max's, and then later Ben's, school experience, our family grew in new and positive ways. Ned and I became familiar with normal parental school experiences, feeling the pride of a positive parent-teacher conference, rolling our eyes at yet another school fund-raising plea, pitching in with a tray of cupcakes for the bake sale. The everyday demands that came home in the form of pastel-colored flyers stuffed into Max's and Ben's backpacks filled our schedules, giving us a sense of belonging to the town and the world, and tied us to others comfortably.

Because of my growing interest in school matters, I joined the local special education parent advisory council (SPED PAC) and tried to learn more about how our town managed special education. The more people I met and stories I heard, the more I wanted to effect some changes. I spoke my mind publicly and in my column, and I began to build a reputation as an activist, getting elected to the school committee (board of education) in my town by the time Ben was three. I earned respect in my town as a local expert on autism and on the plight of the disabled. I threw off much of my self-doubt, and felt good about the career path I had chosen. I was finally doing what I wanted.

But all was not well. As soon as Benji could talk, he began saying things like "I go a mee-in'" (I'm going to a meeting) and then hiding behind a door, thus showing me what my new public life felt like to him. At this point, I was attending one or two meetings every week, and a year later, when I was elected to the school committee, I was away from home even more. And so I had to wrestle with the working mother's challenge of how to do many jobs well. Many afternoons, I felt too tired to play with the boys. Their independent personalities didn't necessarily require me to, but not feeling up to it to it made me feel guilty. And I started to wonder: Were they *too* independent? If I had been a more available mother, would they have been different?

Whatever the answer was, I would have to live with it. I didn't feel I could give up the advocacy and political work, which fulfilled a deep need of mine to make a difference in the world. Nor could I dump things like laundry and cooking on Ned; they were not at all his strong suit. I also couldn't afford a housekeeper or regular child care for Ben. I was doing it all at once, juggling home, children, activism, and writing, with no set hours for any one of my jobs. By now, Ned and I barely had time to talk anymore. I also couldn't stop worrying that on some level my kids were being neglected. Something had to give.

When we did talk, many of our conversations were about what was not working in this new situation, and what was. It took a year to begin to resolve our problems, and even today they are not all resolved. I will still sometimes find myself yelling at Ned for taking me for granted and for not talking to me enough, and he becomes grouchy about my yelling or about too many nights of takeout food (and the resulting strain on our budget) and not being able to get his work done because he is taking care of the kids in my absence.

Ned's credo, a codicil to the Sweetie Treaty, has always been "Find one thing that you can change right now, and do just that." This is good advice when we can follow it. I found that when I could figure out just a few improvements in the way I do things, short of making sweeping changes in the kind of person I am, I was indeed happier, and so was everyone else in the family. If I needed to spend more time playing on the floor with Ben, I had to pick a time during the day when I could do it most comfortably, and then I had to really do it, with no interruptions for phone calls and no obsessive checking of e-mail. Or if I was spending too many nights out, Ned and I had to settle on an agreeable number. (We eventually agreed on a maximum of two, and preferably one.) I also started to talk to the kids more about my work, explaining to them that Daddy's job was during the day, and Mommy's job, aside from being their mommy and taking care of the house, was sometimes at night.

At this point, during my first years of advocacy work, Ned, who was doing so well in his career, found that he was often feeling frustrated. He started saying things like, "There's not enough time to do all the stuff I need to do." He would be grumpy with me and short with the boys, slogging through the bedtime routines with them but never looking up and smiling as he used to do.

For so many years of marriage, Ned had been the rock, while I had been the one with a therapist, the one who openly sought help. I talked about feelings enough for the two of us— at least, that was the joke we used to have. But Ned's downcast behavior was no joke. He was every bit as much in need as I had ever been. Maybe he wasn't a "therapy type," as he said, but who cared, if therapy was what he needed?

"Maybe you want to talk to someone about how you're feeling, someone other than me," I told him one evening. "Maybe someone else will have insights" (*and the neutrality and energy to pay better attention to you,* I thought but did not say).

Ned did not disagree. He could see that his moodiness was dragging us down and that I didn't have the skills to help him, no matter how hard I tried. Eventually I asked my therapist for a referral for him, and he went into therapy. He told me that his sessions only skirted his unique childhood, focusing more on what was bothering him now. He talked a lot about Nat. He talked a lot about how sad the autism made him. But he also talked a lot about not getting to do what he wanted—assuming he could figure out what he wanted—especially with the other two boys but also for himself.

At first, I was surprised to hear that the bulk of his sessions dealt with finding time and identifying needs. The problem seemed so basic, so easy to me. Thinking about it, I realized yet again just how different we were. My issues were not Ned's, and his weren't mine. He needed to connect with himself, something I found easy, and he needed to find a way to express what he wanted, once he discovered what it was. He needed, quite simply, space and time. Once again, I worked hard on letting him talk, just as I had done several years before, when Nat had first been diagnosed. And I took on some of Ned's evening routines, so that he could go off and be alone, writing software for himself (not for work), reading, or playing the piano. He even started a web log, an extremely satisfying pursuit for him, leading to connections with fellow geeks (a term he himself uses), to interesting events out in the world, to old friends in other parts of the country, and sometimes even to job offers.

Getting Our Rest, Taking Our Space

When Ben was a little over a year old, we were offered an all-expenses-paid trip to the Bahamas. Ned's company had just shipped a major product, and as a reward, they were sending all employees to the Atlantis Resort on Paradise Island.

On first hearing this, we couldn't believe our good luck, but our euphoria did not last long. We struggled with the question of bringing the boys along on such a long flight. Ben was hardly more than a baby, and Nat was still not that easy to fly with. Nor did we know how much the boys would actually be able to enjoy the resort, with all of them in such different phases of development. We felt a Bahamas trip would probably be equal parts fun and challenge, and that proportion did not seem good enough. But when I told my mother we were turning down a free trip to the Bahamas, she said, "Why don't you and Ned go alone? We'll watch the boys." I said, "Are you sure? It's four days." But she continued to push me, and so I accepted her generous offer.

In the days leading up to the trip, guilt and fear shadowed me even while I read up on the resort and planned where we would eat and what we would do there. I couldn't stop worrying about leaving the boys for so long, being so far away and in a foreign country. To make sure my parents and the boys were prepared for the challenge, I wrote out three cheat sheets, one full page on each boy, describing where the boys should be each part of the day ("Nat: Friday morning, speech therapy, 830 Boylston Street. Then school. Max: Saturday morning, soccer at Lawrence Field. Ben: Nap, hopefully, 1:00–3:00 P.M."). I also described each boy's little habits, routines, and expectations in areas such as playtime, food, and friends.

For the boys, I made a book spelling out what they'd be doing on each day we were gone, ending each day with Grandma and Grandpa putting them to bed. The last day of the book had us returning and Grandma and Grandpa saying good-bye to them. I also devised a daily calendar for Nat so that he could check activities off as he finished them ("Get on bus; spend day at school; take bus home; arrive home, where Grandma gives you ice cream"). Even if every day was virtually the same as the last, I think it comforted him to have the book and for it to culminate in our return home.

Despite these preparations, an oppressive feeling of worry clung to me all the way to Paradise Island, until I was in our hotel room and called home. Once my mother reminded me of all the fun activities she and my father had planned for the kids, I felt lightened and empty, ready for our adventure.

For three days, it was like being kids again. Ned and I had nothing to do except play. This was certainly the place for playing, too. At the resort there were huge water slides leading into lagoons fed by waterfalls, swaying rope bridges, pretty tropical flowers, all set against the background of the green and blue ocean. With inner tubes under our arms, Ned grabbed my hand as we scurried up a beige stone staircase again and again to the top of a water slide that shot us down through a black watery cave then into a clear tunnel that ran through a shark tank. We floated down the resort's simulated river on our backs, ate outdoors overlooking the beach, and went to parties with Ned's fun-loving coworkers at night. We let ourselves relax fully and forget about what we had left behind, though I still called the boys every night at a designated time, as promised.

At the end of the four days, I didn't want to leave, except that I couldn't wait to see the kids. I had to hold Ben, barely more than a year old, and talk to Max and kiss Nat. I knew I would have to find a way to come back here with them (and we did, four years later). As it turned out, the boys had a great time without us. My parents threw themselves into babysitting with such determination that by the end of the week they were exhausted and nearly ill. Yet they were also full of funny stories to tell us the moment we walked in the door. In fact, they had more to tell us than we had to tell them!

Living Well: Not Letting Autism Cramp Our Style

When Nat was ten, he went through another difficult period. It got to the point where I had to put some of my writing on hold while I advocated for a better school situation for him. The change in Nat and the need for Ned and me to regroup as a couple became apparent over February vacation. We were staying in a high-rise resort hotel in Bal Harbour, Florida. We had paid a lot of money to get a large suite facing the ocean with enough room for the five of us and all the amenities the kids would need to have a really great time.

The boys had their own room with a balcony. "Nat will jump off the balcony!" Nat began to tease, as soon as he noticed this feature of the room. "Nat will fall off the balcony and hit your head! Yes!" He slapped his head for emphasis, his indigo eyes flashing.

TIPS ON LEAVING YOUR CHILD
WITH OTHERS

- Put together information on your child's habits and expectations: favorite/hated meals; friends to play with; suggested after-school activities. Also provide directions to important locations: supermarket, therapy clinics, and so forth.
- Create a book for your child explaining the routine that will be followed while you're gone and depicting whoever will be caring for him or her.
- Create a daily calendar for your child. We put together a special calendar for Nat so that he could see what his activities would be each day, check them off, and see when we'd be coming back.
- When you're away, be away. We tried not to talk too much about the boys while we were on vacation, except in general, philosophical terms. (No pining, no whining!) We made a point of trying new things and doing activities that we could not have done if the boys were around, like parasailing, jet-skiing, or just lying on a raft all afternoon and drinking a little too much alcohol.
- Make contact with your child at prearranged, regular times. We called home daily at a designated time so that there were no surprises. Surprise is the enemy of the autistic family!

"Oh, no, Natty, what would happen then?" Ned asked in mock despair. These playfully threatening conversations were a new development in our relationship with Nat. After our initial horror at the thought that he would actually try something dangerous, we realized that such talk was merely a way for him to tell us about his fears and his wonderment concerning the world around him, and to get reassurance from us: You fall off a balcony, you hurt your head. This never varied, and it was just the kind of certainty and predictability Nat craved.

"Head will bleed and bleed," replied Nat, eyes flashing, joyfully imagining the agony and drama of it, ever more ecstatic that our dialogue about this was perpetually the same.

Nat had also started to talk a lot about falling out of airplanes, walking on railroad tracks, and jumping in front of moving cars. He never actually made any attempts to do these things, and we figured he wouldn't jump off the balcony either. Whenever he threatened to do something like that, we tried to draw him out about it, and we were stunned and even moved by what we learned about his thought processes.

"Nat, what will happen if you walk on the tracks?" one of us would ask.

"The train will come and hit you! Boom!"

"Yes, and then what?"

"Head will bleed and bleed. Go to the hospital."

"Yes, and what will happen at the hospital?"

"Have to sleep there. Mommy will cry, Daddy will cry, Max will cry, Ben will cry."

"And Nat will cry."

We loved the glimpses these discussions gave us of Nat's preoccupations, even if they were a bit macabre.

Later during the vacation, however, he did get involved in mischief on the balcony. We found this out one afternoon, when Max noticed that several of his Beanie Babies were missing. As Max became more and more upset looking for the toys, Nat began laughing, and we put two and two together. I went out on the balcony to have a look. Below, spread across the lawn of the neighboring resort, was a tragic, colorful array of tiny stuffed animals: Max's Beanies!

"Hey, look at this!" I yelled to everyone. I was angry at Nat for laughing and for what he had done; but then before I knew it, I was giggling at the bizarre spread of toys way down there on the grass, and Nat, so proud of what he'd done, and also so transparent, that in the end we all laughed, even Max. Max was learning to appreciate the absurd humor this family had to offer, and as long as we could keep Nat from throwing Max's toys off the balcony again, he was OK.

After that incident and for the rest of the vacation, we were careful to lock the balconies. Still, a small chill settled over me as I realized that these new violent fantasies and mischievous behaviors might foreshadow something worse. Sure enough, when Nat returned to school after this vacation, he began to behave in ways that threw our family into a crucible of upheaval—one that eventually made us stronger than we'd ever been.

8

HANDLING THE
WORST OF TIMES

ONE OF THE SHARPEST PAINS for a parent is seeing your child struggle. Watching Nat struggle to understand the machinery and rules of the world, hoping it wouldn't chew him up and spit him out, I suffered along with him. I wanted so badly to soften the sharp edges for him, to make others more compassionate. For Ned and me, our challenge was not that we lacked an understanding of the world, it was that we knew its ways all too well. And so we moved from grieving over his disability to over grieving what lay ahead for him. Little by little, we came to the painful realization that only through regularly resisting toward some of his most natural tendencies would he be able to succeed on his own.

And yet with this new realization, there came a release from some of the old pain; it was easier to be angry at the world than to be angry at Nat. This shift in my focus, away from the injustice of Nat's disability toward the indifference of the world, actually bonded me more strongly to Nat. *OK*, I said to myself. *Now we know what we're up against and what we have to do*. Insofar as possible, we had to make Nat into some-one with the skills to succeed in this world.

A New Phase of Understanding and Action

Starting when Nat was around eight years old, as he moved from one school placement to another, improving in some ways while stagnating in others, "Push for more" became our creed. We sought to thrust him ever higher, to strengthen all his abilities. Every time we learned of a new resource—a medication, a special diet, a better school, a smarter doctor—we felt compelled to pursue it. We were always looking for the thing that would "make a light go on" for Nat.

We heard about a particularly good autism program in a school system in a suburb about twenty miles west of us. It was funded, actually, by a conglomerate of school systems that had pooled their resources and space to run a great variety of special education programs. I spoke to the director of this collaborative on the phone and liked his warmth and his sense of humor. He told us that there might be an opening in the autism classroom we had heard about, and that the head teacher was a young man. I was intrigued by the possibility of Nat being taught by a man. A male teacher could be a terrific role model. He would offer a different chemistry, and that might be a good thing for Nat's occasional aggressive outbursts.

After a visit with the teacher, we decided to send Nat to this program. It was a wonderful fit, with a small class of around seven kids with abilities similar to Nat's, and two assistants in addition to the head teacher. The children occasionally mixed with the typical students in the school, for assemblies or lunch, and this was a positive experience for Nat because he got enough support to make it work. Nat smiled a lot that year, in addition to progressing in literacy, math, and social skills. I came across the class picture the other day, and seven years later, Nat can name every person in that room.

For two years this setup worked well for Nat, even when the

> ## FURTHER SUGGESTIONS ON FINDING THE RIGHT SCHOOL PROGRAM FOR YOUR CHILD
>
> - Visit at least two different programs whenever you're considering making a change. Look for peer matches and role models, children in the programs who seem like your child or slightly higher in functioning. Take note of how well the children are treated—we look for patient staff with compassion and a sense of humor—and which educational techniques are used.
> - In addition to assessing classroom personnel, try to assess the degree of supportiveness and flexibility in the program director and the building staff, as well as their receptiveness to parental input.
> - For further information see *www.nichcy.org*, the website of the National Dissemination Center for Children with Disabilities, *http://rsaffran.tripod.com/schools.html* for a superb survey of ABA (applied behavioral analysis) programs throughout the world; and *www.nap.edu/books/0309072697/html*, where you can browse the book *Educating Children with Autism*, written by a committee of the National Academy of Sciences.

head teacher left and Nat had to adjust to someone new. It began to look to us as if Nat were a higher-functioning child than we had realized. I felt sweet hope course through me as I talked to the director about the prospects for Nat's third year with the collaborative.

By the end of the second year, Nat would be too old for this classroom, so he would have to move on. The collaborative offered two new programs for us to choose from. One emphasized prevocational experience and a pragmatic curriculum, offering subjects like money skills. The director told us that the children in the program were lower-functioning than Nat and that some also had behavioral issues. If Nat went to this program, he would be one of the higher-functioning kids there. Hearing this made me a little depressed; I felt Nat could do better.

The other program was farther away, and it had higher-functioning, developmentally delayed kids, most of whom did not have autism or aggressive or destructive behaviors, just social and cognitive skill issues. If Nat went to this classroom, he would be the most challenging, lowest-functioning kid there. I wanted Nat to go to this classroom because I wanted to believe he would adjust to its challenges, that he was ready to stretch.

"Well, he has some behavior problems," I told the director, "but I'd like him to try the higher-functioning classroom."

Ned was silent. He was worried, he told me later, that this placement would not be a good fit for Nat. But he saw how badly I wanted Nat to attend the program, and he, too wanted to believe that Nat could handle it. Anyway, we both believed that the program would help him somehow. It was a special education program, after all.

"Just how bad *are* the behaviors?" asked the director.

I knew the right answer was "not so bad." But the truth was, Nat could be difficult, throwing things in class, intentionally spilling things and messing things up, and even sometimes hitting teachers or classmates. At the end of the last year, he had even overturned one of the classroom computers, yet his teachers had not shown much concern; after all, Nat had never done it before. But I didn't tell any of this to the director. Instead I asked, "With the right kind of teacher and a lot of structure, wouldn't we be able to avoid trouble?" As I said this, however, I felt a twinge of fear. In retrospect, I should have listened to the fear.

"You know," the director said carefully, "in a program like this, the expectation is for *no* behavior problems. That's a lot to ask of a kid like Nat. But if Nat can make it in this kind of program, a lot of doors will open for him."

Oh, how I wanted those doors to open! I was like a stage mother, pushing her unsuspecting child toward a difficult but shining, desirable new role. "I think he can do it," I said.

After the meeting with the director, Ned expressed his doubts to me about Nat's ability to succeed in the new program. I understood his concerns, but I couldn't let go of the dream of Nat in the "better" classroom, which was how I had begun to think of it. "Look," I said. "He's shown that he can do the academics that this new classroom would offer. He needs better role models than the kids in that other program would be; the kids in this better program are higher-functioning and more social! He might even make some friends."

Ned was still doubtful. "It's going to be a hard change for him," he said.

I did not want to hear this. I wanted to see Nat continue progressing the way I saw him progressing now. I didn't want him to be a "low-functioning" kid. I knew that these labels were limiting, and I wasn't going to let anyone tell me who my child was or was not. I realized I was pushing Nat, but I thought it was appropriate for him at that stage. In the end I persuaded Ned and myself that with the good staff ratio, the reasonably small class size, and the supportive program director, Nat would be fine.

Ned and I often have opposing views about what is best for Nat, and this stems from a basic philosophical difference. It's not that Ned doesn't believe in Nat's potential, it's just that he wants to be practical and work on the things that Nat can actually succeed in while avoiding the things he's more likely to fail at. I, on the other hand, want to make sure that we never close off any avenue too soon, that we are never guilty of saying, "He can't do that," only to find that he could have done it with the right support. Sometimes this dynamic between us is maddening, and we often have long, impassioned arguments before we reach an agreement. In this case, however, we both agreed fairly quickly that it would not be a huge risk to try the higher-functioning program.

Looking back on it now, I wish we had prepared for this placement more thoroughly. It would have been good to have the principal meet Nat so that he could get to know our son and understand what kind of support he needed. We should have observed the peer group in the new classroom to identify whether there were any good matches for Nat, or if the children were much higher-functioning than he. We could have requested additional behavioral backup to help with Nat's transition difficulties—for example, asking the new teachers to spend some afternoons alone with Nat so they could get to know one another, paying them for their time if necessary. Knowing that Nat had some behavioral problems, we could have determined beforehand how the school dealt with disruptive behavior. Also, it probably would have helped give us a basis of comparison if we had visited the other program option before deeming it too low-functioning for Nat. We eliminated it just on the basis of how it was described to us, without observing it ourselves. In short, we were blinded by the glow of the higher-functioning program.

Trouble

Nat started attending the new program that summer, to get to know some of his classmates and one of his teachers for the following school year. When Nat walked into that classroom with us on the first day, I could tell by his sudden, darting movements that there was going to be trouble. He was anxious, the way he often is when he steps into a new environment. He may also have sensed that no one was in charge here in the same confident, competent manner that his previous teachers had been, and this probably made him even more anxious. At the same time, he may have felt a need to test what the limits were in this new place, as a way of getting to know it. Limit-testing is part of Nat's character, something he does because he has no natural, internal sense of what is appropriate in a new situation. Beginnings, middles, sides, and ends must be spelled out to him. I knew this from the time I wrote the first Nat Book. So why didn't these teachers understand this? And why were they giving him Twizzlers every few minutes?

"Chewing can calm him," one of the aides explained. "It gives him sensory input in his mouth."

"Chewing sugary candy *calms* him?" I asked, incredulous. I knew enough to realize the aide's technique came out of the sensory integration (SI) school of therapy, in which neurologically challenged children are encouraged to chew rubbery or crunchy items as a way of gaining a particular kind of sensory stimulation that can calm them and even elicit better language skills. But SI therapy doesn't usually involve sugary candy. This was bribery, not neurological therapy or behavior modification. In fact, the personnel in the new classroom had gotten the behaviorist approach exactly backward: When he acted out, they would try to "calm him" with candy, which I'm sure he understood as a reward and an incentive to behave badly again.

Ned patiently explained this dynamic to the teachers, adding that Nat was used to being rewarded after he had exhibited *good* behavior. They seemed to understand, and we relaxed. And indeed Nat had few problems for the rest of the summer.

The fall went well, too, at least to begin with. Even though the head teacher was a rather brittle, meek woman, Nat thrived academically. He participated in all group lessons and progressed in all subject areas on his education plan. He did have some outbursts of hair-pulling, destructiveness, and other difficulties, but the reports always described them as isolated or "out of the blue." The teachers didn't recognize any patterns or cause and effect in his behavior because they weren't looking for any.

All was not well, however, when we looked just below the surface. The teachers, particularly the speech-language pathologist and occupational therapist, were cold and unfriendly toward Nat. As long as they could help him make progress, it didn't matter, or so I told myself. Still, I wondered if they resented him for some reason. But why? Perhaps they perceived him as very different from the other kids in his class because he had autism and somewhat difficult behaviors, while the rest of them were only cognitively or developmentally delayed. We did not take up the issue of coldness this time, hoping that their distant affect would fade in time. We also hoped that the behavioral blips would prove to be isolated events. But when it comes to Nat, letting certain things go can be destabilizing, and it can give him the wrong message as well (that the boundaries set up are weak and inconsistent). In hindsight, we should not have been so complacent, but rather, we should have reconvened our special ed team as soon as Nat started misbehaving in his new class.

At the same time Nat was starting in this new school program, he had a home tutor, a college sophomore named Dani, who was working very well with him. Dani understood that Nat had trouble communicating, and she focused on his gifts: his sense of humor, his passion for Disney movies, his easygoing nature, his mischievousness. She got him to tell her his usual jokes, the ones that contained errors that we were supposed to catch and correct. She also worked with him on all sorts of academic skills, like categorizing and riddle-solving. She even started to teach him mathematical word problems. So even with his behavior problems at school, Nat was on an upward trajectory of accomplishment.

We were feeling so good about Nat's ability to do things we hadn't dreamed him capable of that we signed him up for a gymnastics class offered by the Special Olympics at the Massachusetts Institute of Technology. The Special Olympics runs largely on donations and volunteers, yet it manages to offer many effective and amazing classes and events, attracting compassionate, empathic people to coach, and taking some of the most severely disabled people and helping them master athletic skills and feel like stars.

Nat's gymnastics class had several autistic kids in it, as well as some girls with developmental delays. The young woman who taught the class was an open-minded, smiley college student who was more than willing to listen to the parents about what the kids needed. She had to, because the class was a disaster at first. In early class sessions, the autistic boys were bouncing off trampolines, running away, swinging from the climbing ropes and flapping their hands. Many of the parents were skeptical that these kids would be able to make it through the two-hour sessions, let alone learn any gymnastics. But we pulled together and taught the coach how to deal with the kids, and many of the parents helped her coach, as well. The autistic boys, we told her, needed consistency, repetition, and simple instructions. She understood quickly and made sure that the class was the same each time. Nat started to learn routines on the mats, the rings, and the parallel bars. Each routine had a structure that Nat could comprehend and be reassured by, and so, to our delight, gymnastics became a favorite activity for him.

The Winter of Nat's Discontent

Overall, Nat seemed to be doing well. But when winter arrived, his misbehavior in the classroom escalated dramatically. We had recently switched him to Paxil, a newer drug similar to Zoloft, and had increased his dose. Unfortunately, we were discovering that when the dose is too high, drugs like Paxil and Zoloft can disinhibit Nat to the point where he becomes nearly manic. Thus, we suspected this new manifestation of increased destructive behavior probably had something to do with his medication. Even though our psychopharmacologist was an excellent and responsible doctor, treating autism with psychoactive medication was still so new that it often relied on trial and error.

When we got back from our vacation in Bal Harbour, even with this escalation in difficult behaviors such as pinching and hair-pulling, we were not yet alarmed about the situation. His spirits were good, we loved how animated he seemed, and the reports from the school staff were still characterizing his misbehavior as having come from "out of the blue" and saying that Nat was otherwise "fine."

In late February, however, the school's attitude changed from unconcerned to angry and intolerant. By early March Nat seemed to be unraveling. His aggression had intensified dramatically. He was jumping up and hitting teachers and students, and even attacking them when their backs were turned. The director began calling me to the school—an hour away—to take Nat home. The first time this happened, I was indignant. Could the school really send home a disabled kid for acting out because of his disability? I took Nat home that first day, but I immediately expressed to the program director my concern about Nat's rights. That day I consulted one of the state's most formidable special education lawyers, who told me that, yes, the school could suspend Nat for up to ten days. If a pattern of misbehavior persisted, however, and the misbehavior was determined to be linked to the disability, there was supposed to be a team meeting where we discussed how best to help him. But when the school sent him home several more times, the lawyer told me we should probably start looking for a new placement, even though we were about to have a team meeting.

The Functional Behavioral Assessment

On the advice of our lawyer, we had the school do a functional behavioral assessment (FBA) of Nat in the classroom. Schools are required by federal law to do an FBA if a child with a disability is exhibiting disruptive behaviors, particularly if the child has been suspended. In an FBA, a behavioral specialist, or behaviorist, looks for problems in the classroom dynamics by interviewing the child's parents and observing the child, the educational setting, and the staff's interactions with the child. Then the behaviorist recommends ways to improve the situation, recommendations that the child's team is supposed to follow.

In our case, the behaviorist felt that Nat required more consistent responses to his behaviors and more structure in the form of one-on-one teaching. He also urged that the program

---

How I Covered My Bases
When Nat's School Began Sending
Him Home for Disruptive Behavior

- I familiarized myself with the applicable sections of the law by visiting *www.wrightslaw.com*.
- I enlisted the help of an experienced special-education lawyer. See the Federation for Children with Special Needs website for links and resources (*www.fcsn.org*).
- I kept a paper trail of all correspondence and e-mails.
- I contacted the program quality assurance people at our state department of education and began a formal complaint. See the website from the Minnesota Governor's Council on Developmental Disabilities: *www.partnersin policymaking.com*. Click on "online courses" to learn more about advocacy.
- I had my town hire a well-recommended behaviorist to do the functional behavioral assessment (FBA) required by law in the event of disruptive behavior that may be a manifestation of disability.
- I brought supportive professionals to our meetings with the school.
- Though I did not control my outrage, I should have. It is always easier dealing with others when you're not acting furious. I should have begun looking for new placements from the first time the school sent him home.

---

add a behaviorial support person for a few weeks to train the staff in behavioral techniques to help Nat get back on track, phasing him or her out once Nat's behavior had settled down.

But the collaborative refused to add yet another staff person to the class. This was not supposed to be a "behavioral" kind of program, the program director reminded me, instantly severing the warm connection I had felt with him. Without his support, I was beginning to feel scared that we were going to lose this placement without having another one line up. Unlike the behaviorist, the staff believed it was solely Nat's medication that made his behavior aberrant, unpredictable, and uncontrollable.

Nat's behaviors are not unpredictable at all, the behaviorist told the team at the meeting we attended at the school toward the end of March. He showed us data on Nat's actions and the staff's inadequate responses. For example, the staff was mostly reactive, rather than preventive, in dealing with Nat, responding after a transgression rather than taking the time to set him up with transition time and expectations beforehand and rewards afterward. He would hurt a teacher, and she would show her distress, which would reinforce the behavior. None of the staff seemed to have a sense of any antecedents to the action, thus guaranteeing it to happen again.

While Ned and I believed that Nat's drugs played some part in his new behaviors, we saw the teachers' interactions with Nat as more significant. I had witnessed their reserve, their coldness, their inability to connect with him, and I had no doubt that these had contributed to the terrible behavior dynamic they had with Nat. The things they said at our team meeting reflected the negative way they saw him. A glaring example was the occupational therapist angrily complaining that Nat had attacked her from behind, and that this was particularly dangerous because she was pregnant. The way she said this made it sound as though she hated Nat. I was mortified by the story but also by her reaction to the incident. What had happened was terrible, of course, but Nat could not have targeted her *because* she was pregnant; he lacked that kind of awareness and malice. Yet this is what she seemed to believe on some level. The other teachers also seemed to see Nat only as a threat to their classroom and to their safety.

As I listened to them talk, I detected another issue, a subtext to their complaints: They felt that Nat was a threat to their program. One remark by the director implied that his program would not be allowed to remain in this school if the school principal felt that the children in it were dangerous. As building managers, the principals have the final say over who stays and who goes in their schools, and the interplay between system-wide directors and principals is complex and often politically charged. And so upon hearing the director's remark, I understood this placement was effectively over for us. It didn't matter what the law said, and I certainly didn't want to fight to keep him where he wasn't wanted. Still, I was heartbroken by the way the program personnel had been so quick to abandon Nat, and my heartbreak quickly morphed into fury. *They called themselves a special needs program, yet they would not deal with Nat's special needs! How dare they!*

Nat returned to school with the provision—though I protested this—that there would be no additional support for him and that they would call me to pick him up every time he misbehaved. He lasted a day or two more under these conditions. Early April was last time I was called in to bring Nat home. I walked into the principal's office, where the director was waiting for me with the principal. Looking at me coldly, they explained Nat's latest act of aggression. I looked at them with contempt and said, "I'm taking Nat home, and we won't be coming back. Shame on you."

I took Nat from the class without a word to the teachers, saying, "Come on, darling. We're leaving this place." I felt like Mrs. Jumbo, the mother elephant from *Dumbo,* one of Nat's favorite movies, when she takes her son Dumbo away from the bullying kids. Like her, I was full of self-righteous anger; and like Mrs. Jumbo and Dumbo, Nat and I now had no place to go.

An "Alternate Placement" for Nat at Home

As it turned out, our troubles were only just beginning. A few days later I met with my town's special education director and the assistant superintendent of student services to find out where in town Nat's new placement would be. But they told me that there was no place for Nat in our town's schools either because he was "too dangerous."

"Dangerous!" I was livid. "He's not dangerous! He just needs a behaviorist with him," I said, referring to the functional behavioral assessment. "He needs the right support!"

The SPED director tried to calm me, but she had just crushed our last hope, the hope of getting Nat into the recently created autistic-spectrum classroom at a school in our town. I told her I knew several kids in the autism program, and he was very similar to them.

"There's no space in there," she told me. "It wouldn't be a good fit, anyway."

"Then where will he go?" I said frantically.

She hesitated, then said, "You will have to homeschool him until something else opens up."

I railed against this decision. I complained in a letter to the local newspaper. I complained to the superintendent of schools. But in the end, we had no choice but to keep Nat at home and try to use our tutors to educate him until a placement opened up in another program. The law may have guaranteed Nat's right to be educated alongside his peers to the greatest degree possible, but our town could not (or would not) find him a place, and so we had to keep him home while he deteriorated.

We knew that we could have sued, but we didn't want to completely destroy our relationship with our town. And what would we win if we used the courts to force Nat's way into a classroom where he wasn't wanted? Another set of unwilling teachers, and more difficulties for Nat? Instead of fighting, I decided, I would conserve my energy for the coming days of having Nat at home, which were bound to be difficult.

Despite the aggressiveness that had caused Nat so much trouble at school, one area of our lives remained hopeful: the Saturday Special Olympics gymnastics class. Nat attended regularly, mastering routines on the mats and on the parallel bars.

His gymnastics coach even came to our house several times while Nat was being homeschooled. She would take him to the nearby park where he could practice his routines, using playground equipment as a substitute for the gym equipment. In her mind, he was preparing for the State Special Olympic Games in June. Ned and I did not dare hope that Nat would be able to compete there, but we were happy to let her work with him. Nat rarely misbehaved with her—at least she never reported anything to us. He probably restrained himself because she was so gentle and positive, and because she so clearly believed in him.

Despite his progress with gymnastics, Nat became increasingly difficult to manage as the weeks went by. Occasionally he lunged at me, pinching, scratching, and hitting. Ned and I were at our wits' end. To help me handle Nat's behavior, Ned started working from home a great deal, even taking a whole week off at one point because I was so depressed about Nat and frankly so scared of him and what he might do. I cobbled together a homeschooling program using four part-time tutors, whom I had found by placing ads in the newspaper. One by one, they stopped coming because Nat would hit them in the head or pull out handfuls of their hair.

Then one day, Dani, our last remaining tutor, was with Nat and I heard her scream, "Nat, stop! Sue, help!" I came into Nat's room just in time to see Nat, with a tight grip on Dani's hair, getting ready to hit her. I grabbed him and tried to restrain him, not knowing what to do next. He seemed like a wild, rabid animal.

Dani told me that he had jumped at her when she had asked him to do the same academic exercises (like word problems and sentence construction) that he had been doing for months. He must have been feeling more and more insecure as his homeschooling routine became less and less predictable. He probably felt the need to test everyone around him in every situation to see what the rules were, and to see whether his tutors would become fearful and frantic toward him, like his former teachers from the collaborative classroom. I also wondered if he craved the drama and certainty of those negative responses, if they were somehow addictive for him. *Like a killer after he has had his first scent of blood,* I could not help but think. Whatever the answer, I could no longer ask Dani to work with Nat; it just wasn't safe for her. With no one to teach my increasingly aggressive child, I was beginning to face the prospect of seeking residential care for him.

Broken Connections

During this period, I began feeling distant from Nat, unsure of him, and I was certain he could sense it, and that he felt I was not on his side anymore. I now believe that this broken connection played a critical role in Nat's further descent into aggressive behavior. I also believe that his experience in the collaborative classroom had touched off a cycle of anxiety— Nat's uneasiness due to his teachers' lack of skill, then heightened staff anxiety, then Nat's aggression, then even more staff anxiety—and he brought this elevated state of uneasiness home, where the cycle continued. I just didn't yet know what to do about it.

By six weeks into Nat's homeschooling, things had become very scary. One day, I took Nat and Ben for a little outing into the city on the subway. Nat loved the subway, which he'd been taking into town occasionally with Ned. But that day, we took a different route from the one Nat was used to. Of course, I took pains to explain our new route; I knew I had to, especially the way Nat had been behaving lately.

As we pulled into a station, I anxiously told him, "We're going to get off here because we have to take a different train. Then we will get on another train and go home, OK?" Nat looked at me clear-eyed, and so I thought he was going to be fine. But as I prepared to get off the train, taking Ben out of his stroller and folding it up, Nat attacked me head-on, clawing at my arm again and again with a painful pinching grip. I was holding Ben with both arms and the stroller was hanging from my forearm, so I wasn't able to restrain Nat. I was terrified that he would go after Ben next, or cause me to drop him. I struggled to speak in a measured voice and to hold back my tears but he was really hurting me. "Nat, calm hands. Nat, calm hands."

By now people were staring. I managed to loosen the stroller from my arm, letting it rest against my leg, and to shift Ben to one arm so that I could reach out and defend myself against my ten-year-old. Nat was nearly five feet tall then, just seven inches shorter than I was, and surprisingly strong. His eyes were dilated to black, and he looked terrified, as I guess he was; it's frightening to lose control of yourself.

I finally did reach him, however, by speaking very sharply. "NAT, STOP!" I said, my eyes flashing with anger. Luckily he did stop, although he'd already left a bruise on my arm.

I was shaken by this incident, and I absolutely feared Nat, my own child, and worried that any connection we would make in the near term could only be limited and shaky. He was a stranger to the family again, and I felt our family life closing in on itself once more. Hopes and dreams were giving way to living moment by moment, just trying to survive. We shifted into siege mode once again, worse than we'd ever known.

The Light at the End of the Tunnel

After the incident at the train station, we knew we had to do more for Nat than we had been doing. I called our psychologist to talk about temporary hospitalization and residential placement.

"I can't believe I'm having this conversation," I said dully. "How can I send him away?" I imagined Nat, packed up in the car, pleading, "Go home, go home. Go home. You be good." I could not stand the thought.

"Think of it as the best way to help him," our psychologist said gently. "If he needs a higher level of care than you can provide, then this is what you should do. Besides, you ought to know that if you're thinking of placing him in an adult residence after he turns twenty-two, then you often have to start with such a placement much earlier, like in his early teens."

"Oh God! This is too much! I have to go." I hung up and immediately called Ned at work. Sobbing, I told him about my talk with the psychologist.

Ned said, "I don't know, it sounds like overkill to me." I started to calm down, but then he added, "Maybe Nat does need more, though. We'll have to deal with the fact that he is extremely difficult to manage *and* that one day he will need to live in a residence."

How can we send him away? I wondered. But, *how can we continue to live like this?* I called my parents. "They're recommending that we send him away," I cried. "I can't do it. I just can't."

My father said calmly, "You don't have to send him away; you know what's best for him. You and Ned. He'll be all right. Try that medication your doctor mentioned."

"Resperidone?" Nat's psychopharmacologist had been urging us to give Nat this drug, an antipsychotic medication that was having wonderful results among children with aggressive tendencies. But we had shied away from it because of its harmful potential side effects, including tardive dyskinesia, involuntary ticlike movements of the mouth and tongue, which, though rare, can be irreversible. (Another, more common side effect is weight gain.) Though we understood that tardive dyskinesia was unlikely and weight gain would not be a problem with a skinny kid like Nat, we had held off because it was a drug with more harmful side effects than Paxil or Clonidine.

"Yes. See if Resperidone helps," my father said. "One step at a time."

By saying this, he reminded me I could still be in charge and restored my faith in myself.

Though our psychologist did find a temporary residential placement for Nat, Ned and I, reflecting on my father's words, decided not to use it. Whatever Nat was going to do, we would deal with it as a family. This firm resolve helped us feel better because it put us back on Nat's side and stopped the cycle of fear and mistrust. Once again, I could see him as simply my son, in a lot of trouble and needing me more than ever. Once again, it was Nat *and us* against the world.

With this realization, love, relief, and determination flooded through me, and I felt it deep in my bones. I think Nat felt it, too. Now that we had finally agreed to put Nat on Resperidone, our doctor told us that we'd see results almost immediately. He explained that Resperidone would likely relieve the intensity of our situation, and that he didn't think Nat would have to be sent to a residential placement.

Within a few days, we found some blessed relief. Nat was definitely slower to strike us. At the same time, we located a new behaviorist agency, having concluded that we needed a professional to work with Nat at home, not tutors or college kids. The agency sent Lisa, a middle-aged, bespectacled behavioral therapist. I thought: *This auntie-type is going to deal with Nat?* When I warned her that Nat would become aggressive, she smiled kindly at me, with a look that said, "So?" She was very warm but no pushover.

After her first hour with him, all she said was, "He's very bright. His reading ability is incredible." I could have cried; this was the first positive thing anyone had said about Nat for months. When he knocked her glasses off her face in the middle of their session, she just stood up and crossed his forearms in front of his chest, holding each of his hands gently at his sides. He looked surprised by this maneuver. "A light basket hold," she quietly explained to me. I felt a softening in my gut and wondered what it was—it had been that long since I'd been able to relax. My relaxation would improve my relationship with Nat, and that, in turn, helped our family life start to expand outward again.

Seeing Lisa's confident way with Nat, I knew our ordeal was finally over, just like that, as happens with siege mode. For the first time in a long while Nat was under control. In combination with Lisa's approach and the family's supportive

embrace of him, the Resperidone helped decrease Nat's aggression substantially. With Lisa coming in for just a few hours
a week, Nat's days suddenly had a dependable structure, and
even more importantly, he now had a dependable, unflappable
teacher who believed in him. Soon Nat was doing everything
she asked him to.

Our One Bright Light Becomes a Torch: The Special Olympics

That summer, against all odds, Nat and his gymnastics team
competed in the 2000 State Games, and we invited around fifteen friends and family members to watch. The kids performed
beautifully: They waited their turn, followed their routines, sat
patiently when necessary, and finished each routine with the
Special Olympics flourish of the arms held up in the shape of
the letter "V." They had uniforms, a parade, and they even got
medals for their efforts. Max seemed very proud of Nat and was
appropriately envious of the medals—this kind of normal sibling envy is a rarity for Max. Afterward, our friends and family
members joined us at home for a celebratory meal. This was the
first time we had an achievement of Nat's to share with others,
and our guests were ecstatic about his accomplishment.

Our experience with the State Games convinced us we
should take even more risks with Nat, hoping that they would
lead to more good times for the family. As hard as it might be,
we wanted to keep amassing happy experiences and quiet triumphs to counterbalance all the bad experiences, which we
now knew could occur with terrible intensity. Nat's difficult
period at home had left us sore, fearful, and almost hating him
at times. We were nearly beaten down by his autism. But then,
just as we were ready to give up, Nat's success at the Special
Olympics seized us by the heart and helped us to take joy in
him once again.

As it turned out, because of everything we had just gone
through with Nat, on the day of the State Games we were al-

most too tired and discouraged to take him. But Ned said to me, "Let's risk it. What have we got to lose? We can always go home. But think how good it will feel if it works!" And there, in that dimly lit, stuffy gym, as we watched him prancing around the mats, eagerly following his routine, his long ivory limbs stretched out with perfect precision, I felt my heart fill up again, and I was ready for anything.

9

OUR MOST
IMPORTANT DISCOVERY

He's Trying to Connect With Us

⟶

B Y MAY, NAT HAD BEEN PLACED in a private behavioral day school similar to the one he had attended when he was five. We had decided to go back to the highly structured, regimented approach that had worked so well in the past. Nat settled in to the familiar behavior-modification classroom very well. His behavioral situation was finally feeling comfortable for us again, and our maturing family was reaching a fairly stable state. Even though we sometimes chafed at the limitations, the behaviors, and the slow pace that autism forced on us, we began to feel that we could—or should—do more together as a family. Ned would point out that it wasn't fair to Max and Ben for us to stay home so much. They needed to grow up in a setting where autism didn't always dominate. But how could Ned and I make this happen? How could we make Nat try activities that were new and uncomfortable to him? Or was it OK simply to leave him home with a sitter? Leaving him out of things made us feel sad and guilty, but we had to do more as a family or we would start to feel stunted, and our other kids would miss out on the things normal families do, like going to movies, concerts, and museums together. We were going to have to figure out a balance of activities we could all do together and activities the rest of us would do without Nat. With luck, it would strengthen our family life.

This was easier said than done, however. Even the well-trained professionals at Nat's new school had problems tamping down Nat's aggression. To keep him busy and structure his school-vacation time, we signed him up for a Christmas-break program. But the program director had called me within a few hours of my dropping Nat off there. "Maybe you want to come and get Nat."

"Why? What's going on?" But I already knew.

"He's been a bit aggressive, and, well, he says he wants to go home."

"I'll be there in about a half hour." *Damn.* Now I would have to get Nat and rearrange the whole day to accommodate him. I gathered up Max and Ben, who rolled their eyes at the disruption, and we got in the car.

The Christmas-break program was held in a huge gym, and when I got there kids (of varying disabilities and ages) were sitting in the middle of the floor. A college-aged boy told me, "Well, he got kind of agitated, and we tried to get him to go for a walk. When we got back inside, he started hitting."

"He *hit* you?"

"Yeah." His expression was blank, but I was feeling pretty bad for him. I looked questioningly at the young woman in charge of the program. She repeated the story.

I didn't have the energy to try to talk the staff into giving him a time-out, or rewarding him for having tried a new thing with a break or a piece of candy. Time to cut my losses. I took Nat and Ben by the hand, and we left, with Max not far behind. OK, we would do something else today.

In the car, I found I was choked with tears, muttering, "I just can't deal with this stuff!" The grief and self-pity overtook me like a sudden downpour, and as I sat behind the wheel, I started

---

STRATEGIES FOR THE
HARD AND HOPELESS DAYS

- Adjust your expectations for the day. When times are tough and I start to feel hopeless or overwhelmed, I ask myself if I'm trying to do too much right now. I look just at my boys and nothing else. What do they need, right now? I stop thinking about bills, meals, or laundry, and focus only on getting through this difficult moment with them. I think of lowest-common-denominator activities: something we can all do together. Baking is warm and comforting. Watching a video together is soothing and a good excuse for snuggling.
- Think in small increments of time. What activities will help you and your child to get through the next hour? I usually stay close to home. It's easier to contain behavioral blowups at home, and it's safer to be there than out in public when Nat is difficult to control.
- Get emotional support. Once the boys are settled, I call Ned, my mother, or a friend—someone who gets it. For a helpful glimpse into the life of another family dealing with autism, see the blog at *www.genrecookshop.com*. Reading other peoples' stories can help you feel less alone.

---

to cry in ragged sobs, my tears splashing down. I gave in to it this time, an almost delicious self-indulgence, although with the feeling that I was going to have to pull myself together soon. *I shouldn't do this in front of the kids,* I thought. *I have to be strong.* But I just kept crying.

Max sat next to me, frozen, no doubt embarrassed, but wishing to help without knowing how. Nat shifted around uncomfortably because he hates it when I cry. He becomes sad at first, and if it goes on too long, nervous and then giggly. He may feel vaguely responsible. Little Ben was playing very loudly with his bear, probably trying to drown me out. *OK, get a grip. You can't do this.*

I put on my sunglasses and swallowed hard. I took a deep breath. As I drove home, I considered the options before me: videos, family Candyland, baking. *With hours of nothing planned, we could do gingerbread,* I thought. *A house, even.* I remembered the gingerbread houses we'd made in the past, the painstaking hours making the dough, waiting for it to chill, rolling it out, waiting for it to bake, then at last, the delicate leaning together of slightly warped brown pieces. By the time you got to frosting and decorating it, your teeth ached from having licked so much sugar, and your back ached from standing bent over for so long. But it was something the three of them liked to do: Max liked the architectural part. Ben liked pretending it was a real house that gummy bears live in. Nat eagerly followed the recipe—a familiar set of rules—and just as eagerly awaited his reward: getting to eat the raw dough. We would have a home day together, and it would be fun.

Our Most Important Insight

Nat's lack of social skills had always been a hole in our family's fabric. How could we repair such a thing? Why did he resort to aggression at times? The two questions were connected somehow, and Ned and I were determined to find the answers so that we could better understand Nat and improve our family life.

Our way of getting at a problem is to talk about it at length and place it at the forefront of our consciousness, observing, experiencing, and analyzing it until the answers come to us. This time, we began to notice that Nat went through negative and positive phases of several weeks each. We noticed, in addition, that negative phases occurred most frequently in the winter, and they also seemed to precede bursts of physical growth.

But we wondered whether other factors were involved, too. One revealing episode occurred when Nat was twelve years old and had resumed his habit of fake hysterical laughter, like the laughter that began before he was first put on Clonidine. It felt terrible, and perverse, to have to tell our child that he was laughing too much, but Nat did it expressly to annoy people. It got so that the moment we heard him laugh, we wanted him to stop it.

One evening the kids were getting ready for bed. While Nat was showering he began laughing loudly for long stretches at a time, and Ben, who was nearby in his bedroom, took the bait.

"Nat! Stop it!" he screamed.

Nat responded by laughing even louder. Hearing this, Ned stormed upstairs to the bathroom, unable to stay calm and neutral the way he usually does—it's hard to remain neutral when it feels as if Nat's out to get us. Sooner or later, one of us is likely to lose our temper.

"Start acting like a person," Ned snarled, giving him a time-out by shutting off the shower temporarily. Max and I were downstairs in the living room reading, and we could both hear what was going on.

"Ned, come on!" I yelled, as I ran up the stairs. "We can't talk that way to him!"

I found Ned in our bedroom.

"What's the point of this?" Ned asked, as he flung his arm out in the direction of the bathroom and then sank heavily onto our bed. His anger was already evaporating, though, and I could see below it his frustration and sadness. "It just seems like he's getting worse," Ned complained. It was true that the laughter was hard to take, but Nat was *not* getting worse overall.

"Oh, come on." I sat down next to him. Outside I could hear Nat giggling to himself in his room now as he put on his pajamas, having doubtless been made more nervous and excited by the tense exchanges with Ned and Ben.

See, that's why you shouldn't yell at him, I wanted to say to Ned, but I bit my tongue.

"Quiet, Nat!" Ben called out from his room.

"Ben—pretend you can't hear him," I coached from my bedroom. Ignoring Nat is a strategy that still sometimes works.

"But I don't like it when he laughs," Ben explained. Without seeing him, I could somehow tell his arms were folded and that he was frowning.

"I know, honey," I said. In a minute I'd go next door to Ben's room and try to help him. Meanwhile, I put my arms around Ned and leaned my head on his shoulder. "The school says he's doing great. Do you ever open his backpack? You have to look at his notebooks when he comes home from school. Then you'll know he isn't getting worse at all." Ned would not be convinced, however, and just sank deeper into despair. Finally, I became angry with him. "If you'd look at the goddamned notebook once in a while, or actually called his teachers, maybe you'd know that he really holds it together in school, and that home is his downtime!"

"Well, that's hard! He's always trying to bug us!"

While we quarreled in our room, the boys all kept their distance, playing quietly, each in his own room. But our argument ran out of steam pretty quickly. We both recognized the familiar pattern. That evening, it was Ned who had lost it, and I had held on. But the situation could easily be reversed the next time. We knew that this frustration and despair was something that would come and go for both of us and that we would trade off being the strong one. It was our old "happy cop, sad cop" routine. Eventually the boys heard us talking more quietly, and one by one, they emerged from their rooms like tentative birds after a storm.

A few weeks later, Nat was sitting on the living room couch when he began the laughing again. This time, however, I happened to be feeling more relaxed, and as I looked at him I saw his wide, goofy, braces-filled grin. Just like that, because he was so dear, my heart filled up, and I plopped down right next to him.

"Natty, what is so funny? What is so funny?" I asked playfully, tickling him and poking his ribs. He kept laughing, but now it was in response to my actions and my voice. He was so adorable just then and I felt so much love for him. And then in a few moments, I noticed his laughter dying down in a natural way. He was looking at me warmly. Now my throat was burning—this had cracked me wide open. *Oh my God,* I thought. *He really does it to connect with us. He just doesn't know how, other than to annoy us.* I knew this was so because of the way Nat had stopped laughing naturally and on his own. This revelation permanently shifted how I viewed Nat's difficult behaviors thereafter, allowing me to see more of the person inside and to relate to him in a more satisfying way.

Later I told Ned about this pivotal discovery of mine, and it made perfect sense to him. He told me how, on one recent afternoon, Nat was getting worked up and it looked as if he were about to pinch him. Instead of tensing up, jumping back, and defending himself, Ned decided to stand his ground and to try to connect with Nat. He focussed on his compassion for his son instead of his fear of being hurt by him. "Suddenly I felt so strongly that he's my kid, and I've got to be on his side even though he's not on mine, " Ned told me. Apparently Ned had managed to convey something strong and positive to Nat because Nat relaxed and did not pinch him.

Nat's behavior with others reflected, at least in part, Nat's sense of how a given person felt toward him, how much respect, tolerance, or love the person had for him and how close a connection there was between them. We were beginning to appreciate just how powerful Nat's need for connection really was.

My epiphany about Nat's laughter would mark a profound, positive change in how we dealt with Nat *and* how he responded to us. From then on we would try to understand all of Nat's actions as human expressions of the need and desire for social contact, rather than simply annoying manifestations of autism. We had had inklings of this truth for years, but all of our emphasis on behavior modification had made it hard for us to see. When you respond neutrally to undesirable behaviors in order to decrease their frequency, you may succeed in the end, but you are also cutting yourself off from the person whose behavior you're trying to modify. In your eyes, he becomes a collection of behaviors to reward or suppress, and on some level, he stops being a person to you.

I'm not blaming our behavioral therapists or Nat's teachers for neglecting this truth. I'm just saying we gained an understanding of Nat that moved us beyond their model. He had grown, and we had grown. We would still use behavior modification to deal with certain more malleable behavior problems, such as tantrums, for example, or to get him to try a new academic skill or a novel food. But we now had a larger view of Nat as a person whose need to connect to other people often manifested itself in irritating, difficult behaviors. It was up to us to remember that, to focus on the underlying need more than the annoying act. The loud laughing, for example, was an attempt, however misguided, to share his happiness with us. It was up to us to laugh with him, to talk about what was funny and what was not, and to help him take pleasure in us appropriately. And we did.

Increasingly after this shift in thinking, Ned and I were able to appreciate Nat in new ways—for example, we realized that he freed us from the restrictive norms and standards of family life. More and more, we embraced our unique, eccentric style and took pride in ourselves as a family. We took pride in Nat, too. Watching his tremendous efforts just to behave "normally," I was often struck by what an amazing, strong person he is inside, and I would find myself reenergized. Every time he used his words instead of screaming, or let his hand dangle instead of pinching, I felt he had succeeded. Sometimes Ned and I would feel so much pride and empathy for him that we would just leave him alone, his ultimate reward, just letting him be Nat and not trying to make him part of our world.

Ned and I had always been fairly solitary people, living in our own orbits, working side by side in the evenings on our separate projects. Having Nat in our lives merely amplified our tendency to exist alone but together. Sometimes I felt it was our own desire to be alone that helped us understand Nat's extreme solitude. If we were often happy by ourselves, why must he be pushed to be with others? But I also understood that he *must* be pushed, in order to develop properly.

Max and Ben also have rich inner lives filled with time to themselves, drawing comic books, reading, playing dress-up. Even as babies they would have "crib time," as well as "Mommy time." They got used to my sitting at the computer, writing in short bursts while they played at my feet. They learned to entertain themselves.

Nat was, of course, the most unto himself of any of us. Frequently as a teenager he wanted nothing other than to watch a video. Or he would sit alone in his favorite spot, in the very center of the white living-room couch, staring at a book and talking to himself. He still talked his silly talk, though we had accepted it by now instead of trying to suppress and redirect it. Silly talk gave us insight into Nat's thoughts, describing bits and pieces of his day and his favorite songs with the words stretched out or shortened. We also understood that Nat needed silly talk to help him feel better in a world that jangled his nerves. Once we understood how important Nat's silly talk was to him, and that he could still use functional language when necessary, we even began to find it endearing.

On a recent quiet Sunday he came into the playroom, where I was at my desk, looked at me briefly, and then looked for a long time out the sunny bay window, softly talking about quiet and Mommy, saying: "Mommy, hew. Ssh—window. Hee, window." He straightened the pillow on our yellow chair, without sitting down on it. Then he looked back out the window, watching the birds fly by.

I said, "What's up, Nat?"

He said, "OK."

He still does not engage in real conversations, but it's clear that he thinks, observes, listens, and feels. That day in the playroom, I could feel that he was completely with me, a whole person, just like my other boys, only more quietly so. In his silly talk, he notes our moods and reactions, smiling to himself based on what he has discovered. "Yelling, hee," he says. "No talking, ssh." He talks to us using recognizable English when he needs something, like food, and in this way he is not that different from when he was a little boy.

Helping Max and Ben to Cope

Shoot first, ask questions later—this is often Ben's method of dealing with people, and it's something he's learned from watching us deal with Nat. He has learned to be tough from his—and our—difficult interactions with Nat. Most of the time, he's suspicious of Nat. He's seen Nat destroy Max's things, he's heard us tell Nat to stay out of Max's room, he's heard us accuse Nat of doing things that he has done and things he hasn't. Unlike Max, Ben did not grow up with Nat right alongside him, sharing a double stroller, a bathtub, bedtime stories, and bunk beds. Max had gotten to know Nat first as his silent peer, and then as someone he could help. To Ben, Nat has always been the source of trouble, the one who puts the family under siege. Max has always been compassionate, while Ben is more fiery and concerned about right and wrong. To Ben, you are either a good guy or a bad guy. A big boy or a baby. A Max or a Nat.

"Someday Nat's not going to be my brother anymore," Ben announced once. It pained me to hear this, but I knew I had to put my discouragement aside and let Ben have his feelings without being judged. So I just said, "Why do you say that, Ben?"

"I don't like it when he does mean things and when he laughs at me."

I'm glad Ben can express his feelings, but I wish that I could cool his anger toward Nat. From my own therapy, I know that you need the freedom and safety to express your feelings, but at the same time, you can't just go around expressing all of your feelings all of the time. And this is what Ben started doing at around four years old. I was afraid that he hated Nat, and I didn't know what to do about it.

Somehow, in my grand scheme of increasing our family's happiness with the addition of Ben, I didn't figure on Ben's being adversely affected by Nat's autism. By the time he was four, Ben had started to notice Nat's odd behavior, and it upset him. There was little room in such a young kid for empathy toward Nat, not only because of the things that Nat broke just to make Ben cry but also because Nat seemed broken himself. Ben had the four-year-old's contempt for broken cookies, torn pictures, and anything uneven or simply not right. With his artistic temperament—he has always drawn well, creating Chagall-like images of robots floating over buildings—he would dictate to me the exact shape of his cheese slices or his peanut butter sandwich. Uncompromising and precise, he knew exactly how things should be—and that included his brothers.

Every now and then, Ben realizes that he and Nat have similar interests, and a tiny connection forms between them. One morning, Ben came into the living room and found his teddy bears were undressed, their clothes unceremoniously strewn about on the coffee table. Ben usually finds nudity intriguing, in true little-boy fashion, but there was something about this undressing that must have seemed disrespectful to him. Ben was angry, and he knew whom to blame. "Nat took off my bears' clothes," he shouted, looking for Nat so he could yell at him directly.

But I had a flash of inspiration this time. "Maybe Nat wanted to see them naked, just like you do."

A smile spread across Ben's serious face. "Nat wanted to see the bears naked," he said, delighted. He went running to find Nat. "Hey Nat! The bears are naked!"

I don't think Nat paid much attention, but this time I had managed to defuse Ben's anger and turn the incident into something positive.

In general, though, I wonder what toll Nat's sieges take on Max and Ben. During those hard times, my heart is just not in parenting. I sit on the floor with Ben, helping him build a Lego volcano, but my stomach is churning as I wonder where Nat is at that moment. I'm asking myself, *What's bugging Nat these days? Why does this happen every winter? Will he ever grow out of it?* Ben can probably tell that I'm not completely with him at such moments.

The thing I didn't fully realize when I set out to have another baby and "double the joy" was that I was more than doubling the work. My third child demands just as much of me as my first. And my second child I worry about because he demands so little. And so, when Max, at the age of ten, suddenly starts crying heartbrokenly because snow has gotten in his shoe, or because his broccoli has gotten mixed in with his potatoes, I let him because I know it's not really about that. I know that his feelings have to come out somehow. You can't live in a family like ours and be completely at peace.

I frequently tell Ben and Max that if they hate being in this family sometimes, it is OK. I tell them life is hard, but it shouldn't be *this* hard, especially for people as young as they are. I also try to tell them that having Nat in the family allows us to experience the world from a different perspective, and gives us the chance to really appreciate life when things go well. I think this helps them a tiny bit.

Meanwhile, Nat just goes on doing his odd things all day long, but mostly they've become part of the normal background noise in our home. Sometimes Ben even imitates Nat's silly talk, in an effort, I think, to get Nat's attention—and maybe also to connect.

"Hew heem," Nat says one night, while sitting at the dinner table, picking at his food, separating chicken from vegetables.

"Hoo heem," Ben says, smiling, leaning toward Nat from his seat at the head of the table.

"Ben will go away," Nat says, looking right at him. In other words, silly talk is Nat's domain, his secure island. Others are not supposed to trespass.

Ned and I grin at each other, pleased to hear Nat being so

direct, and also to see that Ben understands enough about his brother to know how to get to him. Ben has to get him back sometimes, after all.

"Nice telling him, Nat," I say, in praise of his appropriate talk. "Ben, did you hear what Nat said to you?"

Max is smiling, too, by now because it's kind of a special event when Nat uses language to communicate with his brothers, even if he's communicating something negative. Max says, "Nat, you don't want Ben to do silly talk?"

"No Ben silly talk!" says Nat, who by now has started rocking a little. Rocking is another behavior he uses to soothe himself and help block out whatever is bothering him.

"OK, darling, he won't do it," I say, my eyes meeting Max's across the table in friendly conspiracy. We are all touched by Nat's expressing himself, moved, in fact, but we don't want to go too far.

We've taken special care with Ben to make sure he works through his anger about Nat as he grows up, which is a task that has weighed heavily on me. He has always felt things very strongly, particularly anger. When he was around four, I took this concern to my therapist, who suggested I validate his experiences as much as possible. Whether he was being Spiderman or a dead mummy, we dared not smile at how cute he was. "Don't try to kiss him when he's Spiderman," my therapist wisely instructed. When Ben was very young, from ages two to five, Ned and I talked with him about Nat in a roundabout, indirect way, using ourselves as examples. For instance, I would say, "Look at Nat talking to himself. I wonder why he does that? I think Nat has trouble figuring out how to talk to people. I wish he could talk to me sometimes." The best I can say is that my way of helping Ben is still evolving and that I will watch for signs that he needs more help and then get it for him.

Once, when Ben and I were walking together to a toy store, he suddenly turned to me and asked, "Mommy, do we all speak the same language at home?" His class had probably been talking about languages at his preschool, acknowledging how families can be different from each other, or something like that. "Yeah, of course, Ben," I said, and then I asked him, "Do you think Nat speaks our language?"

Ben was silent for a minute, sucking his thumb. I thought he was going to be angry at me for changing the subject to Nat, or that he'd want to talk instead about the toy he was thinking of

---

*HELPING SIBLINGS COPE
WITH THEIR FEELINGS*

- Acknowledge that there is indeed something difficult, painful, and unusual in their lives, but that this is nobody's fault. Remind them that everyone has struggles in life. We are not the only ones with something challenging to face.
- Consult one or more of the following books: *Views from Our Shoes* edited by Donald J. Meyer, *Being the Other One* by Kate Strohm, and *Talking to Angels* by Esther Watson. Also, see *www.our-kids.org/Books/kidbook.htm* for a great list of books for young siblings of children with special needs.
- Encourage siblings to express how they feel about family life in their own words, to identify their feelings as best they can. Remember that these feelings often come out in unexpected ways.
- Offer praise for siblings' efforts to form a positive relationship with their autistic sibling. I applaud Max and Ben for how well they get along with Nat, when these moments happen. We also encourage Ben and Max to speak directly to Nat, and Nat to respond directly to them, rather than mediating for them. (See *Siblings Without Rivalry* by Adele Faber and Elaine Mazlish.)

---

buying, or maybe he wouldn't answer my question at all. But he finally removed his thumb from his mouth and said, "Yeah, but I don't think he can do it very well." I smiled, closed my eyes, and sighed, happy that Ben could talk about Nat calmly, without anger.

We recently saw a clear sign of Ben's progress, at six years old. "When I grow up," he blurted at breakfast one day, "I'm going to have an autistic son."

---

continued

- As much as possible, treat all your kids in a balanced and fair way. I give Nat household responsibilities and have expectations of him just like I have of Max and Ben. Nat's disability doesn't mean he can get away with bad behavior or that he gets his way all the time.
- Keep up with research on the emotional effects of growing up with a disabled sibling. See the Council for Exceptional Children's website, which has an information center on disabilities and gifted education (*http://ericec.org/faq/siblings.html*).
- Look for therapeutic opportunities and support for siblings, especially if they seem persistently angry, sad, or withdrawn. I have frequently consulted with the public school's guidance counselor for ways to discuss Nat with the boys, and we found a wonderful therapist, through a friend, to do play therapy with Ben. Group support helps children, too. Look for a "sibshop," a sibling workshop, near you. See the sibling project of the Association for Retarded Citizens at *www.thearc.org*, or read Donald J. Meyer and Patricia F. Vadasy's workbook, *Sibshops: Workshops for Siblings of Children with Special Needs*.

Ned and I were startled, even though we had become accustomed to Ben's stark and unusual remarks. "Why do you think so, Ben?" I asked.

"Because a family's a family, no matter how much autism," he answered. Then he went back to eating his cereal.

Sputtering, I explained that he would probably not have autistic children, that it was something he shouldn't worry about.

Then Ned said, "It's true, Ben. A family's a family, no matter how much autism."

"You don't need to worry about that stuff, though, sweetheart," I reiterated. But I could see he was already onto the next thing, the funny picture on the back of the cereal box and why it had been drawn that way.

Nat Hits Adolescence

With the onset of Nat's puberty, we began to talk to him about the importance of privacy. One surprising result is that Nat learned to refer to masturbation as "making privacy." The first time we heard him use this phrase, we couldn't help but laugh because were so pleased that he had found his own way of describing the activity to himself. It showed a kind of understanding of the issue, and it was so Nat.

One thing we taught him about masturbation was to do it in his room, but sometimes he did it in Max's room instead—with Max's pillow, unfortunately. He probably did this to annoy Max, and also in an obtuse effort to connect with him by getting his attention. In his own room, he didn't realize that he needed to close his door, either. Once, I came upstairs looking for Nat and found him undressed on his bed, door wide open. Max was standing in the doorway, and a friend was in the hall behind him. I concluded that Max had just discovered Nat and was blocking the view of him.

I quickly closed Nat's door, reminding him of the need for "privacy." Then I shot Max a look of empathy. "You OK?"

He nodded, and I went back downstairs. A day in the life. But from now on, I would have to be more aware of where Nat was when visitors came to the house. This was one burden that I didn't want Max to have to take on.

The Ongoing Challenge of Family Activities and Social Events

The question *What do we do about Nat?* was giving way to another question as Nat became a teenager: *Can we connect with him more often and get him to go along with us on new family activities?* Sometimes we could, but not as often as we would have liked, and sometimes when he did come along, we would have to find a way to enjoy the trip if he acted out. On a trip to an art museum, Nat threw tantrums the whole time we were there, probably because we wanted so much for this trip to work that we couldn't stay connected with him sufficiently to keep him on our side. He kept saying, "After the paintings, go home. After the paintings, go home." Even when he stopped repeating his autistic mantra, he wandered around the museum in apparent agony, sucking his thumb. To him, the museum was as senseless a place to be as the playground. What are the rules? What do you do there? When will it end?

Max watched Nat's tantrums silently, adjusting his own expectations of this outing, understanding that we might have to cut it short. But Ben argued for staying. "No, Nat, we want to stay at the museum—right, Makth? We don't want to leave." Max, who always takes his cues from Ned and me, waited patiently for us to forge ahead to the next exhibit, while Nat's cries bounced off the high museum ceilings, mingling with the clamor of all the happy museum-goers.

Should we give in to him? I asked myself. Ned and I considered the two main options: we could try to withstand Nat's truculence to please Max and Ben. Or we could call it a day and find treats to eat, pleasing Nat—easier but dissatisfying. And we'd only been there for an hour. In the end, we pushed ourselves because we were feeling strong that day. We decided that Ben and Max would each get to see one more thing they were interested in: the armor for Ben and the Egyptian tomb for Max.

In the end Nat endured the added exhibits, and we celebrated our success afterward with pretzels and mustard outside on the museum steps. I still don't really look forward to bringing Nat places, but it did get easier as he approached thirteen. Maybe it was that he was finally settled in a good school program and the fact that we'd been able to stay connected with him. In any case, Nat started to show more understanding of— and seemed even to enjoy—social visits and parties, so that he no longer felt the need to cry or scream on those occasions, nor did he say, "No party!" when we told him we were going to one.

He seemed more inclined to enjoy himself at events where no one expected him to talk. He liked being among other people in a different house, watching his videos on the host's television. That way, he could experience something familiar but in a slightly different setting, stretching himself just a little bit.

I would watch Nat with both pride and nervousness as he navigated new social situations, greeting people monosyllabically, watching them respond to him with curiosity, bewilderment, or admiration. I never knew how much to explain him to strangers, or if I should at all. Ned always said we didn't have to. But that's the way he is, willing to ignore the looks we get from others. "Other people shouldn't define you—or Nat," he would say. He was right, but it wasn't so easy for me to forget what other people were thinking of us. Newer friends of ours would hear about Nat's autism, and when they invited us to their homes, I wondered what they were expecting—maybe a wild child who would tear up the place like the Tasmanian Devil from Looney Tunes.

One of Ned's coworkers met our boys for the first time at the big company party. While greeting the other two boys politely, he began covertly studying Nat. But all he saw was a handsome, quiet preteen boy who looked like a stretched-out version of his two younger brothers and who hung around the food table, sniffing the barbecue too deeply and then zeroing in on the chips and salsa. Once Nat had finished all the chips, he asked to watch his Disney video in the host family's playroom. "Watch it," he said, pointing to the *Pinocchio* tape he'd brought and was holding in his hand now. After he was set up with the video—and after the little kids settled in around him, looking at him curiously (why was a big kid watching a Disney video?)—he was fine. There he stayed for the entire party.

Fortunately, there were always certain family outings we could count on, islands in the storm, places where we could take Nat and relax because we knew he would be accepted as he is. My family is one. Last summer, we went to the seashore to visit my sister and her family, who were staying in my parents' house there. As soon as we arrived, I felt certain that something was going to happen, probably because all the way up, Nat had been anxiously repeating the rules about visiting, as if he were working hard to convince himself not to do the things he wasn't supposed to. After we all greeted each other, we settled outside on the deck to have drinks and catch up. I thought Nat had stayed behind in the living room to watch a video. Some time later, I checked, and he wasn't there.

"Where's Nat?" I asked everyone warily.

John, Laura's husband, went to check the kids' room, and a moment later, he called me. When I got there, I saw Nat hastily pulling up his pants. "What's going on?" I asked John, but I already knew. "Was he . . . ?"

John nodded.

Laura came in and asked what had happened. Then she remembered what I had told her about Nat's latest phase, and I saw her face fall.

Red-faced and sighing, I took Nat by the hand. "You cannot 'make privacy' here," I told him sternly. "Only in Nat's room." And then I realized where we had gone wrong: When we stay in this house, this room *was* Nat's room! How was he to know that right now, it was his cousins' room?

"Stay at Grandma–Grandpa's house," he begged, thinking

that now he would have to leave. His eyes were fully dilated. I imagine his heart was pumping fast, and his bloodstream was filled with adrenaline. He understood that he was in trouble again, and probably was not fully sure why.

I knew I had to bring him back down. As hard as it was to put aside all of my anger and nervousness, I tried to open up to him. "Oh, Nat," I murmured, looking in his eyes. "We're staying. Just be good."

He saw that things were suddenly OK again. "Sorry I yelled at you," he prompted me to say, using his familiar, unique, and poignant grammar. Nat, who had learned to talk by memorizing books and scripted language, never learned correct pronoun use and eternally, ironically, called himself "you."

"Yeah, I'm sorry, Nat. Just be good," I said, pushing strands of his blond hair away from his eyes. And he behaved wonderfully for the rest of the visit.

Later on that afternoon, Laura and I took a walk around a nearby pond. "Sue, how's it going with Nat?" she asked.

I was glad she had brought the topic up. "You know, that—what happened before—is exactly why I was reluctant to come here."

"Yeah, I know. It must be hard traveling with him, not knowing how he'll behave."

"It is. But I appreciate that John didn't say much to him, and left it to me to deal with the problem."

"Oh, he wouldn't interfere. We're just so glad you're here. We love Nat. And he's doing so well!" Her big grin told me she absolutely meant it, despite the "privacy" incident.

Being understood like that was like lying down in a big, soft bed and taking a long rest. "Thanks," I said. "I'm glad to be here, too."

Expanding Nat's Leisure-time Repertoire

By thirteen, Nat was constantly learning to do new things (like attending parties and comfortably eating dinner in a

EASING SOCIAL VISITS FOR YOUR CHILD

- Tell your child where you're going and who's going to be there. Show him pictures of the people you'll see, if you have them.
- Remind your child that he does not have to talk to people. Tell him where he can sit and what he will eat there.
- When you arrive, ask the host where he can watch a video or be left in peace.
- Tell your child when you will be going back home, and how he'll be able to know that it's almost time to leave. Be sure to give him an adequate warning to help his transition to anything new at the social event: mealtime, changing the video that he's watching, the end of the visit.
- Decide what reward he'll get for good behavior and "quiet hands." Remind him of it before and during the event.

restaurant), which was good for the family, but each new thing he learned to do was still tinged or shaped by the autism. And he succeeded with it only to the degree that we could join with him in doing it, and keep ourselves focused on what was important: his responses, rather than other people's.

We had concluded by then that the Resperidone did indeed make Nat more flexible, less violent, able to take in more of the world, try new things, and as a result, develop new skills. I imagined that this drug helped stretch out his reaction time so that he now had sufficient time between an incoming stimulus and his response to restrain an impulse to act out. This probably made him feel much happier and calmer when dealing with people. I came to see Resperidone as a miracle drug, though Ned and I have periodically worried about its serious potential side effects. Ned admitted that if he had to choose between the side effects and taking Nat off the drug, he didn't know which he would choose because the Resperidone has helped Nat so much and given us so much more of a life. We hope it will never come down to such a choice, but you never know.

At this point, with Nat's behavior under control, we rediscovered something fun to do with Nat: take the subway to the city and go for walks. Ned began taking him on subway trips nearly every weekend. These jaunts stimulated a lot of language for Nat. He loved to discuss hitting people on the train, walking on the tracks, and other kinds of mischief that we now knew he wouldn't actually do because the Resperidone made him less likely to attempt violent or dangerous acts. Still, it was difficult to expand his conversation beyond these predictable, danger-filled statements. We wanted to know so much more about what interested him. But he had a deep need to hear again and again the consequences of his threatened actions; he derived immense comfort from our telling him the same answers: if you hit people, you would have to leave the train; if you walked on the tracks, you would hurt yourself. This made him unusual, although certainly not unique. After all, many nonautistic teenage boys are fascinated with violence and mischief.

Ned told me that on one particular subway trip that ended at the Public Garden, a park in Boston, Nat suddenly got very verbal, hopping around, almost doing cartwheels, he was so excited. He pointed at the sky and said, "You jump out of an airplane! Head will bleed and bleed. Get a shot at the hospital. Alcohol. Sleep in the hospital room with the door closed . . ."

Ned was trying not to laugh; it was so funny, amazing, and joyous hearing Nat speak so much, even this sort of idiosyncratic talk. Nat's odd outbursts were endearing to us, becoming part of our family lore and our shared humor. "Ssh, Nat. Yes, that's right," Ned whispered, chuckling nervously.

Ned and Nat would also walk from home to our town

PREPARING YOUR CHILD FOR NEW EXCURSIONS AND ACTIVITIES

- Start by asking yourself, *What's in it for him? Is this something he will enjoy, once he gets over his aversion to its newness?*
- Think of a small step toward the goal and always have support when trying something new. Nat's early subway trips were to nearby locations, and Ned and I stayed in touch by phone. Ned knew he could always call me to come get them in the car if something went awry.
- Carefully explain the new activity to your child and keep it clearly defined so that he understands the beginning, middle, and end,
- Let your child control the parts of the trip that he can. On the subway rides, Nat chose the destination, the route, and the duration of the outing.
- Observe how your child is doing that day. If he's behaving unsafely (hitting, spilling, ripping) or inappropriately around the house, chances are he's not ready for a new experience somewhere else.
- Stretch your child bit by bit. Our subway trips became longer as Nat proved he could tolerate them; the trips to the library became more frequent as he demonstrated that he could be quiet and well-behaved there.

center, where they would visit the library, after which they would stop somewhere for a candy bar. Nat got his own library card, signed with his scrawled, illegible but legitimate signature. He had to show a fair amount of self-control on these trips. Not only did he have to be quiet in the library, which was tough for him; he also had to keep his hands to himself. Once, when he and Ned were standing in line to check out some books, he noticed a large-breasted woman in the next line. In the past, Nat's impulsive behavior had included breast-grabbing. So when Nat suddenly turned to Ned and whispered, "Nat will pinch private parts in the library," Ned acted quickly, interposing himself between Nat and the woman. Nat peered around Ned to leer at her, but luckily she seemed oblivious, and Nat never touched her. Ned claimed a victory, and we had a good laugh about the episode later. In the face of autism, laughter has held us together probably more than anything else.

Sometimes we would split up for family activities, getting a sitter for Nat or taking the other two somewhere while Nat was still in school (he has a longer day at his school and very few school vacations). I would take Max and Ben on an outing, and it amazed me how easy it was to have fun on these excursions. This must be the way my friends feel, I thought, those with typically developing children, although I was increasingly realizing that their grass was not much greener than my own. More likely I just relished the experience of normalcy far more than my friends did because, unlike them, I didn't take it for granted. I used to feel a little guilty about the pleasure I took in being with just my two younger boys, but I came to see that spoiling them with an easy, comfortable outing without Nat was essential to their well-being as well as my own.

When Max told me during a recent spring that he couldn't wait to see the ocean again after our long winter, I took him and Ben on a spontaneous trip to Cape Cod during their April vacation, while Nat was in school. It wasn't warm enough to swim, but the sun on the sand was surprisingly strong. The two of them frolicked up and down the beach while I just sat there, warmed by their easy friendship and the early April sun.

"Makth! Look at this rock!"

"Wow, cool, Ben!"

Together they spent a while stacking up rocks and then burying the stack in sand, layer by layer. It was a perfect mini-vacation that made me look forward to more trips as a three-some.

A Sea Change for Nat

Summer vacation after summer vacation, when all Nat would do was pace the beach, snack, and eventually look for mischief, we had a tough time enjoying ourselves. But one summer all that changed. For years we had stuck to beaches on the bay side of Cape Cod, where the water was warmer and the waves were gentle. But like the park or the museum, being at the bay lacked a clear set of structured activities for Nat. Nat didn't feel happy building sand castles. To him, it was a pointless, meaningless chore.

One day we found boogie boards at my parents' beach house, and we went to the ocean side of the Cape to try them out. Immediately Nat was captivated. The drama of the ocean spoke to him. The dependable ebb and flow of the waves appealed to his need for predictability, and the heavy salt smell and the crashing of the surf seemed to break through the sensory stew in his head.

Ned decided to take Nat and Max into the water with the boogie boards. I watched with my heart in my mouth, but both of them seemed to know what to do as if they had been doing it all their lives. Paddle out, watch for the wave, ride it in. Even when Nat wiped out, he went right back in the water and tried again. We wondered whether his autism deprived him of a normal sense of danger, or if this was simply Nat's personality. Perhaps he was just daring and had a high threshold for pain. He was crazy about the waves; we had never seen him so happy, so lit up by anything. For the rest of the vacation, his silly talk was peppered heavily with the word "ocean," a sure sign of his enthusiasm. He would stand at the shoreline, watching the waves crash around his feet or roll over a swimmer's head, and he would laugh and laugh with joy.

Max was more cautious than Nat, taking longer to actually go in the water, but just as willing to try again. The difference in their attitudes seemed appropriate, because Nat was older, after all, and would be expected to have more self-confidence. Seeing Nat and Max go off into the surf like any other pair of brothers made us feel wonderful, as if we had it all. That summer, I said to Ned, "On a boogie board, there is no autism." We were ecstatic that we had taken this risk.

This past winter, hoping to build on our success with boogie boarding, I got it into my head that we should all try skiing. I had heard of adaptive ski, instruction that is tailored to people with disabilities, so I began to build a case to Ned, the way I always do. "Look," I said, "Nat likes thrills. He likes amusement park rides, the ocean, sledding. He is athletic. If we could get him past the awkwardness of the heavy, immobilizing boots . . ."

"A big 'if,'" Ned said. "And then there's Ben."

It was true. Ben could be stubborn and moody. I could just imagine Ben refusing to try this unfamiliar activity. Nevertheless, on the day after Christmas, when we were up in New Hampshire visiting Ned's father, the fresh powdery snow that covered everything and the bright sunlight made me want to try skiing that same day. Impulsively I sent Ned off with the boys to an indoor pool, while I went out and bought whatever snow clothes we were lacking.

Later in the car, as we got within a mile or two of Mount Gunstock, as it loomed ahead of us, I began to lose my nerve. *What had I been thinking? How was this family going to ski?* I had to break the news to Ned. "Hmm," I said tentatively.

"Hmm?" he said, smiling. He already knew what was coming.

"Well, it feels a little scary that we're going to try this. What if getting on and off the lift is too hard for the boys to figure out?" I said. "What if I can't explain to Nat how to stop himself on skis? What if . . ."

Ned laughed and shook his head. "This is so like you, to

push us all to do this big thing, and once we get going, you start to have doubts!"

I laughed, too. "OK, so?"

"Well, how about this: We go to the mountain, and we just go tubing. Maybe that's enough."

"Yay!" shouted Max. For him, tubing was much less scary than skiing, even though he'd been willing to try either one. Just sit in a inner tube and slide. Perfect for the laid-back Max—and his shaky family.

So we went tubing, and it certainly *was* enough. The rope pull was a challenge in itself for Nat, who managed to stop the machinery on every single run. He never did master rolling out of it the way you're supposed to, and by his sixth or seventh run, the lift operators were stopping it for him every time they saw him. Still, time after time, he went down the slope with Max, and he even went down several times by himself. It was wonderful to see the two of them run to the line together. They had so little in common, so few things they liked to do together. Now they had tubing to add to the list.

Unfortunately, unlike his older brothers, Ben went down only once, after which he cried for a solid hour. He was too tired from our Christmas celebration the night before, and he couldn't make the transition to this new and unusual outing. Also, the day was brutally cold, and he probably wasn't dressed warmly enough, despite the layers I had piled on him. So I stood with him at the bottom of the mountain and watched everyone else come down. I finally turned his tears into laughter by telling him that the mountain's nickname was Naked Butt Hill (a made-up nickname, but I was desperate to make him happy). That, and my happiness about Max and Nat's bonding, carried us through Ben's discouragement.

After two hours, Ned and I declared the day a success and left for home, triumphant. In addition to the fun had by Nat and Max, I felt this day had taken us one step closer to skiing by getting everyone used to a ski lift, waiting in line, being out in the cold, and the ski resort environment. We had usually taken warm weather vacations, in Florida or on Cape Cod, so this was our first inkling that we could enjoy wintertime right here in New England as a family.

Ned Creates "Nat's World"

Even after our successes on the beach and at the ski slope, Ned and I still wished there were more things the family could do together. This is probably what led Ned to invent a new family activity, using his skill as a software engineer to tap into Nat's interests. Ned's invention is a computer game called Nat's World, which allows Nat to go anywhere he likes, to see the ocean and the people he loves, all via computer. The idea for Nat's World came to Ned after he bought his first digital camera. He would upload pictures from the camera and e-mail them out to family and friends, or just keep them as files on his computer. Nat, who loves family photos, soon began using Ned's computer to look at them.

"Go to Grandma-Grandpa's house," he would say, pointing at pictures of my parents' house that were displayed on the computer screen. "Nat will go there." Nat would try clicking on our pictures, hoping this would take him through a door or around a street corner depicted there, as he had learned to do with computer games. Noticing this, Ned developed a program that linked the photos with others he had taken of the same location, allowing Nat to take himself around corners or through doors, at least in his imagination. Over time, Ned has honed the program and the photos so that Nat can travel all the way to several favorite places, including the subway, the ocean, my parents' house, and the town library.

Max also plays a role in this activity. He goes with Ned on picture-taking walks, shooting scores of pictures of different routes to Nat's favored destinations, which Ned then uploads into Nat's World. Max loves to take pictures—he's planning on a career as a movie director—so he takes a lot of pride in getting shots that will work out especially well in Nat's World. In this way, Max also gets into his brother's head and imagines what Nat likes to see. Because Nat loves to watch the credits roll on videos and at the end of computer games (it's their most predictable aspect, after all), Ned taught Max how to make Nat's World credits that roll when the game ends.

One of Nat's favorite images in Nat's World is a desktop photo of all of us. He loves to stare at our faces in this photo, where we're safe and unchanging. Nat's World is the perfect unifying family activity, equally loved by Nat and the rest of us. The images of Nat's World give him the predictability he so intensely craves, something our actual mutable faces can never provide. See Ned's website, *www.nedbatchelder.com,* for the software Ned created.

In addition to occupying his time in a pleasant way, photographs can also stimulate Nat's language in ways we never thought possible. On the last evening of our most recent Cape Cod trip, the five of us clustered around Ned's computer to view the digital photos we had taken during the week. Nat was riveted, as were we all, by the images of us having fun on the beach: the wide expanse of cold, blue-brown ocean; the hills of sand rising behind our beach gear; the honey-colored backs of Max and Ben, coated with sand and salt. Impulsively I said, "Nat, are you happy to be going back home?"

Immediately he responded without really thinking, "Happy to go back home."

But then, more quietly, he said, "Sad to go back home. Sad to leave Cape Cod." And he started to cry, which I'd never seen him do before.

What could I do? I was sad to leave, too. We cried together.

The other day I asked Max to share his thoughts and feelings about Nat. I was surprised by how readily he took me up on the invitation. *If he's this articulate on the subject, he must think about it quite often,* I realized.

"When we were little," he said, "it was hard to see him not being able to do that much. But now he can read and stuff, do gymnastics . . . I wish he could play with me, though, because Ben's too little. And I don't like it when he pinches me or . . . takes my pillow for privacy, you know," he added, blushing, eyes down.

Then he shook his hair from his eyes and said, "If Nat wasn't autistic, my life would be different. I might feel like any other person. Having an autistic brother makes me completely different from everyone else, which is a good thing. I'm kind of like an expert on it."

10

JUST A FAMILY

Ned RECENTLY TURNED FORTY-TWO. He told me that he used to see his life as a linear trajectory in which he'd climb ever higher. Now that he's forty-two, he told me that he can sense the fact that his life is arc-shaped; he knows the downward part of the curve is ahead of him, though he's not going downward just yet. But he isn't bothered by this; rather, he feels moved by it, at peace with life and its inevitable end.

Not me. I am not at home with going downward or ending. I started enjoying life so much later than Ned. Now, with the dread of autism gone, my anxieties reduced to frail ghosts that still haunt me but only now and then, I love my life and I am fervently nurturing it. I use my time as efficiently as possible because there are usually at least two things I want to be doing at any given moment: writing and being with Ned and the kids.

At forty-two, I'm very different from the person I was at twenty-seven, when I began the journey of motherhood. Back then, I felt so sad most of the time, and I tried to anesthetize my pain through shopping, decorating, or television—until my anxiety over baby Nat forced me to confront my fear and get him evaluated. I squandered too much of my life back then on sadness and fear. I still grapple with the occasional urge to beat myself up over my mothering. "Don't feel bad about feeling bad," Ned reminds me, as always. But it's hard not to; I don't want to waste any more time doing things the wrong way or paying attention to the wrong issues.

Now I know that it's the boys who matter, and it's Ned and I who matter. Understanding ourselves and each other is what it's all about. That's not always so easy, however. Connecting with Nat, for instance, begins with a leap of faith. The rich and joyful feelings I have when I look at him come partly from something that emanates from him and partly from something inside me. Every now and then, when I sit down next to him on the couch, he will lean his head against my shoulder, just barely touching me: my mysterious forest creature, coming for a visit. He doesn't look me in the eye, but he smiles at the floor. I feel it then. Even though he shrinks back the next second, he was there, my boy. As long as I can find him every now and then, I am a happy mother.

Understanding My Children

One of my greatest but least satisfied desires as a mother has been to know whether my children are happy. I have not been given children who are easy to read. Ben, my youngest, is more open than his brothers, but if he cannot find the words he needs, he clams up and gets angry. As for Max, he used to be easy to read, but now he wears the stoic mask of the adolescence. And it's not easy to know whether Nat is happy, either. He doesn't smile much because people usually smile to each other out of social convention. (When he does smile, however, it is truly momentous because it means he is fully cognizant of his good feeling and wants to show it to us.)

I certainly can't ask Nat how he feels and expect to get a meaningful answer. Nat's thoughts seem to come out in impulsive bursts, little declarations of what he would like to do, or what he'd like someone else to do, always in very simple language: "Nat will eat," he'll say when he's hungry, or "Your bus is here," when his bus arrives to take him to school. When someone who interests him walks into a room, he will probably incorporate that person's name into his silly talk: "Grandpa, hewm." When he speaks to us, it is as if a timid forest animal has again ventured over to us to sniff our outstretched hands. It does not last long.

He so rarely comments on the world around him that when he does, it astonishes us and makes us smile. The other day, when I was driving in the car with him and Max, I made a wrong turn and ended up taking a lot of back roads and having to do some backtracking. Suddenly Nat said softly, "Did you get lost." From the inflection of his voice, he didn't appear to be asking a question, something he rarely does, but perhaps he was asking one, after all. My heart stopped for a second because it felt so momentous that Nat would understand what I had been doing with the car, and that he had been able to put his thoughts together so cogently. Whenever he does something like that, I want to pounce on him, hug and kiss him, and make him do it again. But I restrain myself because, having tried that before, I know it scares him off, and he runs back into the forest. However much I want to hug him, it's a form of love he cannot appreciate much, and so I limit the frequency of my hugs, which are mostly satisfying only to me.

Just as I have to guess at Nat's emotions, I also have to figure out whether he's sick or physically hurt. This has been a long-standing problem with Nat. When he was around eight months old, and Ned and I were driving home from dinner at my sister Laura's house, Nat sat in his car seat behind us, whimpering intermittently. I was already used to this understated but persistent whining, which he had started to do whenever I took him to other people's houses, and I was tired, too, so I didn't check on him for quite a while. Finally, when I had had enough, I wrenched myself around to really look at him. What I saw was

Ned's briefcase, suspended from baby Nat's ankle. I reached back and detached it from him. Then Ned and I looked at each other in the new silence created by our child, who was now free of pain, and for that moment we both wanted to die. "Well. I guess I'm going to hell now," I joked, but my voice was tight and rough with sadness. Later I would learn that most other children would have made a far greater fuss. They would have known how to get someone to help them. But not Nat.

Similarly, when Nat was about ten, I noticed him limping occasionally. I called his teachers, and they told me he limped from time to time in the classroom, too. Then I took him to the doctor, who asked if he had been sick lately. I said he had had strep perhaps a month ago. Her eyes widened, and she sent us for an X-ray immediately, hoping that we'd find just a fracture. Instead, the X-ray showed that Nat's hip was inflamed. "We are going to have to get him to the emergency room *now*," the doctor said after studying the X-ray. Nat had fluid in his hip, and the doctors at the ER were afraid it was the result of a strep infection in the joint, which they told us was a serious condition. We never asked how serious. I couldn't have stood to hear it. A doctor would have to draw the fluid out and check it for bacteria. We stayed in the room with Nat and watched as the doctor delicately performed this task. We prayed for clear fluid, which would indicate that his hip was not infected. I stood by him, touching his hand all through the procedure, and willed God to make him be healthy.

As it turned out, Nat was fine. The inflammation and fluid had indeed been caused by the strep (the antibodies that had fought off the infection had also irritated his joint), but the hip wasn't infected with bacteria. But the doctor did mention that Nat must have been in a great deal of pain walking around with this fluid on his hip. All we had seen of it was the limp. He had never thought to come to me to complain or to cry.

Only recently have we begun to feel a confidence that Nat will one day have the skills to communicate fully about his physical well-being. One recent Sunday afternoon, Nat ran to the toilet, making vomiting noises. While I stood behind him, rubbing his back, he went through a series of dry heaves. I figured he was getting sick, and I hovered around him in the bathroom, waiting to see if he'd have more heaves. Ben had just had a mysterious two-day fever, so perhaps some virus was making the rounds.

Nat had no fever, and appeared to be basically OK, especially after I gave him some Pepto-Bismol. The rest of the day passed uneventfully. It wasn't until the evening that Nat began pacing from the kitchen to the living room and looking at me with wide, dilated eyes. "No school," he kept saying, and then, "School tomorrow."

I kept saying, "That's right, darling, no school tonight; school tomorrow."

This answer didn't seem to reassure him. He just kept looking at me and then looking away. Finally, he started making the retching gestures again, while continuing to eye me nervously. After this had gone on for a while, I began to suspect that something weird was going on. He looked shifty, or something. If it had been anyone else, I would have sworn that he was up to something. But Nat didn't play tricks, manipulate, or lie.

At last he said, "If you're sick, no school. Stay home."

How odd, I thought. This was the first time he had ever used the word *if* in a sentence. He had correctly used a conditional clause, whereas we usually had a difficult time getting him to utter even a simple sentence. My heart swelled at the thought of this accomplishment. But then I wondered: *Why such eagerness to communicate?*

And then I put it all together: he wanted to miss school. Nat was upset about going back to school, and he had figured out a way to get out of it: by being sick. Ned and I were astounded by the series of connections he had made.

But we still had to deal with the matter at hand. Ned said firmly, "Nat. You're OK. You're not sick."

Nat immediately stopped the retching behavior and said, "Yes."

Problem solved. He'd have to learn to fake illness better than that! Ned and I looked at each other and laughed for a long time. Fake barfing! What was next? Of course, Nat was fine the next day. And yes, he went to school.

It is easier to tell whether Max is happy, though not by much. He offers us the full array of emotions, where Nat does not. The difficult thing with Max is being able to tell whether he knows his own feelings, and whether he can deal with them if he does. He is a master at fitting in, at appropriate behavior, and, of course, pleasing people.

My wish for Max to be unafraid of his feelings, once he really understands what they are. My fear is that he censors himself deep down, allowing only the "acceptable" feelings to bubble up. I wonder if someday deep anger at having an autistic brother will jump out and seize him by the throat, but it hasn't yet. His misery, if you can even call it that, comes out over minor hurts, small indignities. Once, while leaving the house, Nat rushed to open the door when Max wanted a turn at it. Nat scratched him accidentally as he ran by, and Max demanded three Band-Aids for the tiny wound it left. I try to honor the seemingly trivial upsets, knowing that this kind of attention and understanding will help him to become fully happy one day. It's important for him to feel validated and to find a way to let out his feelings, even if they only bubble to the surface with the little bit of blood from a small scratch.

With Max, as with Nat, I have to wait for moments of revelation, and hope that I will notice them when they arrive. Max will tell me something of great significance to him when I least expect it. One morning while I drove him to school, for example, he started to tell me a long, drawn-out story from the *Animorphs* book series, leaving out not one detail. I followed the tale as best I could while concentrating on my driving. The Animorphs were kids who could change into animals. In the story Max was telling me, one character, Tobias, had turned into a hawk, not realizing that he would never get to be completely human again.

I heard Max's voice break slightly all of a sudden, and realized he was close to tears. *Whoa!* I wanted to slam on the brakes. I wanted to stop time. My mind raced backward a moment or two to retrieve what he had just said, and luckily it was still there, fresh in my head. *The boy, who just wanted to be normal, would forever be part hawk and part human because of something he had not understood.* Something in this had resonated with Max, the horror of the irrevocable, the pain of feeling different, and he had ventured forth out of his private preteen world to tell me. My throat burned with tears, and I nodded in sympathy, agreeing with Max about how sad the story was, wanting to pull him to me and cover him with kisses, to tell him I was so sorry that life was as sad as it was. And also to tell him how proud I was that he could be moved by such a story. But I knew I couldn't do that; it would have just embarrassed him. He only wanted me to hear the story, not to make a big deal out of it.

Ben's emotions, unlike those of his older brothers, have never been a mystery. They run through him in quick succession, dissonance and then bright harmony, arpeggios of major and then minor chords. When Nat slams the door of Ben's room at home, Ben yells, "I did not want you to do that, Nat! That is very bad of you!" I come to talk to him, and he tells me what he's just told Nat. Just as quickly as he flared up, though, he is laughing about some piece of toilet humor or a knock-knock joke, like any six-year-old. I don't know if his anger over Nat is harming him; I think that as long as he can keep telling us about it and, I hope, seeing more improvement in the situation, he will remain an essentially happy person.

In his spare time, Ben sits at the dining room table, drawing storybook after storybook, his paper spread all over the table and washable markers carefully arranged by color, with one for every color of the rainbow and many gradations in between. He sits for hours, his mouth unconsciously working, imitating the movement of the pen in his hand. If I ask him what he's making, he says angrily, "Nothing!" He does not want to be disturbed or moved from his path as he creates his stories. He's our little van Gogh, our tortured artist, at the age of six.

His stories are often tragic, Old Testament–style tales of evil and retribution. "This man hates birds and wants to destroy them," one story begins. The story's characters come to violent ends involving volcanoes and other disasters. The very last page has a drawing of some yellow birds in a nest. Three of them are crying, "Mama!" and a fourth is saying, "I don't think she's coming back."

When I showed this book to my friends Justin and Ann, we all laughed appreciatively at Ben's imagination and drawing skill, and the sharp edge to his art. But I think we also felt rather sobered by the story and how it reflected all that Ben was dealing with. Ben, tan and smooth-limbed, perfect and petite in his long basketball shorts, is a child whom I want to cradle forever and keep to myself, this child I fought to have later in life, but he will have none of it. He pulls away from my grasp, preferring that I tell him a knock-knock joke. And so I do, because that's how we bond these days. With Ben, as with all of my children, I have to take what I can get, the small stolen moments, the teasing glimpses of shared affection. It is never enough, but they are who they are.

Though I worry about Ben and all the true tragic stories he must digest, Ned's sister Sarai, a psychologist, tells me that his books give him an outlet for all his stuff. She is particularly impressed by one book with a full-page illustration of assorted sink drains. "Ah," she said. "See this? He's finding a way to dispose of what he thinks of as his dirty, unacceptable feelings. Very good, very healthy." She reached over and patted my hand. "Relax," she said. "He's fine."

But I can never completely relax with Ben. He is my Ha Ha Kid, the one who gets into trouble, the one to watch for mischief, the one who once swallowed a thumbtack and a penny. It is easy to know what Ben is feeling but not easy to know whether he will be a happy person. Recently I began taking

him for play therapy, to have another and more qualified set of
eyes watching over him. We have started to see a happier, more
relaxed Ben who thinks of his therapist as another play date.

Happiness Is in the Eye of the Beholder

Today, despite everything, we are a happy family. Maybe
we're happy because we tell ourselves we are. We act brave and,
in doing so, we become brave. We believe we must keep trying
to have fun and grow; like Sisyphus, we keep pushing the stone
up the mountain without hope for a different outcome—we're
still a family shadowed by autism, after all.

A couple of years ago, we took the kids to see the movie
Toy Story 2. In preparation we went through all the usual conversations:

ME: Should we take all three boys?
NED: I don't know. Will Nat be able to sit for it?
ME: Will Ben?
NED: Will we have to buy a ton of candy to make it
     all work?
ME: Will it be a boring, silly Disney family movie?
NED: Is it worth it?
ME: Who knows? Should I just take Max and Ben?

And so on, back and forth. And then, as we get close to de-
ciding that I should take Max and leave the other two boys
with Ned, we start to feel remorse.

ME: Nat loves the first *Toy Story*.
NED: Yes, he does.
ME: We shouldn't always just take Max and Ben. These
     movies are made for families; other kids are noisy,
     why can't ours be?
NED: Let's just get one big popcorn, two sodas, and one
     bag of M&M's. Whatever happens, happens.

So we went to the movie. We settled into our seats, all five of us in a row very near the front, Ned on one end and I on the other, near the aisle—just in case. The theater darkened, and all three boys turned expectantly, and silently, toward the screen. Ned looked down the row and winked at me. Then he leaned across the boys and whispered to me, "Look at them, Sue. I don't know how this is going to turn out. But right now, at this moment, it's all good."

Nat's Bar Mitzvah

We continue to press onward, trying to make our life meaningful and as close to normal as possible. And so we decided to have a bar mitzvah for Nat. A bar mitzvah is a traditional Jewish ceremony and celebration for boys when they turn thirteen years old, a rite of passage from childhood to adulthood. The bar mitzvah had been my idea, one that germinated suddenly but struggled to grow because of fear and pessimism. It took a lot of determined coaxing and care to make it happen.

I had been raised Jewish, and when Ned and I got married, we decided our family would be Jewish, too, because religion meant more to me than it did to Ned. Ned, who had been raised with an assortment of customs, already knew quite a bit about Judaism, and he was very open to the idea. As Nat approached thirteen, all my Jewish friends were in the throes of planning their children's bar or (for girls) bat mitzvahs. I felt a stabbing sense of loss every time I heard the details, and they finally stopped telling me about them to spare my feelings. Though Nat had attended religious school between the ages of seven and eleven, we no longer belonged to that synagogue. But I had long suspected that Nat had some kind of amorphous spiritual affinity. He willingly attended temple and recited the Hebrew prayers effortlessly. Maybe it was simply their structure and repetition that attracted him. But what if it were more than that? Shouldn't Nat have the opportunity to explore his spirituality?

I took the bar mitzvah idea up with Ned. "Why do you want

this, Sue?" he asked me, sounding a bit mystified. Frustrated that he didn't see the point right away, I heatedly explained my feelings. I told him we could make Nat's bar mitzvah work, that we could create our own service and that all we needed was a rabbi, a Torah, a few prayers, and people to celebrate with us. I described it as a chance to stretch our notions of religion, to redefine the bar mitzvah on our terms. To achieve something great where others might feel defeated.

"And look at all we have to celebrate," I added. "Look how far Nat has come since the last special Jewish occasion, his *bris* [ritual circumcision]! Look how far since the diagnosis! How far we've all come. Shouldn't we proclaim to our family and friends that we are doing just fine, that Nat's autism was no tragedy—well, it is, but it isn't—and in fact, we have plenty to be grateful for?"

"Well, I guess so," Ned said slowly. "As long as we really can call the shots. And find a rabbi who will do it our way." That was a bridge I was going to cross a bit later. I didn't yet know any rabbis in the area with whom I wanted to have this conversation.

After talking to Ned, I brought the bar mitzvah idea up with my mother. "You don't belong to a temple," she reasoned, "so how will you do it?" She had let us know before how unhappy she was that we no longer had a synagogue.

"Mom, it doesn't matter. There's no rule saying it has to be done a certain way, or even in a temple. We'll make it work, but will you help us and support this thing?"

"Of course we will. What do you want us to do?" Soon enough, she and my father became excited about the prospect of a bar mitzvah for Nat, even offering to help pay for it. Then they figured out how they would participate. At a typical bar mitzvah grandparents are called to the altar to say a little blessing before the bar mitzvah boy's Torah reading. My parents decided they would read a special blessing during the placing of the prayer shawl on Nat, and my father would give him his old prayer shawl, the one he'd worn to his wedding.

"Wow," I said, "I didn't know you still had a prayer shawl." This idea made the whole thing suddenly tangible. I got off the phone excited.

When I told Ned's father, Batch, about our plan, he was more hesitant than my parents had been. "What is he even going to get out of it?" he asked.

My heart sank, but I understood why he had asked. Yet I believed that Nat *would* enjoy it, perhaps more than a typical thirteen-year-old would. After all, luckily Nat was free of the cultural baggage many Jewish teenagers carry around with them, so that things like bar mitzvahs are "uncool." What was more, Nat had a special affinity for ritual and repetition, things he would get plenty of at the bar mitzvah rehearsals and the bar mitzvah itself. I asked Batch to think about how he might participate. It could be anything he wanted because of the inclusive and unique ceremony we were planning. I added that, because he wasn't Jewish, we didn't expect him to recite a Hebrew prayer.

Ned and I threw ourselves into the bar mitzvah plans. We decided on a fairly brief service, in keeping with our custom of setting reasonable expectations for Nat (and often fairly low ones). "Declare victory and get the hell out," as Ned said. With help from a local rabbi, we compared bar mitzvah ceremony programs and got an idea of the basic components: greeting the guests; putting on the prayer shawl; reciting the Sh'mah, the most basic Jewish prayer; reading from the Torah (the first five books of the Hebrew Bible or Old Testament); a speech by the bar mitzvah boy; and a closing song and benediction.

For the Torah portion, we chose the passage from Exodus at the burning bush, where Moses, after being appointed by God to lead the Jews out of slavery, asks, essentially, "Why me?" Apparently Moses had a speech impediment, and he didn't understand why he should be the one designated to speak to Pharaoh and lead the Jews out of Egypt. But God insisted that Moses was indeed the one, and that he should look to his brother Aaron for help. I got chills when I thought about the parallels:

Nat, like Moses, greatly challenged but buoyed by his family, leading us to a whole new way of life.

We would not have Nat read the Torah passage, as most bar mitzvah boys do, though; we would leave that to the rabbi. We decided that he or she would have to be someone special, without a controlling personality. Someone open-minded who understood the priority we were putting on Nat's comfort and on having a meaningful ceremony, whether or not it followed Jewish tradition to the letter. We decided on Bob, the rabbi who had married us and was my father's oldest friend.

Bob had an "anything goes" view of Judaism that fit in with our wishes for the bar mitzvah. He told us that whatever Nat could manage would be fine, and he would do the rest. So we decided that, while Nat wouldn't read from the Torah, he would do most of the prayers in the hour-long service. I had already trained Nat over the years to recite the blessings over candles, wine, and bread, and to say the Sh'mah. Now he would also have to learn, through memorization, the special prayers preceding Torah readings. As a study aid, a bar mitzvah tutor created a tape with Nat's prayers on it.

We decided to go all out for the event, booking a small ballroom at the Fairmont Copley Plaza, the same hotel where we'd honeymooned ten years before, after our second wedding. I wanted the very best for this occasion; no quiet, somber celebration would do. We would have a light luncheon buffet, and classical music would be piped into the room. I chose my outfit carefully, feeling like the mother of the groom at a wedding, and we took Nat to Brooks Brothers for his bar mitzvah clothes. He looked wonderfully handsome in a navy blazer, yellow shirt, and khakis.

In the weeks leading up to his bar mitzvah, Nat would come home from school each day and consult his calendar, from which he'd read the words "Do bar mitzvah tape." Then he would run upstairs and listen to his prayers with me. When the cue came for him to join in, he would look at me, earnest and wide-eyed, and repeat his lines. He learned them so fast that I was even more certain that I'd been right all along, that he'd be able to take part in the ceremony, even though it seemed like a lot to expect from someone so disabled.

As the date drew near, we began to rehearse more intensively, going through the ceremony and having Nat try on his special clothes so that he would learn to feel comfortable in them. The second time through the ceremony, he tried to pinch Ned, but Ned ignored this and stayed connected to Nat, and we pressed on.

Despite our confidence that Nat would perform well, we still were sometimes nagged by doubts. The stakes were high: We were inviting sixty friends and family, and some would have to travel from far away. Whatever Nat did that day, he would do it in front of all those people. As June approached, and with it the bar mitzvah, we grew increasingly nervous, knowing at the same time that the more nervous we felt, the more nervous and disconnected from us Nat would feel—an emotional state that nearly always led to difficult behaviors.

Concerned that we were nearing dangerous behavioral territory, I decided to take action. I told family and friends that they couldn't count on staying at our house during the bar mitzvah weekend because I needed to keep the household routine as normal as possible for Nat and to keep myself from having to focus on hostess duties and thereby risk breaking my connection with Nat. He would need me to be all there for him.

When the day came at last, I awoke to a driving rain. I wrapped my hair in a bun, something I wouldn't have normally done for a fancy occasion. But I didn't want to have to think about how the humidity was making make my hair look. I could not afford to weaken my link to Nat because of something so trivial.

We drove to the Copley and waited in the lobby while our guests arrived. We had invited many people—our closest friends, parents, aunts, uncles, and first cousins, and five of Nat's teachers. My parents were ready with their brief prayers and the prayer shawl, and my father-in-law, Batch, came with a special gold bowl, a century-old family heirloom that had made it to every significant ceremony in the long family history (includ ing our wedding). This was undoubtedly the gold bowl's first bar mitzvah, however. It adorned the altar where Nat stood. With the Batchelder bowl and my parents and their prayer shawl, I felt we were surrounded by talismans and love.

When we were ready, we filed into the golden ballroom. The rabbi, Ned, Nat, and I took our places, standing at two long tables facing the rows of guests. The room was hushed; every one waited eagerly and nervously for us to begin. Nat seemed just fine, a little soft-spoken with his beginning prayer. At one point, we asked him to repeat himself because we hadn't been able to hear, and he willingly complied.

And then he started to giggle.

I glared at him, which never works when he is having a laugh attack. *Oh no, Nat, don't start that,* I thought, starting to panic. What would we do if he just kept laughing all the way through the ceremony? *That damned laugh!* I thought. We've never been able to stop it after we get really upset about it. I felt my jaw clench. I saw that Ned had noticed my tension, too.

But I knew I couldn't give myself over to anger. I had to find my way back to Nat. Nat, who was trying so hard; Nat, battling his malfunctioning nervous system; Nat, so adorable in his jacket and tie and his Tweety Bird eyes. I focused on Nat and how much I loved him. *Well,* I thought after a while, *so what if he does laugh the whole time? Who here doesn't know all about Nat? And after all, he wouldn't be Nat if he didn't laugh inappropriately!* My tension dissolved, and I smiled warmly at him. And soon Nat calmed down and followed through with the ceremony very skillfully, if a little quickly.

After the Torah portion was over, I looked out and saw peo ple dabbing their eyes. I was supposed to give the bar mitzvah speech, but every time I started, I began to cry, so Ned had to do it for me, reading from my prepared text, which described what Nat had gone through to prepare for this day and what it

234 • JUST A FAMILY

all meant to us. At the end, Ned subtly cued the guests to leave Nat alone after the ceremony, saying, "We will be happy to accept your good wishes on Nat's behalf." It was a perfect way to balance Nat's dignity and feelings with our guests' needs. So after the ceremony, Nat sat next to us with his boom box and CDs and played his *Lion King* songs while friends and family swarmed around us, carefully sending Nat their love from a safe distance.

For a long time after the bar mitzvah, the five of us floated in a haze of happiness and newfound hope. Bar mitzvahs are supposed to give boys their first occasion to act as men, and Nat had indeed given us a glimpse of the man he could become. He had shown us that he had unimagined depth and ability. He had employed that wonderful memory of his, honed to perfection by his autism, along with his hunger for repetition and consistency, and he had triumphed. He seemed to be aware of his triumph, too, for in every picture of him taken at the bar mitzvah reception, he is smiling knowingly and, miraculously, is looking straight at the camera.

What Autism Has Taught Us

We can do many things to prepare Nat for adult life, to help him participate in the world, and yet it's painfully clear that the world still is not ready for him. Ultimately, that's our challenge; after all, we're his primary advocates. Ned and I must continue to try new methods, even strange ones, return to old ones, combine approaches, water down certain strategies so that they are useful to us (i.e., not too demanding, considering the needs of our entire family). We compose the Nat Books, family songs, computer games. We experiment with Nat's tutoring program. We rewrite the IEP, bring new ideas to the school, wheedle, cajole, and plead with program administrators to make exceptions, to do special, unusual things that happen to be right for Nat. We reconfigure behavioral techniques and other established strategies to fit our erratic home life. We go on vacations and spend too much money to make sure we have everything we need for a happy time. We're not consistent but dynamic, impulsive, and creative in approach. Like a family should be. Our approach is to do what good cooks do: increase the ingredients you like and discard those that don't seem to add anything, keeping the basic structure of a recipe intact. There's a balance, a give-and-take to making it work.

Nat's brothers continue to buzz around him and grow beyond him, interacting with him differently with each new phase of theirs. I still try to find a common denominator for all three. Last summer, discovering that they liked water fights, I excitedly bought three huge Super Soakers at the drugstore because I knew that for around thirty dollars I was going to get at least a good hour of all three brothers playing together.

But while Max and Ben sprayed each other playfully, Nat seemed startled every time they got him. He didn't even think to squirt them back. He just kept squirting his water onto the grass, mesmerized by the stream. Then he'd get hit in the face by Ben or Max, and he would look up, puzzled, and wipe his eyes, returning his glance to the stream of water from his own gun.

Finally I said, "If you don't like it, Nat, squirt Max!"

Max repeated the instructions, and so did Ben. "Yeah, Nat, squirt us!" After more coaching from his brothers, Nat figured out how the game was played. But we could tell he still preferred to watch the water stream out of the gun onto the grass. *It's OK,* I thought, *as long as he's out here, doing basically the same thing as the other boys.* I said as much to Max and Ben, and I think they appreciated Nat's playing with them even this much.

Max and Ben's relationship with each other helps heal some of the pain and disappointment they may feel about Nat. Lately, they've started making movies together, a skill Max has honed in the last few years. We sent Max to an arty summer camp where he learned new techniques like animation and Super 8 filmmaking. Last year, he saved his money and bought a digital video camera, and we chipped in and bought him editing software. Max and Ben make their movies during summers and weekends whenever friends are scarce. Ben often comes up with the story idea and willingly acts in these films. Max directs and does the camera work and then spends days at the computer, editing and adding special effects, Ben looking over his shoulder. I try not to worry that they spend so much time inside, in front of screens. Once they even cast Nat in a movie, in the role of a hostage to "Dr. Evil." I did the camera work that time, while Max (Dr. Evil) and Ben (Star Sabre) fought over the hostage. Considering the effort, it was an Oscar-worthy film.

Their latest creation, *Loo,* is a parody of the 007 movies (*Loo* is what you get when you flip over the numbers 007). This short film contains a body double made out of a pillow wrapped in a bathrobe, fade-outs, music, and sound effects. Last summer, Max copied one of Ben's intricate robot and machine drawings and animated it using Flash software. It's posted on Ned's web log (at *www.nedbatchelder.com*).

As Ben's interests and personality continue to unfold, we watch for special talents and affinities, just as we do for Nat and Max, and we find summer camps and after-school programs that will expand his world beyond the confines of the family. My guess is that drawing and painting will figure heavily in Ben's life, along with mechanics and creative writing.

I hope Max and Ben will one day have rewarding relationships with Nat. The other day, when I pulled a painting out of Nat's backpack, a dark yellow image of a sun with heavy brushstrokes that nearly filled the page, both Max and Ben said in unison, "Ooh, that's good, Nat!" and neither seemed to notice or mind that Nat never responded.

"Nat, say thank you," I prompted, as always.

Ned and I must keep acting as Nat's representative with his brothers. We must continue to remind them that he is there despite his silence, that he counts, that he feels. We also must be able to turn to them and do the same when they need it. No one brother is more important than the others, but each needs support at different times. Nat, of course, needs support most of the time, but sometimes, like the day when we went tubing, it's

Ben who needs the most help. At times when Max is sad because we lost a favorite toy from years past, it's he who needs support the most. As long as we all know for certain that whatever it is we are feeling about this family is OK—no matter how ugly or unbearable it seems—and we will be OK.

Our Ride Together

Last year, after I became a bicycling enthusiast, it wasn't long before I began to feel like I wanted this to be an activity for the entire family. What better way to enjoy our Cape Cod vacations, than to ride the Cape bike paths? But, as always, there were obstacles to consider. Ben did not like riding on the back of a bike in a seat, and he didn't like bikes with training wheels. And even though Nat had learned how to ride when he was seven, he had been unwilling to get on his bike for the last few summers. When he had last tried, he had spent the entire fifteen-minute bike ride yelling "All done with the bike ride! All finished! NO MORE RIDING!"

But I knew that with Nat, phases come and go, and I decided last year to try again. One morning in late spring, when I was feeling particularly courageous, I asked him to come riding with me, just on our street. He jumped off the couch immediately, always a good sign. We rode up and down the street, and even around the block a few times. It felt good. Nat really seemed to want to be there. He was focusing outward, looking down the road, and braking just right, too. And when a car approached, he swerved over to the sidewalk, without my even warning him. *Hmm,* I thought, *he really looks good.* My family-bike-ride fantasy began to seem like a possibility.

When we got to Cape Cod for our vacation, we waited until the first cloudy day to try it. We visited the bike shop and chose bikes for everyone, including one with a special tandem attachment that would allow Ben to pedal behind me. He was very happy not to have to ride in a bike seat or use training wheels. Then I turned to Nat, to get him ready. I explained in

simple, repetitive terms that we would be riding our bikes on a
long ride, and at the end we'd get ice cream. Structure, repetition, reward. But also, connection. I looked at him full-on, in
the eyes, so that he could see that however he felt about it, I was
with him.

"Yes, OK." He looked away.

"You'll ride, a long time, and wait for the ice cream?"

"Yes, OK, yes."

"You'll be calm."

"Yes."

I was satisfied. In my mind, we would probably only do a little, not even all the way to the halfway point on this path (three
miles). It would be a small victory. I didn't want to set myself up
for disappointment. My parents joined us. We amassed at the
beginning of the bike path, then fell into line. Nat and my father were at the head, with Nat listening to my dad's directions,
as he always seems to. Ned rode behind them, then me, with
Ben, who thought he was pedaling for both of us. Max was behind me, then my mother.

I was in a sweat because of how much Ben was making the
bike lurch. I was also nervous about how Nat would do as we
pressed on. So I pulled up next to him and looked at his face.
He was smiling. I sighed and unclenched my fingers, and tried
to relax. So far, so good. Maybe this would work. We pushed
on, up a very big hill that seemed to be hard only for me, because of my extra wiggly load.

Finally, to my delight, we actually had made it to the halfway
point, the three-mile mark, and it had been easy (except for
me). We all got off our bikes to take pictures. I reviewed the
plan with Nat, reminding him of the ice cream. "OK, yes. Get
ice cream after the bike ride," he said enthusiastically.

The trip back was uneventful, with one moment's trepidation as I watched for Nat to successfully apply his brakes as he
went down that big hill. This time I rode in between everyone,
having handed off Ben to my father so that I could keep a better eye on Nat, although he didn't seem to need me to. The

path ahead was easy now, and very straight. Nat and Max took the lead together, passing Ned. I fell back behind them. My bike tires hummed as they spun. Soon I realized I was grinning: There were my two older sons, riding companionably together, faster than their father, just as it should be. And nothing but ice cream on their minds.

Unexpected Gifts

When he was a baby, I saw Max as my gift from God, and thought he should have been given Nat's name, which has that meaning. But Maximillian, which means "the greatest," is also apt for him, because he is physically the biggest of our three sons. Moreover, he seems better equipped than any of us to rise above our misfortune and find contentment. Ben became my next gift, the fulfillment of my faith in God. As the "right hand of God," the Hebrew meaning of his name, Ben was like a divine handshake, proof that we sometimes do get what we wish for, and that we were right to wish to for it.

What I've come to understand to be true, though I don't always feel it, is that Nat too is a gift. People tell me, "He's lucky to have you. You were chosen as his mother because you could provide him with such a good life." I hate hearing this. It doesn't make sense to me. I don't believe there was an autistic soul cruising around, looking for a good mother.

In a similar vein, a friend who believes in reincarnation once told me Nat's spirit must have chosen his impaired body for the lessons it would teach him in this life, and that my spirit chose to be his mother. I shook my head in disbelief. While I don't believe that we had any choice in the matter, I do agree that there are things I have learned, and that my family has learned, because of Nat. Nat has shown us in the most concrete possible way that you can't take anything for granted. He has taught us to appreciate small pleasures—when they are so hard won, they become big pleasures. Through Nat, I learned to look at myself and figure out how *I* need to change in order to do what needs to be done and in order to be happy. Also through Nat, Ned and I have learned to rely on each other, to be strong for each other, and to make each other smile, even during the toughest times. We have all learned to revel in our eccentricities, not to be diminished by them. Ben and Max are learning that life is a struggle, especially for those who are very different, and their hearts and minds will grow stronger as a result.

That's the best we can hope for. Sometimes I would prefer to be like the innocents around me, the families who take their normalcy for granted, who complain about homework, car pools, allergies. I will never again be a happy innocent. That is a loss we will not recoup. But the worst loss of all is that I'll never know my child except as, at best, a construct of my own making and, at worst, a heartbreakingly difficult being. And he could have had it all. No, I still cannot let that go. But there is so much we do have, and I hold greedily onto that. We have three beautiful, healthy sons who seem to love being part of our family.

There is no cure for Nat's autism, no one good approach, and no way out. There is only the five of us. We help Nat become the best he can be, and in the process he makes us who we are. Because of this strange and terrible gift, we cannot be typical, we cannot be normal. But this is certain: We are OK. And we stand together, sometimes against the autism, sometimes against the world. But always together, as a family.

EPILOGUE

I STILL FIND MYSELF WONDERING, during my dark times, *What if Nat woke up one morning to find that he wasn't autistic any longer?* I see us all, gathered around his bed, the site of the miracle, eagerly listening to his every word. He speaks so clearly now, in full, effortless sentences. At last, we understand everything. It's as if he has woken up from a coma, or a deep, enchanted sleep. He will have to catch up for all the lost time.

We tell him, "And then you did . . . . Why was that?" We have so many questions for him, as he does for us. And now he can tell us all his secrets. "Oh, I hated it when you would try to make me talk to you."

"Why?"

"Because your words came at me too fast. If anything else was going on, I couldn't pay attention to whatever you were saying to me. The noise in a room overpowered everything else."

"What were you saying with the silly talk? What was 'Feem—sh?'"

"'Feem' just made me feel good. It was *my* word. Because you didn't know what it meant, you couldn't talk to me about it or make me talk about it. And 'ssh' was just that, 'ssh.' I loved the feel of 'ssh.' I loved when people got quiet."

"Why did you hit? Why did you pinch?"

"I don't know. I think that with the pinching, my fingers got carried away. It feels good to squeeze. And once I hit, it's hard to stop."

And then I have to ask the most important question, "Do you love us?"

"Yeah, but it's hard understanding all of your emotions. You can laugh, then cry, then sing, all in the same hour. How can you change moods so fast?"

"Maybe now you'll see," Ned says. "What do you want to do now, Nat?"

"I want to meet some girls."

I wish for a miracle like this so badly that when I really think about it, I can barely breathe. So I close my eyes and let it pass through me. And the more I think about it, the more I come to realize that there are not many fifteen-year-old boys, autistic or not, who actually talk that way to their mothers. Anyway, I do know Nat. I know why he does what he does, the "feem," the pinching, all of it. All in all, as my father once said, he's still our Nat.

So I drop my miracle fantasy and open my eyes and go look-ing for him. There he is, pacing back and forth, living room, hallway, dining room, waiting for his video to rewind, his loud steps reverberating through the house, his hand opening and closing in time with the cadence of his soft silly talk. He notices me immediately, but he keeps moving, probably hoping I will not disturb his comfortable rhythm.

"Hold it, Nat," I say, stopping him between rooms.

He turns and fixes on me with his wide blue eyes, waiting, silent now. He's taller than I am these days, but his hair is still bright blond, the same as it was when he was a baby.

I say, "I just want a hug."

Immediately, he leans in toward me, "OK, yes," he says, so softly it is almost imperceptible.

I kiss his cheek and breathe him in. His long arms are gingerly draped around me, bony and warm. We stand together for a moment, just like that, and my pain recedes, carried away with the tide.

Acknowledgments

There are many people who are part of this book, so many whom, along the way, have helped with material, guidance, support, or love. There are also a great many people in our lives who have helped us succeed as a family. It takes more than a village to raise a child like Nat. There have been so many doctors and specialists in our lives who made this experience humane, bearable, and sometimes even pleasant, but I want to thank Dr. Margaret Bauman, Sheila Currier, and Dr. Janice Ware in particular for their supreme effort. I must also acknowledge the many wonderful teachers we have known along the way, who believed only in Nat's potential, and smiled at his spirit; and the many dedicated tutors in our lives who were so talented, creative, and never minded when Nat pinched, especially Dani Strachman and Sara Huber. There are also numerous friends, who helped by reading and giving honest input, like Nancy Bea Miller, Emily Terry, Beth Teitell, Paul McLean, Sheila Delahanty, Merle Manwaring, and my cousin Eric Marcus.

I must also thank the family: Ned's family, the Batchelders, for being helpful, loving, generous, and always welcoming, especially Sarai, for reading a draft, and for her steadfast support. Special appreciation goes to my parents Mel and Shelly Senator and my sister, Laura Senator, for book input, and of course, for their faith in Nat and in me. Also, my eternal gratitude to my therapist, for being my lifeline and helping me understand and get through it all.

I want to thank my agent, Diane Gedymin, for having the stamina, vision, patience, and loyalty to carry this project through to the end, and my very wise editor, Eden Steinberg, and the caring, collaborative staff at Shambhala for seeing the value in this project and really "getting" it.

Finally, thank you to my three beautiful boys, Nathaniel, Maximillian, and Benjamin, each so different, for sweetening my life, and each teaching me what I needed to know about being a parent. And of course, my deepest thanks to my husband, Ned, for being my partner through it all, for always making me laugh, for letting me cry, for taking such good care of us, for reading all the drafts, for remembering what I forgot, and for being my best friend above all others.

APPENDIX

A Brief Overview
of Treatments and Interventions

The purpose of this list is not to make treatment recommendations but to familiarize you with the main options. Before choosing a treatment for your child, always check whether it is covered by your insurance and seek advice from a trusted doctor and other parents.

APPLIED BEHAVIOR ANALYSIS (ABA): An approach to teaching skills to people with autism that uses positive reinforcement and the collection of data to determine the level of progress in attaining a given goal. This technique is also sometimes referred to as the Lovaas method. See *www.mayinstitute.org*. Click on the FAQs and go to the ABA fact sheet.

AUDITORY INTEGRATION TRAINING (AIT), OR THE TOMATIS METHOD: People with autism tend to have hypersensitive hearing. In this approach, children listen to different musical sounds and frequencies to re-attune their hearing and sensory processing. See the following page at the website for the Association for Science in Autism Treatment: *www.asatonline.org/about_autism/autism_info08.html*.

AUGMENTED COMMUNICATION / ASSISTIVE TECHNOLOGY: An intervention that uses technological devices such as keyboards, voice recognition systems, and communication boards for the purpose of supporting communication, daily living skills, behavior modification, and any other aspect of interaction or independent functioning. See *www.cesa7.k12.wi.us/sped/autism/assist/asst10.htm*.

CRANIO-SACRAL THERAPY (CST): An approach in which pressure and touch are applied to the head and vertebrae. This has been found to relieve autistic symptoms in some patients. See the Upledger Institute website at *www.upledger.com/therapies/cst.htm*.

DEFEAT AUTISM NOW (DAN!) PROTOCOL: A treatment approach that focuses on the connections between autism and diet, along with other physiological issues. This treatment involves a series of medical tests and dietary and nutritive regimens designed to alleviate autistic symptoms. Often a gluten-free, casein-free diet is recommended. See *www.autismresearchinstitute.org*.

FACILITATED COMMUNICATION (FC): A controversial treatment method that may enable an autistic person to communicate in writing, using a computer or other communication device with the help of a trained teacher, therapist, or caregiver who encourages patient expression and responses. Some feel the results may not have been genuine because they feel that, in many cases claiming success, the facilitator was influencing the communications. Others swear by it. See*http://pediatrics.aappublications.org/cgi/content/full/102/2/431*. Also see *www.asatonline.org* to get information on Assistive Technology versus Facilitated Communication.

FLOORTIME: A relational approach to teaching skills to people with autism that emphasizes connecting with the child and engaging the child's attention as the basis for learning. Also known as the Developmental Individualized Relationship-based (DIR) method. See *www.floortime.org*.

HIGASHI, OR DAILY LIFE THERAPY: A treatment method that emphasizes harmony of the mind and body, gaining independence, and community life. Higashi is a strict, non-pharmacological approach, using rigorous physical exercise; healthy eating regimens; regular exposure to music, academics, and art; and strongly reinforced social activities. See *www.bostonhigashi.org*.

PICTURE EXCHANGE COMMUNICATION SYSTEM (PECS): An educational communication technique that builds basic relating and language skills by encouraging the child to use of picture-bearing cards to express his or her needs. See *www.pecs.com/page5.html*.

SENSORY INTEGRATION THERAPY (SI): A therapeutic approach using activities that develop and strengthen the child's physical sense of his own body in space. SI promotes balance and discourages "sensory defensiveness"—i.e., excessive sensitivity to touch, taste, or sound. SI uses actions like swinging the child, physio ball play, and deep pressure to help the child develop the ability to regulate his or her physical, sensory, and even neurological responses to stimuli.

THE SON-RISE PROGRAM: An alternative, relationally-based treatment approach in which the caregiver joins the child in the repetitive forms of play that the child favors, thereby establishing a bond with him or her.
See *www.autismtreatmentcenter.org*.

TREATMENT AND EDUCATION OF AUTISTIC AND RELATED COMMUNICATION HANDICAPPED CHILDREN (TEACCH): An educational approach that takes advantage of the autistic child's need for structure and organization. The teaching methods and the classroom itself use strategic layout, along with rigid schedules, rules, and boundaries to eliminate distractions and focus the child. See *www.teacch.com*.

GLOSSARY

Key Terms
Used in the Special Ed System

core evaluation: The initial evaluation done by the school system to assess a child's needs; the evaluation out of which the individualized education plan (IEP) is developed.

early intervention: Federally supported entitlement programs and services designed and administered by each state and designed to help a disabled child progress until age three, when he or she becomes eligible for public education services and programs.

expressive language: Language that is expressed aloud, for example, the ability to tell a story of answer a question. See **receptive language**.

inclusion/mainstreaming: The federal Individuals with Disabilities Education Act (IDEA) dictates that, insofar as possible, disabled children should be a part of a regular classroom, or in an adapted classroom that follows a regular educational routine, for a segment or even all of their day. "Inclusion" implies that the child must have all supports, adaptations, and services necessary to progress in as typical a classroom environment as possible. "Mainstreaming" is when a disabled child participates, with little or no support, in a typical classroom with typically developing peers.

individualized education plan (IEP): The document produced as a result of a team meeting that lists the child's learning needs, the educational goals for the child for the year, and the methods used to achieve the goals and measure the child's progress. Sometimes the parents are asked to express a long-term vision for the child.

language-based learning: A classroom approach, frequently used for children with autism, that emphasizes the understanding of letters and words. Visual cues and images are placed throughout the classroom to promote understanding of letters and words.

occupational therapy (OT): A common therapy for children with autism, consisting of activities that teach occupation-related skills. In the case of a small child, the activities teach skills like imaginary play, turn-taking, and tabletop play (using Play-Doh or drawing, for example).

receptive language: Language that is taken in and understood; for example, the ability to attend to directions and follow them. See **expressive language**.

service delivery: The provision of therapies and educational programs to the child as spelled out in the IEP—for example, "speech-language therapy, three times a week, thirty minutes a session."

special education (SPED): The adaptations made to a school's regular curriculum and teaching techniques so that children with disabilities may be educated to the greatest degree possible with their typically developing peers.

speech/language therapy: A common service for autistic children. Therapy to improve listening, speaking, reading, and writing.

team: The decision-makers for the child in question. The team consists of parents/guardians, evaluators (specialists), and a team facilitator from the school system, and advocates for the child (optional). The child joins the team after age fourteen.

RESOURCES

BOOKS

On Autism

BARRON, JUDY, AND SEAN BARRON. *There's a Boy in Here.* Arlington, Tex.: Future Horizons, 2002.

GRANDIN, TEMPLE. *Thinking in Pictures: And Other Reports of My Life with Autism.* New York: Vintage, 1995.

GRANDIN, TEMPLE, AND MARGARET M. SCARIANO. *Emergence: Labeled Autistic.* New York: Warner Books, 1996.

GREENSPAN, STANLEY J., AND SERENA WIEDER. *The Child with Special Needs: Encouraging Intellectual and Emotional Growth.* Reading, Mass.: Addison-Wesley Longman, 1998.

HADDON, MARK. *The Curious Incident of the Dog in the Night-Time: A Novel.* New York: Doubleday, 2003.

HOWLIN, PATRICIA, AND SIMON BARON-COHEN. *Teaching Children with Autism to Mind-Read: A Practical Guide for Teachers and Parents.* New York: John Wiley and Sons, 2002.

MAURICE, CATHERINE, GINA GREEN, AND STEPHEN C.
LUCE, EDS. *Behavioral Intervention for Young Children with
Autism: A Manual for Parents and Professionals.* Austin, Tex.:
Pro-Ed Publishers, 1996.
MCCLANNAHAN, LYNN E., AND PATRICIA J. KRANTZ. *Activ-
ity Schedules for Children with Autism: Teaching Independent Be-
havior.* Bethesda, Md.: Woodbine House, 1999.

On Siblings and Family Dynamics

BURNS, ELIZABETH. *Tilt: Every Family Spins on its Own Axis.*
Naperville, Ill.: Sourcebooks, 2003.
FABER, ADELE, AND ELAINE MAZLISH. *Siblings Without Ri-
valry.* New York: HarperCollins, 1998.
HARRIS, SANDRA L. *Siblings of Children with Autism: A Guide for
Families.* Bethesda, Md.: Woodbine House, 1999.
MEYER, DONALD, ED. *Views from Our Shoes: Growing Up with a
Brother or Sister with Special Needs.* Bethesda, Md.: Woodbine
House, 1997.
STROHM, KATE. *Being the Other One: Growing Up with a Brother
or Sister Who Has Special Needs.* Boston: Shambhala Publica-
tions, 2005.

WEBSITES AND ORGANIZATIONS

· *General Information*

About.com: *http://autism.about.com*
Center for the Study of Autism: *www.autism.org*
First Signs: *www.firstsigns.org*
National Alliance for Autism Research: *www.naar.org*
National Institute of Mental Health:
www.nimh.nih.gov/autismiacc/staart.cfm

Support for couples: *www.babycenter.com/refcap/446.html*
Support for siblings:
www.thearc.org/siblingsupport/sibshops about and
http://ericec.org/faq/siblings.html
Treatments and interventions:
www.autism-resources.com/links-methods.html and
www.esd189.org/autism/interventions.html
Zero to Three Foundation: *www.zerotothree.org*

Advocacy

Autism Society of America *www.autism-society.org*
Federation for Children with Special Needs: *www.fcsn.org*
Office of Special Education Programs:
www.ed.gov/about/offices/list/osers/osep/index.html
Wright's Law: *www.wrightslaw.com*

Extracurricular Activities

Special Olympics: *www.specialolympics.org*
Access Sport America: *www.accesssports.org/contact/*
Surfers Healing: *www.surfershealing.org/about/about.html*
Easter Seals: *www.easterseals.com*

Tools for Daily Life

www.mayer-johnson.com
www.autismcoach.com
www.eparent.com
www.abilitations.com

Funding and Grants

The Doug Flutie, Jr., Foundation:
www.dougflutiejrfoundation.org
The ARC of the U.S.: *www.thearc.org*
Social Security: *www.socialsecurity.gov/disability/*

Websites and Blogs by Parents

www.genrecookshop.com
www.mothersfromhell2.org/
www.motherswithattitude.com/about.html
www.nedbatchelder.com
www.susansenator.com

Other Useful Sites

Autism and genetics: *www.exploringautism.org/news*
Information on thimerosal (an additive in pediatric vaccines, which some have linked to autism):
www.fda.gov/cber/vaccine/thimerosal.htm
Our Kids: *www.our-kids.org*

About the Author

Susan Senator is a mother of three, a writer, speaker, and advocate for children and the disabled. Her writing on autism has appeared in the *New York Times,* the *Washington Post,* the *Boston Globe, Education Week, Teacher Magazine,* and *Exceptional Parent* magazine. This is her first book.

For more information on many of the strategies mentioned in this book, visit the author's website at *www.susansenator.com.*